FORSYTH LIBRARY - FHSU
028.9C346c 1982
main

WITHDRAWN

Forsyth Library

CAUGHT IN THE ACT

*The Decisive Reading of
Some Notable Men and Women
and Its Influence on Their
Actions and Attitudes*

Edwin Castagna

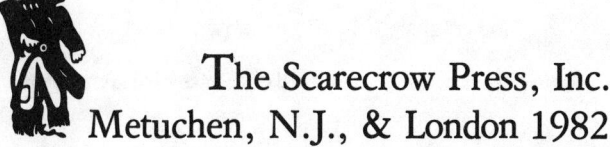

The Scarecrow Press, Inc.
Metuchen, N.J., & London 1982

Library of Congress Cataloging in Publication Data

Castagna, Edwin, 1909-
  Caught in the act.

  Bibliography: p.
  Includes index.
  1. Books and reading. 2. Reading interests.
I. Title.
Z1003.C3 1982   028'.9   82-10276
ISBN 0-8108-1566-4

Copyright © 1982 by Edwin Castagna

Manufactured in the United States of America

- To Rachel -

ACKNOWLEDGMENTS

The author thanks the following publishers for their permission to quote from the publications listed below:

THE DIAL PRESS (New York): *Karen Horney: Gentle Rebel of Psychoanalysis* (1978) by Jack L. Rubins.

DOUBLEDAY (Garden City, N.Y.): *The Life of Teresa of Jesus: The Autobiography of St. Teresa of Avila* (1960).

HARCOURT BRACE JOVANOVICH (New York): *Passionate Crusader: The Life of Marie Stopes* (1977) by Ruth Hall.

LOS ANGELES TIMES (Los Angeles): *Hunt and Peck Not His Type* (Jan. 8, 1978) by Jack Smith.

M. EVANS AND CO. (New York): *Station Identification: Confessions of a Video Kid* (1980) by Donald Bowie.

RANDOM HOUSE (New York): *Memories, Dreams, Reflections,* by C. G. Jung, recorded and edited by Aniela Jaffe, translated by Richard and Clara Winston. Translation copyright © 1961, 1962, 1963 by Random House, Inc. Reprinted by permission of Pantheon Books, a Division of Random House, Inc.

SHEED AND WARD (London): *The Complete Works of St. Teresa of Jesus* (1946).

UNIVERSITY OF CALIFORNIA PRESS (Berkeley, Los Angeles, New York): *Vesalius of Brussels, 1514-1564* (1964) by C. D. O'Malley.

CONTENTS

1. Introduction — 1
2. A Few Examples of the Impact of Motion Pictures and TV on Individuals — 4
3. Decisive Reading of Some Giants of Literature — 13
4. Decisive Reading of Sixteen Religious Leaders from Saint Augustine to Martin Luther King — 38
5. The Decisive Reading of Scientists — 77
6. Decisive Reading of Fifteen Practitioners and Scientists of Medicine — 98
7. Decisive Reading of Freud and Jung, Probers of the Unconscious — 134
8. Books as Armor and Weapons: The Reading of Military Leaders — 147
9. Observations, a Suggestion, and Concluding Thoughts on the Impacts of Reading, Movies, and TV — 173
10. Notes — 179
11. Selective Bibliography — 193
12. Index — 209

Chapter 1

INTRODUCTION

This book focuses on the reading of men and women who have influenced human thought and behavior. Some of them have changed the course of history. It is my intention to catch these great individuals in the act of reading and to inquire into the consequences of that reading. According to some students of communication, electronic technology, with its proliferating developments in storing, retrieving, and transmitting all kinds of information, threatens to reduce readers of books to an endangered species. So this is an appropriate time to examine the significance of the reading of print on paper in human experience.

Although much has been written about reading and the power of print, none of the following publications, which are some of the best known in the field, nor others of which I am aware, come at the subject from my perspective.

What Reading Does to People: A Summary of Evidence on the Social Effects of Reading and a Statement of Problems for Research (1940), a pioneer scholarly study by Douglas Waples, Bernard Berelson and Franklyn Bradshaw, deals mostly with the preconditions, distribution, and content of publications. Information on what reading actually does to people, in spite of the title, is sketchy.

In Books that Changed Our Minds (1938), Malcolm Cowley and Bernard Smith revaluated twelve books, each of which "has exerted a real influence on its own field of thought." The editors were not concerned with personal encounters with books and their impact on individuals.

Robert B. Downs' Books that Changed the World (1956) and Books that Changed America (1976) are, along with his related titles, excellent treatises. But they deal only incidentally with the influence of reading on the individual. Downs' main concern is with the impact of books on history.

When I happened on That Eager Zest: First Discoveries in the Magic World of Books (1961), edited by Frances Walsh, I thought she had preempted my idea. But her anthology is limited to reading done during childhood.

"Research in the Fields of Reading and Communications," edited by Alice Lohrer, in Library Trends, October 1973, a collection of scholarly essays, like the other works cited, does not cover the ground with which I am concerned.

My sources of information on the impact of reading on behavior and attitudes have been mainly autobiographies and biographies. Whenever possible, I have quoted the reader's own words on the reading experience and its influence.

It may be asked, why bother with reading at all when Marshall McLuhan has assured us that the age of print has been succeeded by the age of the electronic media? McLuhan had a lot of fun writing about "hot" books and "cool" television in Understanding Media: Extensions of Man (1964). Linear thinking, based on lines of print, he announced, has become obsolete in the instantaneous world of TV. However, most of McLuhan's ideas are to be found only in the print he so cavalierly dismissed. So the high priest of electronic communication, by his own example, has shown his dependence on the book. In doing so, has he not invalidated his own thesis?

Long before McLuhan, the death of the book was predicted at frequent intervals. With each new fad and enthusiasm that swept the population, heads were shaken sadly over the expected imminent death of reading. It happened with the onset of the ballroom dancing craze and at the introduction of bicycles, automobiles, movies, radio, miniature golf, and TV. Librarians worried that the mass preoccupation with sports would doom the book. And there has been gloomy speculation among publishers lately that we and our hedonistic contemporaries, wallowing in hot tubs and the pleasures of the flesh, will have neither time, inclination, nor energy for the drier rewards of reading.

Still the book lives. Actually, a symbiotic relationship has developed, and books stream from the presses on every new activity, to be read eagerly and collected. The book continues to be a basic tool for understanding and using the complex array of knowledge and opinion upon which our culture depends for its survival. In the next-to-last decade of the 20th century, the book and other printed media-- newspapers and magazines--are still indispensable for much of the population.

But is the survival of reading assured? No one can be certain what is ahead for reading and whether it will be as important in the future as it has been in the past for creative individuals. It is my hope that my investigations of the influence of reading on some of the great minds of earlier times will suggest an answer to the question of the survival of reading.

What John Barth, novelist and teacher, said to a class of "apprentice writers" at The Johns Hopkins University, in comparing the influence of reading and the movies, bears on the question. His statement appeared in the Baltimore Evening Sun October 7, 1975:

> Words written on a page are our greatest source of stimulation and greatest source of limitation. Literature doesn't appeal directly to any of the physical senses. We can go to a sixth-rate movie and weep like a child and still despise the film.
> But literature can shake our lives to the core. Our life can turn around corners by simply reading words on a page. The film is done and forgotten after our weeping. Literature remains the only medium that gets directly inside to our interior life. [1]

In that rather ambiguous statement, in which he judged literature superior to the movies and, by implication, to TV, as "the only medium that gets directly inside to our interior life," Barth spoke out of personal experience and commitment to his own craft, not from a scientific point of view. However, as a highly respected writer and a keen observer of the play of influences on human lives, his ideas are worthy of consideration.

To follow a little further the question of the relative impacts of literature and the other media, let us look, for comparison, at a few pieces of evidence on the influence of the movies and TV on individuals.

Chapter 2

A FEW EXAMPLES OF THE IMPACT OF MOTION
PICTURES AND TV ON INDIVIDUALS

There is an extensive literature on the influence of motion pictures and TV on society at large. However, since the two media are johnny-come-latelies, there is less personal testimony as to their effect on individual behavior and attitudes than there is on the impact of books on readers. As more serious objective accounts of the impact of these media appear, valid comparisons with reading can be made. For now, a few examples will have to do.

Caryl Rivers, in Aphrodite at Mid-century (1973), wrote about Saturday afternoon movies seen with teen-age friends. The Good Guys always beat the Bad Guys, and John Wayne and Alan Ladd

> single-handedly killed more Japs and Jerries, sank more ships, blasted more fighters, slogged through more jungle, than any five regiments.[1]

Along with her heavy Saturday afternoon movie habit, Caryl Rivers was a reader. She said it was her "real education," and "a particularly purple passage" gave her "a certain tingly, melty feeling you-know-where that was decidedly pleasant."[2] So she was susceptible to the appeal of both media. She wrote about the lasting influence of the films:

> The flesh of the creature we knew as 'Saturday afternoon at the Movies' may lie amoldering in the warehouses; but the spirit marches on, somewhere in the collective subconscious of a generation of Americans.[3]

A more conscious reaction to a John Wayne movie was reported in the Baltimore Sun, April 25, 1974. Robert S. Babington saw "one of the few non-horse operas of the Duke's long career."[4] Wayne played an engineer,

> carrying a clip-board instead of the familiar six-gun. He not only designed a bridge and built it single-handed, he extemporized the center span in the face of a rampaging flood by driving a train out onto the incomplete bridge and using that for the final section. 5

So convincing was Wayne as the resourceful engineer--"the kind of guy that does it all himself"6--that Babington followed his rugged example. He became an engineer with more than 100 patents to his credit.

A newsreel triggered Charles Lindbergh's historic solo flight across the Atlantic Ocean. He was bored, according to Dan Carlinski in Modern Maturity, April-May, 1977, with barnstorming and routine flying, and he was in need of a new challenge:

> It came in the autumn of 1926. Giving himself the rare treat of attending a movie (a World War I picture, 'What Price Glory?' starring Victor McLaglen), Slim Lindbergh found his attention riveted to a newsreel report about a three-engine Sikorsky plane being built for a Frenchman and his crew of three, who were aiming for a nonstop ocean crossing. There was a $25,000 cash prize waiting, the newsreel said, for the first pilot or team to go nonstop, in either direction, between Paris and New York. 7

Lindbergh's reaction to "What Price Glory?" and McLaglen is not recorded. But his response to the newsreel made him a hero around the world.

Another decisive response to a film was recalled in revealing detail by Jack Smith, a Los Angeles columnist, in the Tucson Citizen, April 8, 1978. He wrote:

> All of us are what we are in America because of the movies that shaped our characters and lighted our ambitions in our formative years: but few people can single out, as positively as I can, the one movie that was the pilot star of our lives.
>
> My movie was 'The Front Page,' which came out in 1931, when I was a schoolboy, and gave me a call as powerful as the call of the cloth to an altar boy. I wanted to be a newspaperman like

> Hildy Johnson and nothing was going to stand in my way, not even marriage and World War II.
>
> 'The Front Page' turned up on the channel the other night and it gave me an extraordinary chance to examine, from the perspective of what many would call a misspent life, the work of art that fired my clay. It was like that moment of revelation on the psychiatrist's couch, when suddenly a curtain is drawn back and the patient discovers the seed of all his trouble.
> I was naturally dismayed to discover that the man who had been my inspiration was brash, childlike and maudlin, and that the environment that was in my eyes Camelot--a criminal courthouse pressroom of the 1920s--was bleak, seedy and foul.
> However, if it seems improbable that the life of a 1920s police reporter should appeal to an otherwise decent boy, it is necessary to point out that 'The Front Page' had a vitality, drama, suspense and humor that still comes through after 46 years, despite the tattered film and a sound track as noisy as an elevated train. 8

After going on about the attraction of the hardboiled characters, and how he tried to imitate one of them when he got into journalism, Smith reaffirmed his conviction about the power of the movies:

> I think the question of whether the movies actually influence children and adolescents, which is of so much current concern, is clearly answered by my own case history. If I hadn't seen 'The Front Page' when I did I might have gone on with my clarinet lessons and played one day with Bennie Goodman or Artie Shaw; either that or jumped ship in the Fiji Islands, which I almost did anyway, and sunk into a life of fetid dissolution. 9

Granted that Smith was laying it on a bit, there is no question of the film's influence on him during his adolescence. That seems the time of greatest vulnerability to the shaping power of the movies. It will be interesting to see how this compares with the time of life at which reading makes its greatest impact.

Another example of the influence of films on a teenager was reported by Shana Alexander in Talking Woman (1976):

> After Pearl Harbor Bernie quit high school and joined the Navy. The day after the movie-struck boot saw Tyrone Power in Crash Dive, he applied for submarine duty. One fateful night about two years later, many fathoms deep in the Pacific, an accident befell Bernie comparable, in cinema history, to the apple falling on Newton's head. The only movie available ... was Gunga Din, and the crew learned the sound track so well that they could turn the sound off and supply all the Gunga Din noises themselves. Roles were chosen by lot, and several crewmen soon developed highly special skills. One could bellow an elephant love call. Another could sound exactly like a cracked bugle. A third produced rifle fire--nineteenth century British rifle fire. Bernie Schwartz became a whiz at impersonating Cary Grant. Furthermore, he found Grant so exhilarating that he was hooked for life. Even today, when Bernie Schwartz feels uneasy being Tony Curtis, he will metamorphose instantaneously into Grant. This odd habit unnerves some of Tony's Hollywood friends, especially Cary Grant.10

Long before Tony Curtis made it big on the screen, Jack L. Warner had become a tycoon in the business end of the movies. As with Curtis, a movie had shown him where his future lay. In his obituary in the Baltimore Sun, September 11, 1978, the story was told. He was one of twelve children of a Polish immigrant to Canada, when he and three of his brothers were stirred by The Great Train Robbery. At eleven, Jack Warner saw the possibilities of the new medium. Within a few years, he and his go-getter brothers were exhibitors. Moving West, Warner Brothers soon established themselves and operated a big studio. They employed John Barrymore, Humphrey Bogart, James Cagney, Bette Davis, Al Jolson, and Rin Tin Tin. Ronald Reagan also worked for them.

Following these examples of the impact of films on the young, let us look briefly at the influence of TV.

In Station Identification: Confessions of a Video Kid

(1980), Donald Bowie has written the first book I have seen to document the long-time impact of TV on one person. It is a freewheeling account of his domination by electronic media from the time he was a tot. At about three, as he told it,

> ... I inadvertently provided the entertainment, one evening in a restaurant. Seated in my high chair, I spontaneously sang, at the top of my lungs, 'Time out for Dawson's.'... All the customers in the restaurant laughed at me. I had no idea why. I <u>liked</u> listening to the radio; its catch phrases bobbed in my head ...
>
> The radio made impressions that were translucent to my ears: 'Who knows what evil lurks in the hearts of men? <u>The Shadow</u> knows.' Yet radio, however vivid it might have seemed, would pale next to television.[11]

Donald's parents owned the first TV set in their neighborhood in 1949. He recalled its delivery:

> The day the enormous Starrett arrived in our living room was as exciting for me as several Christmases rolled into one. I and four ... little friends ... waited in reverent silence to see the magic. The delivery men took forever, but finally, a little after five-thirty in the afternoon, one of them clicked a brass bezel to <u>on</u>. And in a minute Buffalo Bob appeared. My friends and I were hypnotized on the spot.[12]

In a gross understatement he wrote, "Television had a profound influence on me."[13] It was "only because they were first"[14] that his family had anything to do with molding his personality, which was "fired" by TV "as a freshly painted ceramic piece is set."[15] He said "the radiation from the tube was a kiln that has given me my glazed eyes."[16]

The TV set quickly captured the whole Bowie household. Donald's prissy Aunt Mildred had to defend herself, when teased for watching soap operas, on the ground that they were well acted. Donald, an only child, was lost sight of in the family preoccupation with the set:

> Nobody noticed anymore whether or not I was

> sitting up straight. I wasn't. I was leaning back in my chair, getting slowly round-shouldered in the posture of watching television. Even today I catch myself in a store window walking stooped. And my posture wasn't the only thing about me that television was affecting. As Aunt Mildred might have learned in her psychology course, early influences can be crucial in a child's development. Toilet training <u>counts</u>. I was getting toilet training from television in vivid black and white, impressions that reached the bowels of my psyche. 17

One of the lessons Donald learned from TV, especially from "Clarabell's open bad behavior" on <u>Howdy Doody</u>, was that

> There were two different worlds you could live in ... the world of Aunt Mildred, which was generally prohibitive, and the world of television, which was whatever a free spirit wanted it to be. <u>Unrestrained</u>. All I ever ... understood ... was that television never frustrated me. It encouraged greater liberties than being outdoors. 18

Among the "greater liberties"19 to which David was encouraged were body examinations with Nancy, a friend. They dressed up in loin cloths inspired by "The Lone Ranger." They also mimicked their mothers from what they saw on the tube.

Donald realized later how badly he was hooked. TV "was becoming in my life what a dog is supposed to be to a boy."20 When his father, sobbing, told him of his grandfather's death:

> Silently I went into the living room and turned on the television set. I didn't know what I was supposed to be feeling, so I looked to 'Howdy Doody' for reassurance. I felt particularly alone in the house--and I was. Sitting in front of the television set, I was cut off from my father's grief and my mother's solicitude. I sat there on the rug, suspended in embryonic contentment, isolated in my private world where everything was black and white and happy. 21

Donald Bowie grew up, went to college, evaded the

draft, and lived an unrestrained life with other free spirits like Tube Man, who did nothing but watch TV. He wrote Station Identification at the suggestion of a girl friend. He had told her he was in a dry period, suffering writer's block. She put his little Sony in his lap and told him that was his proper subject: "It is sort of your life story." He asked her, "You mean write about TV?" Her answer was, "Sure. About your relationship with TV. What it meant to you and all."22 So he wrote his book about what TV had done to him:

> What came into my mind was Peter Pan. I remembered how that broadcast had haunted me, how much I had wanted to go, too--to Never-Never Land. The place where dreams are born. Maybe that was what the basic appeal of television was. It persuaded me for a half hour, or an hour, or however long the daydream lasted, that I could be other than myself, that I could actually fly. 23

The irresistible power television had over Donald Bowie seems to be, if not universal among children and young people, at least widely felt. Personal violence, in imitation of TV is, of course, meat for the newspapers, and they give it full play. Headlines are made when a group of girls in San Francisco torture another girl sexually, exactly as they had seen it on TV. 24 A boy in Florida murders an 82-year-old neighbor woman and claims an episode on Kojac made him do it. His lawyer claimed:

> This is a documented case of an immature boy who, at the moment of this crime, could not know whether he was acting out a TV crime drama or was committing a cold-blooded, premeditated murder ...
> When he was unable to keep up socially with his classmates, he turned to the one friend he had--television--with its Barettas and Kojacs and Police Woman. 25

In 1979, when Battlestar Galactica was canceled, a 15-year-old boy committed suicide by jumping off a bridge in St. Paul. His parents said "the boy's whole life was wrapped up in the television space show."26

Not only lurid programs, but commercials, come in

for a lot of criticism. There is no question about their influence. Many of them are cleverly made by skillful manipulators of words and images. The most persuasive commercials--the ones that gull multitudes into buying for big prices products that are not only unnecessary but quite possibly dangerous--can make millions for their sponsors. Such enormous profits are irrefutable proof of the overwhelming power of the medium to persuade.

Psychologists have learned that serious conflicts are set up in children seven to ten years old by "misleading" advertisements. The children "begin to perceive various forms of adult hypocrisy."27 After a few more years, the children "simplify the problem by accusing all advertising, like many other aspects of the adult world, to be a total pack of lies."28 These findings, reported in the Baltimore Sun, November 12, 1975, were made by Thomas G. Bever, professor of psychology and linguistics at Columbia University. Dr. Bever said television commercials "may represent one of the first examples of the institutionalized hypocrisy."29

Between the long hours of trash that befouls the airwaves there are, of course, some inspiring and intellectually challenging programs, both on public and commercial TV. Here is one example, as reported by Martha Mather in the Baltimore Sun, March 23, 1979. A group of six medical students at Harvard in talking together found that they were all drawn to medicine by "Mr. Wizard."

> He was the neighbor we dropped in on every Saturday, just to see what wonderment he'd concoct in his backroom laboratory. He'd taught millions of us young busting-to-learn kids about what causes ripples in ponds, why the wind blows, what it's like to travel in space, why volcanoes erupt and why starfish have survived for generations. 30

"Mr. Wizard," in real life a distinguished science editor, reported feedback from countless children who had seen his show and were decisively influenced by it.

One of the most obvious facts of our time is that TV is a mighty force exerting both positive and negative influence. It appears to be the most powerful of the mass media in its immediate impact on human behavior. And as with movies it seems to make the strongest impact on the young.

To find out how TV affects viewers and to compare it with reading, Peter Crown, a psychologist, monitored the brain waves of readers and watchers. An article in American Libraries, September 1979, described the research. An electroencephalogram showed

> a difference in brain function between reading and watching TV. The size of the TV screen is very small compared to peripheral vision, which is 180 degrees. So when you watch TV, your eyes don't move much at all. This helps with the relaxation response ... where people watched a half hour of television and read Time magazine for half an hour [there was] a difference in brain activity-- and the difference was as you might predict: reading showed a more activated brain wave state than did watching television ... 31

With this glance at a few examples of the influence of movies and TV on individuals, it is time to go to the main business of catching some great men and women in the act of reading.

I will try to discover if, as John Barth claimed, reading really does shake lives "to the core" and cause life to "turn around real corners." Whether "literature remains the only medium that gets directly inside our interior lives" may not be provable. But consideration of the effect of reading should be useful in determining the place of printed language as a "time-binder," in Alfred Korzybski's word, essential to the transmission of the thoughts and ideas basic to an advanced culture.

Chapter 3

DECISIVE READING OF SOME GIANTS OF LITERATURE

It is the nature of artistic genius to produce something unique. Certainly the literary masterpieces of Dante, Chaucer, Cervantes, Shakespeare, Goethe, Whitman, Melville, Flaubert, Tolstoy, Mark Twain, and James Joyce each bear the unmistakable stamp of the author. They are not easily confused with each other. However, the writers had much in common. All were superbly skilled in transforming the products of their imaginations into imperishable writing that still speaks, after centuries or generations, to literate people everywhere. They have added immeasurable intellectual capital to civilization. They are giants beyond question.

Since the influence of these writers has been so pervasive, enriching and often changing the lives of countless readers, an inquiry into their most decisive encounters with books should throw light on the power of print and how it is received and transmitted by literary geniuses.

- DANTE ALIGHIERI, 1265-1321 -

When, in the first canto of The Divine Comedy, Dante recognized Virgil as his guide, he exclaimed:

> o honor and light of the other poets! may the long study avail me and the greater love, which made me search thy volume? Thou art my master and my author; thou alone art he from whom I took the fair style that has done me honor. 1

This is one of the most deeply felt acknowledgements by one writer to another of the influence of his writing.

Florence, as Dante knew it, was alive with literary

activity. His other refuges during his long exile were also centers of learning and culture. He was familiar with the ancient Latin writers as well as the works of his contemporaries. Dante's early schooling was under the guidance of two Latin masters, Brunetto Latini and Guido Cavalcante. It was Brunetto, Dante said, who taught him "how man becomes eternal"[2] through his writing. The influence of the Sicilian school and of Guittone d'Arezzo was strong in Dante's early poetry. And his La Vita Nuovo shows traces of Boethius, Cicero, Saint Augustine, and other ancient writers.

After the death of Beatrice, his ideal woman and symbol of spiritual love, Dante came under the spell of Virgil, Ovid, Lucan, and Statius. The religious works of Aquinas led him to Aristotle. Medieval authors who stirred him were Albert the Great, Saint Bonaventure, and Averroës. A Provençal troubador, Arnaut Daniel, made a strong impression on him that was reflected in The Divine Comedy. Such was the reading of his early maturity that moved him and left tracks in his writing, according to Francis Ferguson in Dante (1966).

The "new sweet style,"[3] popularized by Guido Guinizelli of Bologna also affected Dante's writing. It was heard in the sad words of Francesca da Rimini, when Dante found her and Paolo among the lustful sinners in the first circle of hell. Francesca sighed, explaining how they died together because of "Amor, che cor gentil ratto s'apprende," or "Love which quickly lays hold on gentle heart."[4] Guinizelli had a line so similar it must have been Dante's source: "Amore e'l cor gentil son una cosa," or "Love and the gentle heart are a single thing."[5]

It is clear from these few examples that Dante's reading, wide in scope and time, placed him in debt to many writers.

- GEOFFREY CHAUCER, 1343-1400 -

The evidence of Dante's "incalculable" influence on Chaucer was stressed by John Gardner in The Life and Times of Chaucer (1970). He wrote that Dante's

> genius would cast strange reflections in Chaucer's poetry--the sublime landscape of the Commedia becoming the burlesque-sublime scenery of the

House of Fame, the precise, often tragic characterization in, especially, the 'Inferno' and 'Purgatorio' becoming the comic and satiric portraiture of the Canterbury Tales--but however transformed by Chaucer's art, Dante's powerful influence would from now on always be visible. 6

That influence is unmistakable in The Parliament of Fowls where Chaucer, at the entrance to the garden of Love, repeated three times, "Thorgh me men gon into that blysful place,"7 as Dante had repeated at the Inferno's entrance, "Per me si va"8 (Through me one goes.) As the Italian poet showed compassion for Francesca's excessive love, Chaucer was indulgent in Troilus and Cressida toward the passion of Troilus. More evidence of the Florentine's influence is found in Chaucer's favorite line, "For pitee renneth sone in gentil herte,"9 which he used five times with slight variations. It came from Dante's already cited "Amor, che al cor gentil ratto s'apprende," which, as we have seen, came from Guinizelli. Chaucer put an amusing twist on Dante when, in The Parliament of Fowls, he had himself dragged into the garden by force, 10 whereas Dante entered Hell under the reasoned persuasiveness of Virgil. 11

Like Dante, Chaucer was at home in both ancient and current literature. He had been schooled in the classics at Southampton and London. According to Marchette Chute in Geoffrey Chaucer of London (1964), he found in Ovid's Metamorphoses a model of lively storytelling in a clear style, a fascinating account of the gods, and good lessons in Latin. Young Geoffrey also was deeply impressed by the New Poetry of Geoffrey de Vinsauf. He called him his "deere maister"12 in The Canterbury Tales. Gardner found "the key element in Chaucer's education" was Boethius' Consolation of Philosophy, "the most important single book of the age."13 Chaucer translated Boethius's book from the Latin and drew on it for several of his shorter poems. He took whatever struck his fancy from any source.

Chaucer acknowledged that he learned from Petrarch, when he had the Oxford clerk tell the Canterbury pilgrims that the story of patient Griselda came from Petrarch at Padua. And Gardner showed that traces of Boccaccio were to be found "in the plot and general approach of major poems." The "easy going irreverence, the unabashed delight in obscenity," which "makes the erotic in Chaucer so much more vivid, in fact so much more healthy than the erotica of our day,"14 Gardner found coming from Boccaccio.

Another writer to whom Chaucer proudly proclaimed his indebtedness was Virgil. He paid this tribute in the Legend of Good Women:

> Glory and honour, Virgil Mantuan,
> Be to thy name! and I shal, as I can,
> Folow thy lantern, as thou gost biforn,
> How Eneas to Dido was forsworn.15

Here the English poet has subtly acknowledged the influence of both Dante and Virgil. Chaucer's use of his broad reading, recycling it in his own unique way, fully justifies calling him "a prince of borrowers."16

- MIGUEL DE CERVANTES, 1547-1616 -

Imprisonment has been important in the careers of a number of famous writers. One of these was Cervantes. He seemed to have a special affinity for jails. During his youth he was captured by Turkish pirates and held for ransom in Algiers. Later, when he was working in Seville, provisioning ships of the Spanish fleets, he was several times incarcerated for alleged mishandling of money. He was then around fifty years old, a scarred graduate of the school of hard knocks. Some of his writing had already been published, but it created no great stir.

During Cervantes' most momentous jail term, a fellow inmate was another down-and-outer named Mateo Alemán. The two became good friends. Alemán had written a book which he was convinced, according to Francisco Navarro y Ledesma in Cervantes: The Man and the Genius (1973), "was to be one of the most enlightening ... ever composed in Spain."17 He read it to Cervantes. It was grandiloquently titled The Panorama of Human Life, Adventures and Life of the Rogue Guzmán de Alfarache. The idea of Don Quixote came to Cervantes while he listened to his cell-mate's wild tale in that dismal Seville prison. When Cervantes walked out to freedom he carried some manuscript sheets under his arm. He gave credence to this strange story in the preface to his masterpiece, when he apologized to the reader for not making the book "the fairest, gayest, and cleverest that could be imagined."18 But, he explained, it was "begotten in a prison, where every misery is lodged and every doleful sound makes its dwelling."19

Among the host of authorities Cervantes acknowledged,

including Aristotle and Xenophon, the most prominent was Amadís de Gaula, a textbook of medieval chivalry. For Cervantes, it was both inspiration and target. In Don Quixote he tried to lampoon chivalry to death. Navarro y Ledesma assumed that young Miguel had sharpened his reading skills on the ballads that were hawked in the streets of Valladolid. Later, at school in Madrid, where he was taught the Latin classics, he became well acquainted with Ovid, Horace, and Virgil. But after wrestling with Aeneas, he would "turn exhausted to his beloved Amadís de Gaula."[20] Some years later, the spell ended. Amadís was no longer "beloved" and became ludicrous. Cervantes obviously enjoyed telling how poor, dotty old Don Quixote argued with high seriousness the merits of Amadís over all the other knights. He made fun of the don's all-night orgies with books about his hero. He was transported by the fabulous feats of the legendary knight, so that, "with little sleep and much reading his brains got so dry he lost his wits."[21]

Cervantes recognized the power of print. But at the same time he made fun of excessive reading, of which he had done much throughout his life. And most certainly, the reading he heard during his time in the Seville prison changed Spanish culture and the course of the novel.

- WILLIAM SHAKESPEARE, 1564-1616 -

The well-worn question, "What were Shakespeare's chief sources?," was answered at some length by H. R. D. Anders in Shakespeare's Books (1903). Anders wrote that the scope of the Bard's reading included English drama and literature, including popular books. Shakespeare paid special attention to Holinshed's Chronicles, and he was on easy terms with Plutarch, the Bible, and Ovid. Anders might have mentioned also Plautus and Seneca. Shakespeare was as bold in raiding the works of others as Chaucer or any other writer of consequence. But we can't catch him in the act. He left no autobiography. Since his family was prosperous and well placed in Stratford's society, he probably attended the local schools and picked up some knowledge of English history in addition to the classics and English literature.

In A New Companion to Shakespeare Studies (1971), the editors, Kenneth Muir and S. Schoenbaum, asked:

Who would read through Harsnett's Declaration of

Egregious Popish Impostures just to give a few
devils names like Flibbertigibbet or Hoppididance?
We must suppose, I think, that Shakespeare read
widely, perhaps desultorily, but with a keen exploratory interest in the intellectual world in which
he moved and to which he contributed. 22

That seems a reasonable guess. So the place to look
for the evidence is in his writing. Kenneth Muir's The
Sources of Shakespeare's Plays (1978) lets us see Shakespeare putting his reading to precise use. Muir found that
Timothy Bright's passage in Treatise of Melancholie,

the ayre for melancholicke folke, ought to be
thinne, pure and subtile, open, and patent to all
winds: in respect to their temper, especially to
the South, and Southeast, 23

was turned by Shakespeare into Hamlet's

I am but mad north-north-west; when the wind is
southerly I know not a hawk from a handsaw. 24

And Bright's "the braine as tender as a posset curd,"25 in
Shakespeare becomes:

And with a sudden vigour it doth posset
and curd, like eager droppings into milk. 26

Now picture Shakespeare reading these ponderous lines
from The Troublesome Reign of King John:

Let England live but true within itself,
And all the world can never wrong her state.
Lewis, thou shalt be bravely shipped to France,
For never Frenchmen got of English ground
The twentieth part that thou hast conquered.
Dauphin, thy hand: to Worcester we shall march.
Lords all, lay hands to bear your sovereign
   with obsequies to his grave.
If England's peers and people join in one,
Nor Pope, nor France, nor Spain can do them
   wrong. 27

Shakespeare sharpened that into this:

This England never did, nor never shall,

> Lie at the proud foot of a conqueror
> But when it first did help to wound itself.
> Now these her princes are come home again,
> Come the three corners of the world in arms,
> And we shall mock them. Nought can make us rue
> If England to itself do rest but true. 28

These passages and the next are from the investigations of Karl J. Holzknecht's The Background of Shakespeare's Plays (1950). In his comparison of passages from the North translation of Plutarch's Life of Antony with Shakespeare's Anthony and Cleopatra, Holzknecht proved a borrowing based on a careful reading. Here is Plutarch:

> The poop ... was of gold, the sails of purple, and the oars of silver, which kept stroke in rowing after the sound of the music of flutes, hautboys, citherns, viols, and such other instruments as they played on the barge. And now for the person of herself: she was laid under a pavilion of cloth of gold of tissue, apparelled and attired like the goddess Venus ... 29

Here is Shakespeare's purloined version:

> The barge she sat in, like a burnish'd throne,
> Burn'd on the water. The poop was beaten gold;
> Purple the sails, and so perfumed that
> The winds were love-sick with them. The oars were silver,
> Which to the tune of flutes kept stroke, and made
> The water which they beat to follow faster,
> As amorous of their strokes. For her own person,
> It beggar'd all description. She did lie
> In her own pavilion--cloth-of-gold tissue--
> O'er-picturing that Venus where we see
> The fancy outwork nature ... 30

These few examples of the fruits of Shakespeare's reading show how gayly he stole whatever took his fancy. They also show how with his genius he transmuted the excellent into the superlative.

- JOHANN WOLFGANG VON GOETHE, 1749-1832 -

Among his many literary influences, Goethe described that of Shakespeare most vividly. He was a student at

Leipzig when the greatness of the English poet first came home to him. Here is his memory of the sharp impact in his autobiographical novel, Wilhelm Meister (1795-96):

> Wilhelm had scarcely read one or two of Shakespeare's plays till their effect on him became so strong that he could go no further. His whole soul was in commotion.... 'I cannot recollect that any book, any man, any incident in my life, has produced such important effects on me.... They seem as if they were performances of some celestial genius, descending among men, to make them, by the mildest instructions, acquainted with themselves.... The strength and tenderness, the power and peacefulness of this man, have so astonished and transported me, that I long vehemently for the time when I shall have it in my power to read farther.'[31]

Discounting for romantic license, the encounter with Shakespeare was still momentous. Its effects on Goethe were long lasting. They can be seen in his profound grasp of human nature, in his compassion, in his inventiveness of expression, in the universality of his interests, in the storms of his passions, and in his powerful impact on his readers.

As a man of learning, educated in law and letters, knowing several cultures, especially French and Italian, in addition to his own rich German culture, Goethe, of course, absorbed many strong influences in addition to Shakespeare. He recalled these influences in Truth and Poetry from My Life (1811-22). From his childhood, when the family read together, books and ideas were important in his life. At school, he disliked grammar because there were too many exceptions to the rules. The assigned reading was often dull. The New Testament was too easy. However, each school experience left some residue in his mind.

Like most boys, he loved adventure stories. The Adventures of Telemachus by Fénélon, even in a poor translation, had a "salutary and moral effect," and, he claimed, "it gave rise to a sweet and beneficent influence upon my mind."[32] After a strong dose of such reading, including Robinson Crusoe, The Island of Felsenburg, and Lord Anson's Journey Around the World, he wrote, "Now a still richer harvest came before me...."

This "richer harvest" was "a mass of writings ... which could not be called excellent, yet ... bring us many a meritorious action of former times."[33] Goethe was referring to the "Volksbücher" printed in Frankfort. They were on flimsy paper, but young Johann gobbled them up. He considered them "valuable remains of the Middle Ages."[34] One story came home to him with special force. It was Daniel in the Lion's Den by Moser. Its telling of the survival of an upright man through tribulations that almost destroyed him stayed with Goethe during the long years of the composition of Faust.

When a copy of Klopstock's Messiah, a book inspired by Milton's Paradise Lost, was smuggled in by a family friend, Goethe read it in secret since his father disapproved of it. He and his sister memorized "the most tender and the most violent parts."[35] They were especially taken by Portia's dream and "the wild despairing speech between Satan and Adramelech,"[36] and they "seized every opportunity to greet each other with these infernal phrases."[37] Was this the genesis of Faust in Goethe's mind?

Besides his heavy reading habit, the boy was addicted to the theater to which the family had passes. At the time Frankfort was occupied by the French. Racine and other French playwrights dominated the stage. Johann, who took readily to languages, was soon declaiming long speeches from the plays, "in the tone of the Protestant preachers."[38]

While recovering from an illness during his university years, Goethe dabbled in alchemy and mysticism. His physician suggested Welling's Opus Major Cabalisticum, Aurea Catena Homeri,[39] and other occult books. Their influence shows up in the sorcery and black magic in Faust.

At the University of Leipzig, Goethe deepened his interest in the arts. As a boy he had been fascinated by the rich illustrations in his father's folios. Among the books at Leipzig that impressed him were Gottsched's Critical Art of Poetry, Breitinger's book with the same title, and Lives of the Painters by d'Argentville. He began to make poems for the pictures. In this way he helped himself to see them more clearly and to write succinctly about them. He was convinced that through this process, "I came to more reflection, as they made me more attentive to the difference between the arts."[40] The impact of Lessing's Laocoön on Goethe was described by George Henry Lewes in The Life of Goethe (1965):

> Its effect upon Goethe can only be appreciated by those who early in life have met with this work, and risen from it with minds widened, strengthened, and inspired. It opened a pathway amid confusion, throwing light on many of the obscurest problems which torment the artist. It awakened in Goethe an intense yearning to see the works of ancient masters; and these beckoned from Dresden. To Dresden he went. 41

Although it was Lessing's book, which focused on ancient art, that had propelled him, as he began looking at the Dresden collections his eyes were opened to "landscape and Dutch painters, whose subjects appealed directly to his own experience."42 Here we see a book starting a reader in a certain direction, from which he goes off on a tangent.

At the University of Strassburg, Goethe had an experience that showed him a book which is considered dangerous may have an effect exactly opposite to what the censors fear. Baron d'Holbach's <u>Système de la Nature</u> derided religion and advocated an atheistic materialism. It was under German censorship. But when a copy fell into Goethe's hands, he couldn't see why it was banned. It seemed old-fashioned and gloomy. It turned him against metaphysics. Instead of being subverted, he laughed at d'Holbach.

However, his encounter with Spinoza was a milestone in Goethe's intellectual development. He remembered

> what calm and clearness came over me when I first turned over the posthumous pages of that remarkable man. This effect was still quite clear to me, though I was not able to recall the particulars. 43

Then he read a book attacking the famous philosopher. This displeased Goethe, as did the Spinoza article in Bayle's <u>Dictionnaire Historique et Critique</u>. He wrote:

> I therefore hastened to the work again to which I had been so much indebted, and again the same air of peace floated over me. I gave myself up to this reading, and thought, while I looked into myself, that I had never beheld the world so clearly. 44

Spinoza's undogmatic religious attitude in his Ethics made a strong appeal to Goethe and had a lasting influence on his own tolerant beliefs.

After a long life of reading and writing in many fields, Goethe's final hours were spent with books. He had been reading Salvandy's Seize Mois, ou la Révolution et les Révolutionnaires, but he could not see to go on. His last words were, "More light!"45

- WALT WHITMAN, 1819-1892 -

While Goethe was famous in his youth, applauded in his middle age as a universal genius, and, in his later years, sought out and consulted as a sage, Walt Whitman, a boy when Goethe died, was a lifelong wanderer, an outsider, a pal of outcasts, and a scandal to the genteel world of letters. He died in squalor, neglected by all but a few loyal friends. But like Goethe, even though he wrote in "Song of Myself," "A morning-glory at my window satisfies me more than the metaphysics of books,"46 he was a man of books.

Whitman "read with astonishing application for a man so sociable, leisurely in his habits, so deceptively indolent,"47 according to Gay Wilson Allen's The Solitary Singer: A Critical Biography of Walt Whitman (1955). He spent a lot of time in the libraries of New York, making up for his skimpy schooling by avid and varied reading.

Among writers who made an obvious impact on Whitman was Lucretius. Whitman outlined On the Nature of Things in one of his notebooks. Book IV impressed him most. Patterned on Lucretius' lubricious men and women, "held in chains of Venus, while their limbs melt overpowered by the might of the pleasure,"48 Whitman, in "Children of Adam," wrote of

> Limitless limpid jets of love, hot and enormous, quivering jelly of love, white-blow and delicious juice, 49

and of

> Arms and hands of love, lips of love, phallic thumb of love, breasts of love, bellies glued together with love. 50

A less steamy aspect of the nature of things also attracted Whitman. His was a time of great excitement over scientific discoveries, about which the public often learned through lectures. Whitman listened to many such lectures. He was fascinated by new findings on the rise of the human race and speculations about man's place in the scheme of things. His poem "When I Heard the Great Astronomer"[51] seems to show that he heard O. M. Mitchel's <u>Six Lectures on Astronomy</u>. Allen was convinced that from this work "Whitman unmistakably drew ... for facts, ideas and figures of speech in many passages of 'Song of Myself' and later poems,"[52] and that he had read C. S. Rafinesque's <u>Celestial Wonders of Philosophy</u> and used the book's language. Rafinesque had written, "Even the Heavens are not stable, the orbs are ripening or growing or congregating in social clusters."[53] As Whitman put it:

> I visit the orchards of spheres and look at the product,
> And look at quintillions ripen'd and look at quintillions green.[54]

While Whitman looked to the stars for poetic ideas, he was also stirred by a force closer to home. This was the Young America movement. Its organ was the <u>Democratic Review</u>, to which he contributed. The movement's writers included many Jacksonian Democrats or Locofocos. They wanted to free American writers from the smothering influence of English literature. They called for a great People's Poet who would write about "the necessity and dignity of labor."[55] He would celebrate the "native nobility of an honest and brave heart," downgrading rank and wealth in favor of "honorable poverty and a contented spirit." The goal would be the "brotherhood and equality of man."[56] The self-reliant Poet would hold center stage. All these ideas were congenial to Whitman. One cannot read very far into him without finding them. Here is "Me Imperturbe":

> Me imperturbe, standing at ease in Nature,
> Master of all or mistress of all, aplomb in the midst of irrational things,
> Imbued as they, passive, receptive, silent as they,
> Finding my occupation, poverty, notoriety, foibles, crimes less important than I thought,
> Me toward the Mexican sea, or in the Mannahatta or the Tennessee, or far north or inland,
> A river man, or a man of the woods, or of any

> farm-life of these States or of the coast, or the lakes or Kanada,
> Me, wherever my life is lived, O to be self-balanced for contingencies
> To confront night, storms, hunger, ridicule, accidents, rebuffs, as the trees and animals do. 57

Another influence on Whitman's way of life, according to Allen, was the writing of George Sand. He had read her <u>Consuelo</u> and <u>The Countess of Rudolstadt</u>,

> in which a poet labored as a journeyman carpenter and wore the costume of a day laborer as a symbol of his proletarian sympathy. 58

Universal in his enthusiasms, Whitman loved Italian grand opera along with the songs of wild birds. He carried Homer and Shakespeare in his pockets on outings to Coney Island. And he sang the glories of France and the French, along with the magnificence of California and the Californians, both places and peoples not personally known to him. His acceptance of his inconsistency was as American as the <u>inconsistency itself.</u> <u>He explained in "Song of Myself":</u>

> Do I contradict myself?
> Very well then I contradict myself,
> (I am large, I contain multitudes). 59

Among the multitudes he contained were many Greek and Latin classics in translation, some Asian mystics, the Bible, Shakespeare, Rousseau, Tom Paine, Shelley, Hegel, Goethe, Carlyle, Emerson, Margaret Fuller, phrenologists, water cure advocates, and more such self-designated messiahs who reflected the infinite variety of human concerns, wisdom and nonsense.

Whitman's writing is a richly flavored blend of his many literary influences and his sweaty, exuberant American experience.

- HERMAN MELVILLE, 1819-1891 -

Once when he was depressed because he had failed to win recognition for his writing, Melville found comfort and assurance in Hawthorne's <u>Mosses from an Old Manse</u>, which had come out in 1846. Reading it was a crucial experience for Melville. In an essay about the book he wrote:

> The soft ravishment of the man spun me round about in a web of dreams, and when the book was closed, when the spell was over, the wizard 'dismissed me with but misty reminiscences, as if I had been dreaming of him.'60

But before he was dismissed "with but dreamy reminiscenses," Melville had absorbed Hawthorne's essence. He had found "a great, deep intellect, which drops down into the universe like a plummet," and a "power of blackness" which "derives its force from its appeals to that Calvinistic sense of Innate Depravity and Original Sin." This "blackness," he wrote, "fixes and fascinates me."61 Melville, who was struggling to finish Moby Dick, said "Hawthorne had dropped germinous seeds into my soul."62 Those seeds revealed to Melville the allegorical character of Moby Dick. Edwin Haviland Miller, in his Melville (1975), called Melville's essay, Hawthorne and His Mosses, "a love letter, a confession which Melville can safely make within what purports to be a book review." Its reverberations, he said, "were to be heard and felt throughout Melville's life."63

Melville's mother said that Herman was not fond of books at the age of five, but as he grew older, like Whitman, he read widely. And his early reading echoed in his writing, as did his later reading of Hawthorne. Miller found that before he wrote Typee, his first South Sea tale, Melville had crammed on a stack of books loaded with all the available information--geographical, social, and anthropological--on the far reaches of the Pacific. It was said he could have written the book without ever having left home. But he did leave home, wandering the seas as Whitman had wandered ashore. When he wrote the first words of Moby Dick, "Call me Ishmael," he was naming himself. Dana's Two Years Before the Mast helped him prepare for the life of a sailor ahead of him on his several voyages, beginning with his first on the Acushnet.

His seagoing experiences were a few years behind him when Melville wrote Moby Dick. In addition to Hawthorne, the Bible, Milton, Byron, Goethe, Carlyle, Emerson and Shakespeare were all among his intellectual resources as he toiled through the agony of creation. He told of having read Shakespeare "with eyes ... tender as young sparrows."64 The somberness of Measure for Measure and King Lear was within him as he wrote.

- GUSTAVE FLAUBERT, 1821-1880 -

One of Flaubert's crucial literary encounters was with Goethe's Faust in a French translation. As Philip Spencer noted in Flaubert: A Biography (1952):

> Goethe's poetry overcame him like wine; his head swam and his eyes blurred; as he staggered home Rouen was less real to him than the cell of the despairing philosopher. 65

Twenty years after his reading of Faust, some of the poem's preoccupation with good and evil, honor and temptation, and the conflict in values stayed in his consciousness and found its way into Madame Bovary. There were other influences, of course. At least two local incidents suggested the framework of the story to Flaubert. But the wild romanticism of Goethe was there, curiously tamed and transmuted into the rigid order of what has been called the first realistic novel.

Flaubert was suffering through his five-year travail to find the exactly right words for Madame Bovary at the same time that Melville was bogged down in New York, trying to get a government job that would allow him to continue writing. Like Melville, he had been slow in reading, but not because he was dull. He explained to his mother, when she got after him for lagging in mastering the alphabet, "Why bother, since Papa Mignot can read?"66 Papa Mignot, a neighbor, was full of fantastic stories, and little Gustave hung around for hours to savor them. The family maid, when he begged, also told him wild folktales and legends about the witches and magicians of her native valley. So the child's imagination was kept fed.

As he learned to read in school, Gustave quickly went from fairy tales to forbidden books. The classics and authors who wrote with the famous French clarity were pushed by his teachers. They would have been dismayed to know their pupil was gorging himself on Byron, Hugo, Lamartine, Rousseau, Rabelais, Montaigne, Scott, and Shakespeare. He was a committed romantic at fourteen, impatient of any limitation on his choice of books, never guessing that in time his own writing would be game for prissy censors, busy as always, sniffing out and trying to suppress frank truths about life written in a beguiling style.

Like most careful writers who try for convincing accuracy of historical detail, Flaubert relied on factual sources to augment his native imagination. In preparing for Salammbô, he ransacked the libraries of Paris and came away with piles of books and reams of notes. To get it right about the trees at Astarte's temple, he studied a 400-page memorandum on the pyramidal cypress. He perused the ancient writers Silius Italicus, Pliny, Plutarch, Xenophon, and Athenaeus, as well as the monographs of the Académie des Inscriptions. His main authority was Polybius, the historian who was with Scipio when he took Carthage. It was said that when he completed Salammbô, Flaubert knew all there was to know about the period. No wonder he complained, "I am sated with books. I belch folios."67

- LEO TOLSTOY, 1828-1910 -

Like Flaubert, Tolstoy was exquisitely sensitive to his reading. And his most telling reading, like that of his famous French contemporary, has been documented. He kept detailed notebooks for many years and gratefully acknowledged his literary debts. When he was about twenty, he listed these titles as having had "immense influence" on him: The Gospel According to Saint Matthew, Sterne's A Sentimental Journey, Rousseau's Confessions and Emile, Gogol's Vii, and Dickens' David Copperfield. The following had "very great influence": Rousseau's La Nouvelle Héloise, Pushkin's Eugene Onegin, Schiller's The Robbers, Turgenev's A Sportsman's Sketches, Druzhin's Pauline Saks, Grigorovich's Anton Goremyka, and Lermontov's A Hero of Our Times. Tolstoy attributed "great influence" to Gogol's The Overcoat, Ivan Ivanovich, Nevsky Prospect, and Prescott's Conquest of Mexico. Beyond their influence on him, he believed that A Sportsman's Sketches and Anton Goremyka, which for the first time portrayed peasants compassionately, not merely as "a part of the landscape," along with Uncle Tom's Cabin, had helped destroy slavery throughout the world. 68

The books Tolstoy valued were mostly important, and many were classics. However, he said, "It is an odd thing, but reading bad books helps me detect my own faults more than good ones." He claimed, "Good books reduce me to despair."69 He must often have been despairing.

In <u>Tolstoy</u> (1967), Henri Troyat described young Leo's nights when women dominated his lustful thoughts. They drew him with their seductiveness and repelled him as evil at the same time. But during the day he was on a more intellectual level, with Rousseau and Descartes. He was fascinated by Descartes' "I think, therefore I am." He amended it to, "I want, therefore I am."70 When he came to Rousseau, "<u>The Confessions</u> thundered through his brain like an earthquake." It showed him that his "sordid instincts" and secret sins were not unique, and that cowardliness, lying, and cruelty probably were shared by all men. As he read, he felt a shock of recognition: "I thought I was reading my own mind and simply added a few details here and there."71 So persuasive was Rousseau's formula for the simple life that Tolstoy shucked off his dandified clothes, put slippers over his bare feet, and wore a plain all-purpose garment he made himself of coarse linen.

When he went to Kazan to study at the university, he dressed more conventionally. But he asserted his individuality by staying away from classes and choosing his own reading, from which he fashioned rules of life. He would abstain from women, do everything for himself, be good but keep it secret, and live modestly even if he should get rich. He violated all these rules during the following years of libertine excesses in Moscow. But he returned to austerity years later when his fleshly fires burned low.

When Tolstoy settled down, happily married, at Yasnaya Polyana, the family estate, in the early 1860s, he already had in mind the idea for <u>War and Peace</u>. He spent a whole winter buried in books, studying to buttress his knowledge of the Napoleonic period and its main historic figures. His work on this task was demanding. He complained:

> You can't imagine the difficulties of this preparatory work, plowing the field I shall have to sow.... Studying, thinking over everything that might happen to the future heroes of a very big book, devising millions of schemes of all varieties and selecting the millionth part of them, it's terribly hard work. 72

After <u>War and Peace</u> came out in 1869, making Tolstoy famous, he began reading voraciously again. His novel had made him ponder the forces of history and human destiny. He feasted on Kant and Schopenhauer. To a friend he said, "Do you know what my summer has been?... One continuous roar of approval for Schopenhauer." He said it had been "a series of spiritual joys I have never known before."73 He read and reread the complete works of the German pessimist. And although it seems paradoxical that he should have found "spiritual joys" in them, he concluded that no man had been more profound or true about man's sufferings, his struggle with the will to live, or the importance of chastity as the way to happiness.

Another writer whose ideas affected him deeply was Henry George. He caught George's enthusiasm for the single tax, and his own convictions on the evils of great wealth were reinforced by the American reformer.

From these American and European writers, Tolstoy went to the Asians. He discovered some of his own ideas in Confucius, Lao-tzu, and Buddha. He then immersed himself in religion and philosophy, especially in the Gospels, Epictetus, and Marcus Aurelius.

Out of all this reading Tolstoy formulated a new faith, a kind of Christian anarchy. Following his years of self-indulgence, during which he fathered thirteen children and enjoyed the privileges of the master of an estate worked by serfs, he dusted off his rigorous rules for living. He became increasingly ashamed of living so comfortably when his serfs were illiterate and near starvation. He drifted further and further away from the familiar ways of polite manners and customs. He worked in the fields alongside his serfs. Alarmed by his actions and abhorring his radical beliefs, his family saw him as a threat to their security.

When finally he left home in despair and confusion and died in a remote railway station, it was because he had been driven by convictions to which his reading had contributed greatly.

- MARK TWAIN, 1835-1910 -

While Tolstoy wandered physically and intellectually

in Russia, Mark Twain was restlessly exploring the American landscape and a good part of the rest of the world. He constantly studied men and women, geography, culture, economics, and politics. As printer, journalist, editor, novelist, and travel writer, he lived much in the world of print.

His most decisive reading encounter came when, as he reported in his Autobiography, published in 1924, twelve years after his death,

> I had been reading Lieutenant Herndon's account of his explorations of the Amazon and had been mightily attracted by what he said of coca. I made up my mind I would go to the head-waters of the Amazon and collect coca and trade in it and make a fortune. I left for New Orleans on the steamer Paul Jones with this great idea filling my mind. 74

He was then twenty-two years old, still known as Sam Clemens, and highly suggestible. On the voyage down the river, he made friends with Horace Bixby, a pilot. Pretty soon he was taking a turn at the wheel. When he got to New Orleans, no ships were scheduled for Para, from which he intended to ascend the Amazon. His disappointment was cushioned when he began figuring he might just as well try the exciting job of river pilot. So he paid Bixby to teach him the delicate art of steering steamboats through the tricky currents of the Mississippi. The best-selling Explorations of the Valley of the Upper Amazon by William Lewis Herndon was the bait which, when taken, led Sam Clemens not to his original goal of making himself a coca tycoon, but, in turn, to steamboat piloting, to adopting the name Mark Twain, to becoming chronicler of the Far West in its wilder days, and writing The Adventures of Tom Sawyer and The Adventures of Huckleberry Finn. Herndon's book also gave him a start toward becoming a globetrotter, spellbinding lecturer, and world-renowned man of letters, upon whom Harvard and Oxford universities were proud to confer honorary degrees. This is one of the best examples I have come upon of reading that had a result as pervasive as it was unexpected.

In Cyril Clemens' Young Sam Clemens (1942) there is information on the boy's early reading. Although Hannibal, Missouri was anything but a center of culture, Sam Clemens would go some to get a book he wanted. When a Yankee pedlar displayed his wares one day at the town pump, Sam's eye was caught by the bright yellow cover of Judge Halliburton's Clockmaker, a story of the adventures of Sam Slick. It was, Sam considered, "a tarnation bargain,"75 so he cadged some nickles from his cronies and haggled successfully for the book. At Sunday school, he read the books given as prizes, but he found them too pallid and pious for his taste. He liked lively tales such as Marryat's Mr. Midshipman Easy.

As a small-town printer, an occuption of his youth, Sam Clemens set type every week for a chapter from a novel by Dickens, Thackeray, or Bulwer-Lytton. So he came to know popular writers while filling gaps left by his own skimpy schooling. It is possible that this experience turned his thinking toward writing. He was always open to influence. During his printing years, it was said he once picked up a piece of printed paper in the street out of professional interest. It was a leaf from a biography of Joan of Arc, telling of her trial. Was this still in his memory many years later when he wrote Personal Recollections of Joan of Arc?

When Sam Clemens showed up in New York in 1853 to work as a printer and to enjoy the pleasures of the great city, he located himself close to the Mechanics Library. There, in the biggest library he had ever seen--it held over 4,000 books--he plunged in. During many evenings he went through much of Shakespeare, Cervantes, Scott, and Fielding. He was especially attracted to the essays of Bacon, Addison, Johnson, and Lamb. These he read over and over. He did not much care for Goldsmith's The Deserted Village or The Vicar of Wakefield. When he tried Pride and Prejudice, he had to give up halfway through. For him, "any library was a good one, provided only that it contained no books by Jane."76 The strong stuff was his meat. His own wild, exaggerated style and his choice of rough subjects were not inspired by delicacy and refinement.

Back again in the Middle West, after his hitch in New York, he continued his heavy reading. With a fellow worker in St. Louis, he read and argued over Pickwick Papers, Pendennis, and The Decline and Fall of the Roman Empire. In Keokuk, where he spent two years before his aborted Amazon venture, his friends saw that, although he seemed aimless, he always carried books with him. He was often observed reading Carlyle, Macaulay, and Prescott. Obviously Sam Clemens was a compulsive self-educator of discrimination. When a friend asked one day what he was reading, he said it was Phoenixiana. George H. Derby, the author, an Easterner, had beaten Sam Clemens to the West by some years. He wrote funny stories. Sam told his friend, "one of these days I'll write a funnier book myself. Wait and see."77 His friend doubted Sam would do it because he was too lazy. That was way off the mark. The young printer read with care, and he assimilated what he read. He took his own challenge and not only wrote more popular books than Phoenixiana, he borrowed some of Derby's yarns as storytellers cheerfully have done since before Homer.

The influence of Mark Twain, of course, has been pervasive and powerful. One of the most striking comments on the Mark Twain impact was made by Hendrik Van Loon in the foreword to Cyril Clemens' book:

> I first met Mark Twain when I was about twelve years old in a Dutch version of Tom Sawyer ... I liked it but vaguely felt that life in the mysterious country I never expected to see must, indeed, be different from that lived in my respectable land where little boys did not walk about without shoes! The scenes in the cave kept me awake many a night and I thanked the good Lord (with whom I was on intimate terms in those days) for having put my cradle in a land without hills. 78

Years later, when he was past being scared by stories about kids lost in caves, Van Loon was stranded in Warsaw during the 1906 Revolution,

> with nothing to do but read Mark Twain, and I have learned since to appreciate him as one of our weirdest but most useful philosophers. In fact, I have come to have such a personal affection for him that I am almost glad he is not obliged to be an immediate witness of the lunacy and cruelty and bestiality of our present world from fear of his being obliged to weep too much. And today he would have found it very difficult to laugh. I doubt whether he still reads the papers. He probably spends his leisure hours playing chess with Montaigne while Erasmus acts as a kibitzer. 79

Van Loon's tribute, touching as it was, left out an important aspect of Mark Twain's writing: his books on the unfunny qualities of the "damn'd human race,"80 such as The Gilded Age, To a Person Sitting in Darkness, and What Is

Man? These grew out of his own bitter experiences, but they were also influenced by his reading of Gibbon and the newspapers which, during Mark Twain's last years, were full of theft-by-theft accounts of the plundering of America by the robber barons.

- JAMES JOYCE, 1882-1941 -

Joyce was even more restless than Mark Twain. He never did settle down. He was better educated than the American humorist and entranced by the complications and possibilities of language. Where Mark Twain specialized in the simple story, told with riotous but unerotic touches (except in his underground writing), Joyce delighted in complexity and ribaldry, enriched by his deep knowledge of several languages. Both men were omnivorous readers and their reading was reflected in their work.

In his autobiographical novel, A Portrait of the Artist as a Young Man (1916), Joyce wrote of childhood evenings spent with The Count of Monte Cristo. He was haunted by the dark avenger and fascinated by the island cave, of which he built a model. He could lose himself in his reading. He was moved by

> an old neglected book written by saint Alphonsus Liquori, with fading characters and sere foxpapered leaves. A faded world of fervent love and virginal responses seemed to be invoked for his soul by the reading of its pages in which the image of the canticles was interwoven with the communicant's prayers. 81

Possessed of unusual critical ability while he was still a student at University College, Dublin, Joyce recognized the genius of Henrik Ibsen. According to Richard Ellmann in James Joyce (1959), Ibsen changed Joyce from an Irishman into a European. He learned Dano-Norwegian to read Ibsen in the original. He was said to be so knowledgeable about European literature that there were few major works of the late nineteenth century with which he was not familiar. Before he was twenty, he had read Zola, Hauptmann, Verlaine, Huysmans, D'Annunzio, Tolstoy, and many more. He went at Dante so hard that his friend, Oliver St. John Gogarty, called him "the Dante of Dublin."82 Joyce thought Castiglione's The Book of the Courtier had made him more polite, but to Gogarty he had actually become less sincere.

Among the books that seemed to have a perceptible influence on his writing were Horton's A Book of Images and Hauptmann's Hanneles Himmelfahrt. The Horton book was strange and fanciful. In the Hauptmann play, the juxtaposition of a naturalistic setting with apparitions seems to have foreshadowed the Circe episode in Ulysses.

In his search for a style, Joyce went to the French by way of The Symbolist Movement in Literature by Arthur Symons. He translated Verlaine for practice in the use of language as the Symbolists used it.

So it can be seen that Joyce developed his unique and highly mannered style largely under the influence of his voluminous reading.

- OBSERVATIONS -

Most of the eleven giants of letters came from cultivated homes where books were valued and read, and where they heard stimulating talk. Cervantes, Whitman, and Mark Twain were a minority, with little intellectual stimulation in their homes. Only Melville was slow in reading, at least in his mother's judgment. With Flaubert, the slowness was due to laziness. Why bother learning when he could be read to?

About half of the eleven had the best educations available in their times and places. Goethe, who studied at two distinguished German universities, seems to have had the most thorough academic training, and he enjoyed lifelong close association with many of his most gifted contemporaries. There is speculation, but no proof, that Chaucer studied at Oxford. He had many Oxford friends. Dante, Cervantes, Flaubert, Tolstoy, and Joyce were all university men. It is thought that Shakespeare's formal education was limited to the public schools of Stratford. The three Americans, Whitman, Melville, and Mark Twain, had the most limited schooling.

All the writers were heavy consumers of literature. The scope of their reading was broad. Since printing with movable type had not yet come to Europe, Dante and Chaucer were limited to handwritten manuscripts. Dante, Chaucer, Cervantes, Shakespeare, and Goethe were at home with the ancient classics. All five had Latin and, except for Shakespeare, knew some Greek. Both secular and religious books were among their literary fare. Among books common to these earlier writers were the Bible and the works of Virgil and Ovid. From about the time of Whitman, although the classics were still read, usually in translation, the writers read more modern works. The romantics--Byron, Rousseau, Hugo, and Scott--became especially popular. Beginning with Goethe, almost all prized and read Shakespeare. Most enjoyed adventure stories when they were young.

    I was somewhat surprised not to find more examples of decisive reading experiences during early youth. Only about half of such reading occurred at that stage. Dante did not say when he came under Virgil's influence, but he acquired the "sweet new style" before he reached maturity. Chaucer probably discovered Dante during his early thirties on his first trip to Italy, and Petrarch seems to have attracted him at Padua, during one of his government missions. Cervantes received his most crucial literary stimulus in a Seville prison when he heard a wild rogue story from his cell mate. He was then fifty years old. Since Shakespeare seems to have conned his sources for utilitarian purposes, they must have been read when he was already a practitioner of his art. His sources were so many, it is hard to pin down his greatest reading experience. With Goethe it is easier. He was under twenty, a student at Leipzig, when Shakespeare put "his whole soul in commotion" and "astonished and transported" him. Whitman was in his thirties when he came under the spell of Lucretius on love and Mitchel on astronomy. Melville was in his late twenties, back from his Pacific adventures, when he read <u>Mosses from an Old Manse</u> and wrote, "The soft ravishment of the man spun me about in a web of dreams." While he was still in school in Rouen, Flaubert got hold of Goethe's <u>Faust</u>. The "poetry overcame him like wine; his head swam and his eyes blurred." It was an even more powerful and lasting stimulus that young Leo Tolstoy received when the <u>Confessions</u> of Rousseau "thundered through his brain like an earthquake" and pointed the way to the simple life. There was an oddity in the decisive effect the book on the Amazon had on Mark Twain at twenty-two. It jolted him into starting for Brazil and a rich coca coup. But the pull of the Mississippi was strong enough to hold him when he was frustrated in getting to the Amazon. Everything that followed occurred because of the false start the book induced. The force that changed Joyce, while he was still a student, from an Irishman into a European and the most astounding wielder of language of the twentieth century, who dazzled his contemporaries and turned the literary world upside down, was Ibsen.

Some of the writers remarked on the influence of slight, transient, and even trashy books. We don't know much about such reading done by Dante and Chaucer. Books were rare and expensive during their time. Only a small educated minority could read. The secular and religious authorities preferred it so. But Cervantes, picking up ballads on the streets of Valladolid, lived in a time when print was widely distributed. Shakespeare also probably came upon broadsides and pamphlets when he was a boy. Many of them were undoubtedly bawdy. Young Goethe eagerly pounced on the "Volksbücher" in Frankfort. Whitman said "even light reading could fertilize the mind," and he borrowed many light English and American novels from a circulating library. Later he called this amusement "Illusions of youth." Tolstoy, according to Troyat, read "everything that came into his hands."

The great writers considered here have these characteristics: Most of them began reading young in settings with plenty of books that were valued and read. Only about half were well educated academically. Subjective literature, especially poetry, strongly influenced most of them. But they were moved also by learned writings of ancient and contemporary authors. Most of them had catholic tastes. Most also spent time with the popular, even trashy, subliterature they found around them. The most crucial reading was done during the years after childhood up to the middle years. The impact was often cataclysmic and frequently reverberated, sometimes many years later, in mature work. In effect, they carried their reading experiences as time bombs in their nervous systems, or as ammunition to be hauled out and fired when needed.

It would be interesting to see other studies, in greater detail, on the impact of reading on a larger sample of writers of distinction, to discover whether these findings are typical, and also to provide a basis for definitive generalizations about the influence of reading on the geniuses of literature.

Chapter 4

DECISIVE READING OF SIXTEEN RELIGIOUS LEADERS FROM SAINT AUGUSTINE TO MARTIN LUTHER KING

These religious leaders were chosen because of their wide and enduring influence, because their decisive reading has been reported in some detail, because they are religiously diverse, and because their lives span over a millennium and a half. They are, if not typical, at least somewhat representative of leaders in a field that has had, and is still having, an enormous influence on a large segment of humanity.

Consideration will be given to the circumstances and extent of their reading and the impact their reading has made on their thoughts and actions, which so powerfully influenced their successors and followers.

The absence of a number of the very greatest religious leaders may be questioned. Why are there no accounts of the reading of Buddha, Moses, Jesus, and Mohammed? Little is known certainly about the details of the lives of these and other founders of great world faiths. Often the writing about them is so loaded with pious myths and exaggerations that it is impossible to know about their reading, or if, indeed, they could read. Moses, Jesus, and Mohammed seem to have been most strongly influenced and guided by what they saw, what they heard from others, by inner voices, and what they believed to be divine direction. Books, of course, were very scarce during their times. Conversion, always of central importance for a truly religious person, in ancient times seems to have been induced by the fervent preaching of zealots or the performance of what were perceived to be miracles.

With the early Christian leaders like Saint Augustine, Saint Thomas Aquinas, and John Wyclif, who were highly literate and recorded their lives, we begin to have strong

Religious Leaders / 39

evidence on the crucial impact of reading on religious leaders.

- SAINT AUGUSTINE OF HIPPO, 354-430 -

For one of the greatest thinkers of the early Roman Catholic Church, Augustine's beginnings were most unpromising. Born to a pagan father and a Christian mother in a Roman outpost in North Africa, he "loved not study."[1] He did come to love Latin, but he hated Greek. He was attracted to the theater. Stage plays, he said, "carried me away." They were "full of images of my miseries, and of fuel to my fire."[2]

While he was studying for government service in Carthage, he acquired a taste for philosophy from Cicero's Hortensius, which, he wrote, "altered my affections, and turned my prayers to Thyself, O Lord,"[3] But when he began to study the Scriptures he was disillusioned because the writing was "veiled with mysteries."[4] He could not follow it. He found the Scriptures "unworthy to be compared with the stateliness of Tully."[5] He was too proud to give in to the Bible.

Having completed his studies in rhetoric, essential for success in public office, Augustine went to Rome to teach. There, as he told it in his Confessions, the writings of Plotinus bent him toward Neoplatonism. However, he came to see this preoccupation with philosophy as a time of darkness. The philosophers had tempted him. But he became convinced that their "many and huge books" were only an "echo of God."[6] Even Aristotle left him cold. He could not accept a mechanical, statistical view of man. He took stock of how he had been spending his time:

> And what did it profit me that all the books I could procure of the so-called liberal arts, I, the slave of vile affections, read by myself, and understood? And I delighted in them, but knew not whence came all that therein was true or uncertain. For I had my back to the light, and my face to the things enlightened. Whatever was written, either on rhetoric, or logic, geometry, music and arithmetic, by myself without difficulty or any instruction, I understood. Thou knowest, O Lord my God; because both the quickness of

> understanding, and quickness of discerning, is Thy
> gift: yet did I not thence sacrifice to Thee. So
> then it served not to my use, but rather to my
> perdition, since I went about to get as good a por-
> tion of my substance into my keeping; and I kept
> not my strength for Thee, but wandered from Thee
> into a far country, to spend it upon harlotries....
> For what profited my good abilities, not employed
> to good uses.... 7

Augustine was teaching in Milan, unhappy, oppressed by a sense of his sinfulness, when reading completely changed his life:

> So was I speaking, and weeping in the most
> bitter contrition of my heart, when lo! I heard
> from a neighboring house a voice, as of a boy or
> girl, I know not, chanting, and oft repeating,
> 'Take up and read; take up and read.' Instantly,
> my countenance altered, I began to think most in-
> tently, whether children were wont in any kind of
> play to sing such words; nor could I remember
> ever to have heard the like. So checking the tor-
> rent of my tears, I arose; interpreting it to be no
> other than a command from God, to open the book
> and read the first chapter I should find. For I
> had heard of Anthony that, coming in during the
> reading of the Gospel, he received the admonition,
> as if what was read, was spoken to him; 'Go, sell
> all that thou hast, and give it to the poor, and
> thou shalt have treasure in heaven, and come and
> follow me.' And by such oracle he was forthwith
> converted to Thee. Eagerly then I returned to the
> place where ... I had laid the volume of the Apos-
> tle.... I seized, opened, and in silence read that
> section, on which my eyes first fell: 'Not in riot-
> ing and drunkenness, not in chambering and wan-
> tonness, not in strife and envying: but put ye on
> the Lord Jesus Christ, and make no provision for
> the flesh,' in concupiscence. No further would I
> read; nor needed I: for instantly at the end of
> this sentence, by a light as it were of serenity
> infused into my heart, all the darkness of doubt
> vanished away. 8

This encounter of Augustine with Saint Paul's Epistle to the Romans is one of the most striking examples of the power of reading to light up a life and turn it around. The impact was so profound that Augustine gave up teaching rhetoric and devoted the rest of his life to serving his God. Years later, he made in his <u>Confessions</u> one of the most intimate and revealing examinations ever written of the struggle of the mind searching for a faith. The influence of Saint Augustine's writings throughout fifteen centuries has been momentous and pervasive beyond calculation. He has been revered as a doctor of the Church since the Middle Ages. From Saint Bernard of Clairvaux to Paul Tillich, Augustine has inspired theologians who have credited him with getting to the heart of man's relationship with God. His fortuitous Bible reading started it all.

- SAINT THOMAS AQUINAS, 1224-1274 -

Thomas was the son of a family with a small feudal property near Naples. He was schooled as a monk at Monte Cassino, where he studied Latin and Greek. His family hoped he would work up to the abbacy of the monastery. But the monks were expelled and Thomas returned home. Then he studied at the University of Naples, where he had access to translations of ancient scientific works, just then available for the first time in Europe.

Attracted to the Dominicans, who were more democratic than other orders, Thomas wanted to study with them in Paris. But his family objected and held him prisoner for a year. However, he did get to Paris, then the great center of learning in Europe. His master was Albert the Great, a famous scholar and teacher. Thomas' brilliance as a student marked him for a distinguished career.

The influence of reading on that career was recounted in Thomas Pittenger's <u>Saint Thomas Aquinas: The Angelic Doctor</u> (1969). During his detention by his family, Thomas was said to have given careful study to the Bible. And he put in much time on Peter Lombard's <u>Sentences</u>, the most widely read theological textbook of the <u>Middle Ages</u>. Of Thomas' incarceration, his biographer wrote:

> His time spent in study was useful in later years, for it had not only given him a further grounding in the ordinary academic training of his time, but it also developed helpful habits which he

never lost. He learned how to concentrate on his reading. He also learned to read with more speed than seems to have been common at the time, while also retaining what he read.9

As the years went by Thomas won great respect as a teacher and expositor of religious thought. He was called upon to pass judgment on controversies and to revise theological studies. Having mastered almost all religious and philosophical thought of his time, he cited hundreds of works in his Summa Theologica, considered almost as authoritative as the Bible. Some notion of the impact of his reading on his ideas is shown in these paragraphs from Pittenger:

> Thomas spent much time reading Aristotle and hearing lectures about him. The young friar also made a careful study of the classical work entitled The Divine Names ... a study of the way in which human beings may think about and 'give names' to God; that is, how human language may be applied to the divine being.
> The Divine Names represents the Neo-Platonic way of thinking about Christianity, and is opposite from the Aristotelian way of dealing with such issues. Yet Thomas was able to assimilate the views ... in such a way that he could find value and a use for them....
> Another book which Thomas studied is the great Ethica of Aristotle. Once again he worked through it under the guidance of Albertus, who was giving a course on Aristotle's ethical ideas. Some twenty years later, Thomas wrote his own commentary on the same book, in which he shows astonishing mastery of the text and an ability to question it at point after point, even after he accepts the main thesis--that every man, in determining what is good, seeks happiness as his end, although the kind of happiness he seeks will determine the kind of man he is becoming. Thomas takes this thesis and uses it in a specific way. Presumably, he had long been pondering the ideas, since he had read the book as a student. Actually, all of his writing gives the evidence of long thought, careful consideration, and precision in putting down his conclusions.... 10

It can be seen from this passage that what Thomas learned from reading Aristotle, tested by lengthy weighing and questioning in his mind, was the cornerstone of his whole philosophy. That philosophy guided the thinking and behavior of Roman Catholics for hundreds of years. Its adherents converted uncounted unbelievers to the faith, and stimulated the minds of philosophers down to our own day. The reading of Saint Thomas Aquinas was one of history's most momentous influences on humanity.

- JOHN WYCLIF, 1330-1384 -

Like Aquinas, John Wyclif had a comfortable start in life. His status among the elite enabled him to secure his education at Oxford University. As a graduate, holding one of the university's choicest livings, he had everything going his way. But instead of playing it safe, following tradition, he spent his energies in the dangerous practice of throwing old accepted ideas overboard. He could not accept the hypocrisy of Church practices or the meanness of many of the clergy. This inability to accept the status quo, and his belief in his mission to bring the Bible to the people, led to his lifelong troubles and to his immortality. Herbert B. Workman's <u>John Wyclif: A Study of the English Medieval Church</u> (1966) documents many of the literary influences on this tough-minded forerunner of the Reformation.

Wyclif's knowledge was truly catholic. In his writings he quoted Plato; Gratian, the Italian monk who was called the father of the study of canon law; the decretals of Pope Gregory IX and Boniface VIII; John Andreae of Bologna; Thomas Aquinas; Duns Scotus; Grosseteste; and the Arabs, Avicenna of Bokhara, and Averroës of Córdoba. For his translation of the Bible he had to be familiar with its several Latin versions. As to the most respected ancient authority,

> He accepted almost unquestioned, as did all other thinkers of his age, the authority of Aristotle. He commonly calls him, without other designation, 'the philosopher' ... He acknowledges that Aristotle is a 'heretic,' but leaves his ultimate fate to the 'Searcher of Hearts.'11

Wyclif also was under the spell of Saint Augustine, so

much so that his students are said to have called him "John, son of Augustine."12 Workman suggested,

> In this they did right, for Wyclif owed the better part of his teaching to Augustine, whose exegesis and thoughts he repeatedly quotes and whom he praises because he founded his theology on reason and scripture.... He maintained that Augustine knew the truth better than Plato or Aristotle.13

Saint Augustine's truth, as Wyclif saw it, proclaimed that "the king has the image of God as the bishop has that of Christ."14 To Wyclif this meant

> that the king represents the glorified, ruling Christ, the priest the suffering, submissive Christ, or to put it in another form, the king represents the will, the priest the love of God.15

Such fanciful reasoning, common among medieval churchmen, gave Wyclif a solid standing with the King's party while it provoked his denunciation by the Pope. He was indeed indebted to his reading of Saint Augustine for his peculiar role as a pioneer in the gradual breaking of the Roman Church's power in England and abroad.

- JAN HUS, c. 1372-1415 -

Although he was born to a poor family in an obscure corner of Bohemia, Jan Hus made a great stir in the world as the leading Czech reformer of his time, a time when the Church, which was supposed to be blessed by stability, peace, love, and charity, was torn by schisms, abuses of power, and violent contention. Jan entered a Latin school and then went on to the University of Prague, earning his way as a choirboy. After receiving his master's degree, he began to teach in the university. As a student and later, like others aiming for a career in the Church, Jan carefully studied the writings of Aristotle, Augustine, Peter Lombard, and Aquinas.

How he came under the influence of Wyclif, won recognition as an independent-minded thinker, and then was burned at the stake, was set forth by Matthew Spinka in <u>Jan Hus' Concept of the Church</u> (1966). As Spinka reported,

> Knowledge of Wyclif's teaching was carried to
> Bohemia by the Czech students at Oxford.... Hus
> became thoroughly acquainted with Wyclif's books,
> which he read avidly and assimilated substantially.
> He wrote in 1411 that he 'and other members of
> our university possessed and have read these books
> for twenty or more years.' ... Hus even copied
> some of the treatises, namely De individuatione
> temporis, De ideis, De materia et forma, and De
> universalibus. In the margins of the last-named
> book, now preserved in Stockholm, he wrote approving remarks, such as 'Wyclif, Wyclif, you
> will unsettle a man's mind'; or 'What you have
> now read is worth a gulden...'; and 'May God
> grant Wyclif the kingdom of Heaven!'16

Although his reading of Wyclif opened Hus' eyes on many theological points, he did not accept all of the English reformer's radical ideas. The Bible was still his most treasured authority. Among other things, it spurred him to correct his personal behavior. He had been indulging in fine clothes and fun. But he admitted, "when the Lord God gave me the knowledge of Scripture, I abandoned that type of life."17

But his curiosity drove him to continue to read unorthodox books. And they kept him in hot water. He was ordered to surrender his copies of Wyclif's writings. When he delivered them personally to the archbishop, he ironically asked him "to mark any places he found erroneous so he could warn his congregation against them."18 He argued that to recognize and combat heresies one had to know them. And he quoted the Fathers of the Church in his defense.

The Church always had trouble with men who insisted on doing most of their thinking for themselves. Their charred bones were exhibited across Europe as warnings to others who might be tempted to stray from authority. That did not, however, keep those with questing minds, who felt the need for the stimulus of fresh ideas, from choosing their own reading.

It was both shameful and ludicrous that men like Hus were judged by ignorant clerics who could barely read the Latin writings upon which their judgments were supposed to be based. At the Council of Constance, where Hus was tried, his lawyer properly ridiculed

> those cardinals, bishops, monks and others, professors of law, who in four days have read through, examined, and drawn up a judgment on all the books of John Wyclif ... which even a hundred of the smartest devils schooled in all wickedness could not do.[19]

When the prosecutor Stanislav, speaking for the Church, charged Hus

> with willingness to accept the faith only to the degree that 'every faithful and devout Christian is bound to,' he retorted with devastating force that 'even if Master Stanislav were the pope, and all the doctors, pontiffs ... canons, and monks who along with him have pontificated at the Town Hall their conclusions they called catholic, were turned into cardinals, the faithful are not bound to believe these conclusions are the Catholic faith unless they are grounded in Scripture.'[20]

It is easy to see why the Church leaders could not allow a man to teach and preach who clung so stubbornly to Scripture, and was unwilling to accept the word of even the highest ranking clergy if it conflicted with his reading of the Bible. He had to be silenced. In his end, tied to a stake and burned, he was a true martyr to his reading and a witness to the unquenchable power of books.

- DESIDERIUS ERASMUS, c. 1466-1536 -

After attending schools in The Netherlands, Erasmus entered the priesthood. Then, following brief unenthusiastic diplomatic service, he entered the Collège de Montaigu of the University of Paris, where he studied theology with the Humanists, of whom he became the greatest exponent of his time.

In _Erasmus of Christendom_ (1969), Roland H. Bainton traced the intellectual development of his subject with special attention to the part reading played in making him the first scholar of the Northern Renaissance. At the Augustinian priory near Brussels, Erasmus

> discovered the works of St. Augustine in manuscript. He was so excited he took them to bed with him.

The monks were amazed and amused that one of
their number should go to bed with St. Augustine
and could not understand what on earth he had
found in the saint so to delight him. 21

Erasmus was delighted by ideas. He soaked up
Latin classics, especially Terence, Horace, Seneca, Cicero,
and Quintillian. He was "addicted" to Saint Jerome and to
Augustine. He had also read Peter Lombard, Aquinas, William of Ockham, Duns Scotus, and other medieval writers.
As a Humanist, Erasmus was receptive to ideas from many
sources. In his tolerance

> He was not worried over the erotic passages in
> the classics. After all the Old Testament has
> some very dubious stories unless they are allegorized.... Erasmus counselled not rejection but
> selection and that was one of the reasons he undertook to cull from the literature of antiquity the
> gems of wisdom which he called 'adages.'22

His open attitude toward reading, and his own liberating experiences with books of all sorts and persuasions,
led Erasmus to trust the written word, and especially the
power for good of holy literature. He wanted the inspired
word in the hands of "the farmer, the traveller ... the
Turks ... the mason, prostitutes [and] pimps."23 Of those
who worried about making the Bible so easily accessible,
Erasmus asked, "Do you think that the Scriptures are fit
only for the perfumed?"24

This great liberal was famous for his writings before
he was forty years old, an advisor to popes, and the "mentor of Europe."25 But he lived in a time of great danger to
independent thinkers--recall Jan Hus. He was cautioned by
Noel Beda, a high official of the University of Paris: "I
speak out of zeal for your salvation. Much of what you say
gives great scandal to Christian folk."26 But Erasmus, unafraid, answered Beda:

> Most excellent sir ... I am deeply touched by
> your solicitude for my salvation.... But why are
> you worried about those who rail with abominable
> calumnies, manifest lies, and virulent abuse? You
> cover their raging with the tender word of zeal.
> You reproach me for reading the poets. In my
> youth I loved the poets and considered that they
> contribute to a liberal education. 27

While Erasmus did not fear the consequences of his reading and the writing that stemmed from it, the Church authorities did not share his complacency. The liberalism that had inspired him to get out a revised edition of the New Testament based on the Greek text, and to find spiritual refreshment in the ancient pagans, was more than suspect. It smacked of heresy. Fear of the Reformation haunted the hierarchy. So all of Erasmus' brilliant writing, even on nonreligious subjects, was placed on the Index. And this drastic condemnation was ordered by a man who had once been his friend, Pope Paul IV.

In the life of Erasmus we see the strong and benign influence of reading on a sensitive, generous-spirited man of genius, and how his influence led to the banning of his writing. But, as usual with powerful writers full of liberating ideas, Erasmus has affected the thinking of cultured men and women down to our own day. Those bigots who tried to suppress his ideas are remembered, if at all, as enemies of charity and tolerance.

- MARTIN LUTHER, 1483-1546 -

As the son of a prosperous, ambitious Saxon father, Martin Luther was given a good education. After Latin school and a period of Bible study, he entered the arts program at the University of Erfurt, earning B.A. and M.A. degrees. Then he joined the mendicant order of Saint Augustine. He was selected for advanced theological studies at Wittenberg University, from which he received a doctorate in theology.

During his studies, Luther covered the whole range of ancient and medieval literature that bore on Christian thinking. The writings of Aristotle, Augustine, William of Ockham, and Peter Lombard were all familiar to him. His reading gave him models of religious and personal behavior as guides. Roland H. Bainton's Here I Stand: A Life of Martin Luther (1950) reviews some of that reading.

As a curious-minded and dedicated young clergyman, Luther involved himself in intellectual and organizational Church problems. He joined in the arguments between the Nominalists and the Realists that were agitating the theologians. He was also in the thick of the disputes over the degree of strictness and discipline that should prevail among the Augustinians. As one of the monks chosen to go to Rome to present an appeal in this controversy, he was dismayed at the worldly and even depraved lives of some of the highest clergy.

Luther was not only disturbed about the scandalous conduct he observed among the Roman priests; like many obsessively devout men, he was tormented by questions and doubts about his personal relationship to God. Polemical books did not resolve his problems. The authorities and propagandists he read disagreed with each other. He described his dilemma:

> I greatly longed to understand Paul's Epistle to the Romans and nothing stood in the way but that one expression, 'the justice of God,' because I took it to mean that justice whereby God is just and deals justly in punishing the unjust. My situation was that, although an impeccable monk, I stood before God as a sinner troubled in conscience, and I had no confidence that my merit could assuage him. Therefore I did not love a just and angry God, but rather hated and murmured against him. Yet I clung to that dear Paul and had a great yearning to know what he meant. 28

Luther stayed with the problem as his yearning for understanding drove him on. With his Bible open to Paul's Letter to the Romans before him:

> Night and day I pondered until I saw the connection between the justice of God and that statement that 'the just shall live by his faith.' Then I grasped that the justice of God is that righteousness by which through grace and sheer mercy God justifies us through faith. Thereupon I felt myself to be reborn and have gone through open doors into paradise. The whole of Scripture took on a new meaning, and whereas before the 'justice of God' had filled me with hate, now it became to me inexpressibly sweet in greater love. This passage of Paul became to me a gate of Heaven. 29

As a result of this sudden recognition of faith as the essential prerequisite for God's grace, in his translation of the Bible Luther added the word "alone" after "faith" in Romans 3:28, making it read: "For we hold that a man is justified by faith alone apart from works of the law."30

His new faith made Luther value Scripture, as he understood it, above official Church teaching. He suffered, as had Wyclif and Hus, for setting himself up as his own interpreter of the meaning of the Bible. His independence brought about his excommunication and the founding of his new church of protest. Few reading experiences have made the world-wide impact and influenced as many lives as Martin Luther's successful wrestling with the puzzling words of Saint Paul.

- SAINT IGNATIUS OF LOYOLA, 1491-1556 -

Although he came from a wealthy Basque family, Ignatius enjoyed little book learning. He served as a page and then a knight in the retinues of relatives. Knights in those days went to war. Fighting at Pamplona, Ignatius was hit in the legs by a French cannonball.

The Testament of Ignatius Loyola ... Taken Down from the Saint's Own Lips by Luis Gonzales (1900) tells how, during his long, painful recovery, reading changed his life. He had been a self-indulgent young man. His favorite books had been tales of chivalry, such as the famous Amadís of Gaul. So it was to be expected that

> when he felt better in health, he begged for some of those books wherein the wonderful adventures of illustrious men are written wherewith he might while away the time, for he was much given to the reading of these lying and vain romances. There was, however, nothing of the kind to be found in the house; but they gave him a book entitled The Life of Christ, and another called Flowers of the Saints, both in the Romance language.
> From the frequent reading of these books he acquired an interest in the matters therein treated of. Sometimes from this kind of reading, his attention would wander to those subjects whereof he used to read aforetime; at others, his mind was bent only on the vanities which interested him before his illness, and on many similar fancies just as they presented themselves to him.31

Among these distracting fancies was one "with which

his heart busied himself more than with all the rest." The young knight's thoughts ran to "what acts of service would be most fitting for him to offer to a certain illustrious lady." However, as the reverent account went on,

> by Divine mercy, through his recent reading, these thoughts began to give place to others. For when he read the Life of Christ our Lord and the Lives of the Saints, then he thought within himself and considered in this manner: 'What if I did this thing which Blessed Francis did? What if I copied Blessed Dominic in this?' And thus he imagined many things, setting himself difficult and hard tasks: and as he did so he seemed to feel their performance less difficult; and this, for no other motive than can be yielded by the thought: 'St. Dominic did this; therefore I also will do it: this was done by Blessed Francis; then I too will do it.'32

Gradually, so persuasive was the reading of holy things, that religion won over the temptations of the flesh. One night "as he lay awake he saw with open face the likeness of the Blessed Mother of God with her Holy Child Jesus." Ignatius was hooked for good. He intensified his religious reading and abandoned the violent life of a knight to become a pious pilgrim and beggar.

His wanderings took him to Montserrat, to a cave at Manresa, to Rome, and to the Holy Land. Then, his mind made up for a life in the Church, he studied for some years at Barcelona, Alcalá, and Salamanca. Along the way, he attracted a small group of followers. He also spent some time in jail for unauthorized preaching. Deciding to get the best possible education to prepare for his self-assigned mission, he went to Paris. There he worked, studied, and won the prestigious M.A.

From that time Ignatius became a world-renowned man of the Church. His Society of Jesus, his army of Christian knights, went to all corners of the world to bring the Word to heathens. Ignatius kept busy with writing and teaching. Like all who are obsessed with their missions, he was sometimes embattled and in trouble with Church leaders. But the highest authorities in Rome recognized the magnitude of his work and his charismatic leadership when he was canonized in 1622.

The global soul-saving career of Ignatius of Loyola had its beginning when he read about Jesus and the saints while his war wounds were healing.

- JOHN CALVIN, 1509-1564 -

As the son of a prosperous French family, John Calvin was given an excellent education. He attended school in the company of young noblemen in his hometown of Noyon in Picardy. Then he went to Paris to study at the elite Collège de la Marche and the Collège Montaigu. After he received his M.A. degree, his father sent him to study law at the University of Orléans. The course of his education and the evolution of his thinking was traced by François Wendel in Calvin: The Origins and Development of his Religious Thought (1963).

Calvin's first book, De Clementia, a study of a work by Seneca, written during his early twenties, showed the extent of his learning and his reading. His special knowledge of ancient literature and history was demonstrated in this work. In his other writings, Calvin showed he was well grounded in Saint Augustine, Erasmus, Budé, and other Church Fathers and religious philosophers. His education and reading put Calvin with the Humanists.

In his Institutes of the Christian Religion, which made Calvin a spokesman for reform, he told of his reading and what it did to him:

> When we read Demosthenes or Cicero, Plato or Aristotle or some others of their kind, I confess indeed that they wonderfully attract, delight and move us, even ravish our minds. But if we turn to the reading of the Holy Scriptures, whether we will or no they so pierce us to the heart and fix themselves within us that all the power of the rhetoricians and philosophers, compared with them, seems no more than smoke. [33]

As the Bible displaced the ancient philosophers in Calvin's affections, he changed from the tolerant humanist of De Clementia to a dour and strict master of a doctrinaire schismatic group. No deviation, however slight, from the new dogma, was allowed. As the theocratic dictator of Geneva, Calvin decreed punishment for such crimes as possession of

The Golden Legend, a collection of lives of saints. Owning a copy of Amadís of Gaul, the book that delighted Saint Ignatius and drove Don Quixote mad, was a serious offense. At one time in Geneva, the only reading allowed the guests in the "abbeys," that replaced public inns, was the Bible in French. The extremism of Calvin reached a frightful peak when the distinguished Spanish physician and theologian, Michael Servetus, was burned at the stake because he differed with Calvin on the doctrine of the Trinity.

It was one of the saddest occurrences of intellectual history that such a great man as Calvin was capable of such atrocious cruelty in the name of religion, especially when it was reading that made him leave his humanism behind for a life as a merciless tyrant.

- SAINT TERESA OF AVILA, 1515-1582 -

Like some others who became saints, Teresa suffered lengthy illness and uncertainty. She was tortured by a sense of guilt for her "grave sins and wicked life."[34] The story of her struggle for faith and her profound religious awakening was told in one of the most striking and revealing of autobiographies. It was reprinted as The Life of Teresa of Jesus: The Autobiography of St. Teresa of Avila (1960), translated and edited by E. Allison Peers.

Her home, under benevolent and devout parents, was warmed by a spirit of charity and compassion. Teresa recalled:

> My father was fond of reading good books and had some in Spanish so that his children might read them too. These books, together with the care my mother took to make us say our prayers and to lead us to be devoted to Our Lady and to certain saints, began to awaken good desires in me when I was, I suppose, about six or seven years old.[35]

But Teresa, like Ignatius, also was addicted to chivalrous tales. Her father frowned on such frivolous reading. Yet, "So excessively was I absorbed in it that I believe, unless I had a new book, I was never happy."[36] This led to what she later considered an unseemly vanity: "I began to deck myself out to try to attract others by my appearance...."[37] Then, to escape her own wayward tendencies and the influence of a relative from whom "I learned every kind of evil,"[38] she entered a convent. However, after a year and a half Teresa felt she was not cut out for the hard life of a nun. To make matters worse, she began having "serious fainting fits."[39] Then, she thought again about a religious vocation. Her father had been against it. But, she wrote,

> The fact that I had now become fond of good books gave me new life. I would read the epistles of Saint Jerome, and these inspired me with such courage that I determined to tell my father of my decision, which was going almost as far as taking the habit.[40]

Teresa's health continued to deteriorate. The doctors gave her up. She was in pain and feared that "all my nerves had shrunk."[41] In her extremity, she was shored up by memories of earlier reading:

> It was a great help to my patience that I had read the story of Job in the Morals of St. Gregory, for the Lord seems to have used this for preparing me to suffer.[42]

As important as the consolation of Job's story was to Teresa, it was as nothing to what she gained from her most momentous encounter with a book:

> It was at this time that I was given the <u>Confessions of Saint Augustine</u>, and I think the Lord must have ordained this, for I did not ask for the book nor had I ever seen it. I have a great affection for Saint Augustine, because the convent in which I had lived before becoming a nun belonged to his Order, and also because he had been such a great sinner. I used to find a great deal of comfort in reading about the lives of saints who had been sinners before the Lord had brought them back to Himself. As he had forgiven them I thought He might do the same for me. There was only one thing that troubled me, and this I have already mentioned: namely that, after the Lord had once called them, they did not fall again, whereas I had fallen so often that I was distressed by it. But when I thought of His love for me, I would take heart once more, for I never doubted His mercy, though I often doubted myself.

> Oh, God, help me! How amazed I am when I
> think how hard my heart was despite all the help I
> had received from Him! It really frightens me how
> little I could do by myself and how I was so tied
> and bound that I could not resolve to give myself
> wholly to God. When I started to read the Confes-
> sions, I seemed to see myself in them and I began
> to commend myself to that glorious Saint. When I
> got as far as his conversion and read how he heard
> that voice in the garden, it seemed exactly as if
> the Lord were speaking in that way to me, or so
> my heart felt. I remained for a long time dissolved
> in tears, in great distress and affliction. Dear God,
> what a soul suffers and what torments it endures
> when it loses its freedom to be its own master! I
> am astonished now that I was able to live in such
> a state of torment. God be praised, Who gave me
> life to forsake such utter death![43]

After her emotional bout with Saint Augustine, Teresa relied less on reading and more on a mystical union with God. She had worried about the harm she felt had come to her from forbidden books. But she was reassured: "the Lord said to me: Be not distressed, I will give thee a living book."[44] At first she could not understand this. Then it came to her:

> the Lord showed me so much love and taught me
> by so many methods, that I have very little need
> of books--indeed, hardly any. His Majesty Him-
> self has been to me the Book in which I have seen
> what is true. Blessed be such a Book, which
> leaves impressed upon us what we are to read and
> do, in a way that is unforgettable![45]

In a paradox, appropriately mystical, a book showed Teresa how to achieve union with God. During a Pentecost vigil, she went to a solitary spot to pray. Then she opened The Life of Christ by Ludolph of Saxony:

> As I read about the signs by which beginners, pro-
> ficients and perfect may know how the Holy Ghost
> is with them, it seemed to me, when I had read
> about these three states, that by the goodness of
> God, and so far as I could understand, He was cer-
> tainly with me then. For this I praised God and
> remembered a previous occasion when I had read

this passage and when I lacked what I have now; this I saw very clearly, and, as I became aware how different I am now, I realized what a great favour the Lord had granted me. 46

From this reading she fell into a mystical trance. A dove flew over her head. She was one with God.

It is strange that this small woman, possessed by mystical states, plagued by recurring illness, haunted, often hysterically fearful, should also have been one of the great organizers of her time. She traveled constantly up and down Spain, over rough roads, stopping in rude inns, eating rough food. But she never slacked in her mission. She established convents, settled disputes, and was often embattled in controversies. Her contemporaries esteemed her as a holy woman and an inspirational writer who lived an incredible life of devotion and good works.

Reading Saint Augustine was Teresa's turning point. He inspired much of her writing which, in turn, inspired generations of devout men and women to try to follow her example. Here is strong evidence of the enduring power of books in a never-ending chain of persuasion that lights up and changes lives.

- JOHN BUNYAN, 1628-1688 -

John Bunyan came, he said, from the "meanest and most despised of all the families in the Land."47 His father was a traveling tinker. The boy learned to read and write at a local grammar school. Then he had to educate himself.

In his search for enlightenment and entertainment, John read chapbooks and adventure stories he found at the Stourbridge Fair, the model for Vanity Fair in The Pilgrim's Progress. A few decades later, young Isaac Newton would buy a book on astronomy at the same Stourbridge Fair that set him on the way to revolutionize science. Among the books sold in John Bunyan's time were Bevis of Hampton and The Seven Champions of Christendom. These and others like them gave the common people, such as young John, their heroic models. Foxe's Book of Martyrs, with its bloodcurdling woodcuts, especially impressed the boy. He was a serious reader of sermons, moral tales, and admonishments to lead a righteous life. As one would expect, the God-fearing John came to a deep and extensive knowledge of the Bible.

As Bunyan told it in his autobiography, Grace Abounding to the Chief of Sinners (1666), two books in his wife's scanty dowry greatly influenced his way of life. They had "not ... so much houshold-stuff [sic] as a Dish or Spoon betwixt us both."[48] But of Arthur Dent's The Plaine Mans Path-way to Heaven and Lewis Bayly's The Practices of Piety, Bunyan wrote:

> Wherefore these books ... though they did not reach my heart to awaken it about my sad and sinful state, yet they did beget within me some desires to Religion: so that, because I knew no better, I fell in very eagerly with the Religion of the times, to wit, to go to the Church twice a day, and that too with the foremost, and there should very devoutly both say and sing as others did, yet retaining my wicked life: but withal, I was so overrun with the spirit of superstition, that I adored, and that with great devotion, even all things, (both the High-place, Priest, Clerk, Vestments, Service, and what else) belonged to the Church; counting all things holy that were therein contained; and especially the Priest and Clerk most happy, and without doubt greatly blessed, because they were the Servants, as I then thought, of God, and were principal in the holy Temple, to do his work therein.[49]

Even though the two books did not reach his heart, they strongly influenced his writing style. They showed him that racy, down-to-earth language could spice up and bring home to the lower-class man the holy way of life. And he learned to flavor his stories with homely proverbs of the kind he picked up in his study of the Bible.

Distressed by his failure to assure his salvation, Bunyan kept on searching. But in The Book of Joshua he was terrified by the fear that, like those who were not received in a city of refuge, he would "be slain by the avenger of blood." He lamented:

> O! one sentence of the Scripture did more afflict and terrify my mind, I mean those sentences that stood against me, (as sometimes I thought they every one did) more, I say, than an Army of forty thousand men that might have come against me. Wo be to him against whom the Scriptures bend themselves.[50]

After his fright at being excluded from divine grace, Bunyan found comfort when he read in John 6.37, "And him that comes to me, I will in no wise cast out."[51] Bunyan wrote, "Now I began to consider with myself, that God had a bigger mouth to speak with, than I had heart to conceive with."[52] Taking further solace from the words of God, Bunyan said:

> I thought also within myself, that he spake not his words in haste, or in an unadvised heat, but with infinite wisdom and judgment, and in very truth and faithfulness, 2 Sam. 7.28.[53]

The painful ambivalence within John Bunyan was made clear when he wrote:

> I have sometimes seen more in a line of the Bible than I could well tell how to stand under, and yet at another time the whole Bible hath been so dead and drie as a stick, or rather, my heart hath been so dead and drie unto it, that I could not conceive the least dram of refreshment, though I have lookt it all over.[54]

"Drie as a stick" he may have been sometimes as he puzzled over the holy book, but he was haunted and profoundly influenced by it throughout his life. His writing shows this influence in the opening passage of The Pilgrim's Progress:

> As I walked through the wilderness of this world, I lighted on a certain place where there was a den, and I laid me down in that place to sleep, and as I slept I dreamed a dream.[55]

John Bunyan told of another book that spoke directly to him, free of the ambiguities of the Bible:

> Well, after many such longings in my mind, the God in whose hands are all our days and ways, did cast into my hand, one day, a book of Martin Luther, his comment on the Galathians [sic], so old that it was ready to fall piece from piece, if I did but turn it over. Now I was pleased that such an old book had fallen into my hand; the which, when I had but a little perused, I found my condition in his experience, so largely and profoundly handled, as if his Book had been written out of my

heart; this made me marvel: for thus thought I, this man could not know anything of the state of Christians now, but must needs write and speak of the experience of former days.

> Besides he doth most gravely also, in that book debate of the rise of the temptations, namely Blasphemy, Desperation, and the like, shewing that the law of Moses, as well as the Devil, Death, and Hell, hath a very great hand therein; the which at first was very strange to me, but considering and watching, I found it so indeed. But of Particulars here I intend nothing, only this methinks I must let fall before all men, I do prefer this book of Mr. Luther upon the Galathians, (excepting the Holy Bible) before all the books that I have ever seen, as most fit for a wounded Conscience."56

As Bunyan received balm for his wounded conscience from Luther and support from the Bible, the words of which "were the Keys of the Kingdom of Heaven,"57 so his own words comforted and sustained unnumbered readers in many countries. He is one of the most quoted of writers. Coleridge spoke for Bunyan's readers when he wrote on the fly-leaf of his copy of The Pilgrim's Progress:

> I know of no Book the Bible excepted as above all comparison--which I according to my judgment and experience could so safely recommend as teaching and enforcing the whole saving Truth according to the mind that was in Jesus Christ, as The Pilgrim's Progress. It is in my conviction, incomparably the best Summa Theologia Evangelicae ever produced by a Writer not miraculously inspired.58

As Coleridge reckoned, Bunyan may not have been "miraculously inspired." But he was certainly and indelibly influenced by the reading that began with the country fair chapbooks, Foxe's Book of Martyrs, continued with the two books of his wife's dowry, and ended with his searching study of Luther and the Bible.

- JONATHAN EDWARDS, 1703-1758 -

Jonathan Edwards was one of eleven children in a Connecticut pastor's family. He grew up in a pious, affectionate setting "conducive to learning."[59] His writings, edited by Vergilius Ferm under the title <u>Puritan Sage</u> (1953), show him to have been strongly impressed with his reading. His first schooling was at home. At thirteen he went to Yale University, staying on after his basic divinity studies to win his M.A. degree in 1723.

During his career as one of New England's most influential preachers and writers as well as one of the most controversial, Edwards occupied the pulpit of the Northhampton church, second only to Boston in importance. After a theological disagreement with his congregation, he was forced to move on, this time to the frontier town of Stockbridge, where he was a missionary to the Indians.

Although he had studied the works of Newton and Locke and the Cambridge Platonists, who tried to bring Christianity and Humanism together, the Bible made the most decisive impact on young Jonathan. The weight of its moral lessons constantly bore in on him as shown in this passage from his <u>Diary</u>:

> Last Sabbath, at Boston, reading the 6th, 7th, and 8th verses of the 6th to the Ephesians, concluded that it would be much to my advantage, to take the greatest care, never to do any thing but my duty, and then to do it willingly, cheerfully, and gladly, whatever danger or unpleasant circumstances it may be attended with: with goodwill doing it, as to the Lord, not as pleasing men, or myself, knowing that whatsoever good thing any man doth, the same shall he receive of the Lord.[60]

During his youth, Jonathan was troubled by awareness of his shortcomings. In this passage, about two months after the reference to Ephesians, he tried to buck himself up:

> Have sinned, in not being careful enough to pleas [sic] my parents. Afternoon. - I find it would be very much to my advantage, to be thoroughly acquainted with the Scripture. When I am reading doctrinal books, or books of controversy, I can proceed with abundantly more confidence: can see on what footing and foundation I stand.[61]

As Edwards recounted his most decisive reading in the Bible, he overcame the stubborn resistance he had felt since childhood to the harsh idea of election to salvation. It had seemed "a horrible doctrine"[62] that God in his absolute sovereignty could reject some humans at will, "leaving them eternally to perish, and be everlastingly tormented in hell."[63] He longed for a God in whom he could delight without a quibble. Then:

> The first instance that I remember of that sort of inward, sweet delight in God and divine things that I have lived much in since, was on reading these words, I Tim. 1. 17. <u>Now unto the King eternal, immortal, invisible, the only wise God, be honor and glory for ever and ever, Amen.</u> As I read the words, there came into my soul, and was as it were diffused through it a sense of the glory of the Divine Being; a new sense, quite different from any thing I ever experienced before. Never any words of scripture seemed to me as these words did. I thought with myself, how excellent a Being that was, and how happy I should be, if I might enjoy that God, and be rapt up to him in heaven, and be as it were swallowed up in him for ever! I kept saying, and as it were singing over these words of scripture to myself; and went to pray to God that I might enjoy him, and prayed in a manner quite different from what I used to do; with a new sort of affection. But it never came into my thought that there was any thing spiritual, or of a saving nature in this.
>
> From about that time, I began to have a new kind of apprehensions and ideas of Christ, and the work of redemption, and the glorious way of salvation by him. An inward, sweet sense of these things, at times, came into my heart; and my soul was led away in pleasant views and contemplations of them. And my mind was greatly engaged to spend my time in reading and meditating on Christ, on the beauty and excellency of his person, and the lovely way of salvation by free grace in him. I found no books so delightful to me, as those that treated of these subjects. Those words [of] Cant. ii. 1, used to be abundantly with me, <u>I am the Rose of Sharon, and the Lily of the valleys.</u> The words seemed to me, sweetly to represent the loveliness and beauty of Jesus Christ. The whole book of Canticles used to be pleasant to me, and I used

to be much reading it, about that time; and found
from time to time, an inward sweetness, that would
carry me away, in my contemplations. This I
know not how to express otherwise, than a calm,
sweet abstraction of soul from all the concerns of
this world; and sometimes a kind of vision, or fixed
ideas and imaginations, of being alone in the mountains, or in some solitary wilderness, far from all
mankind, sweetly conversing with Christ, and wrapt
and swallowed up in God. The sense I had of divine things, would often of a sudden kindle up, as
it were, a sweet burning in my heart; an ardor of
soul, that I know not how to express.[64]

Jonathan talked with his father about his intensely emotional response to this reading. Had his father been a twentieth-century psychiatrist he might have raised his eyebrows at some of the figures of speech his son used to describe his yearning for God. His terms were definitely sensual. I cannot see how he got comfort on the score of election to salvation from this reading. However, he said his "sense of divine things gradually increased and became more and more lively...." "The appearance of everything was altered."[65] In short, he was consumed with ecstasy.

However one interprets Edwards' reactions to the Bible, they were among the most overwhelming religious reading experiences recorded.

- JOHN WESLEY, 1703-1791 -

John Wesley, the son of a Church of England rector, well educated at home, at the Charterhouse in London, and at Christ Church, Oxford, could have had a comfortable life in a church sinecure had he not fallen in with some Oxford men who methodically studied the Bible and other religious literature. These Holy Club members, or "Methodists" as they were called in ridicule, became John's main companions.

Wesley's Journal (1739), in six volumes, sets forth in great detail his religious and intellectual development and his reading. In the classics, he went through Homer, Xenophon, Horace, Juvenal, Virgil, Terence, Cicero, Epictetus, and Plutarch. His religious reading covered everything from the Bible and early Church Fathers to contemporary writings on all aspects of Christianity. And he was well up on the plays of Shakespeare and other English playwrights, as well as on history, poetry, and philosophy. He was fluent in Latin, knew Greek and Hebrew, and studied German and Spanish.

In the Preface to his Journal, John Wesley told how a book persuaded him to record the events of his life:

> It was in pursuance of an Advice given by Bp. Taylor in his Rules for Holy Living and Dying, that about fifteen years ago, I began to make a more exact Account than I had done before, of the manner wherein I spent my Time, writing down how I had employed every Hour. This I continued to do, wherever I was, till the Time of my leaving England. The variety of Scenes which I then past thro', induced me to transcribe from time to time, the more material Parts of my Diary, adding here and there such little reflections as occur'd to my Mind.... It not being my Design to relate all those Particulars, which I wrote down for my own Use only; and which would answer no valuable End to others, however important they were to me. 66

His editors, out of pious or other motives, have tinkered with Wesley's writing to "correct" it and to create a "pure text."67 Whatever they did, we have a great mass of what Wesley seems to have written. This makes his Journal a revealing record of the thought of a religious leader who, for more than two centuries, has influenced the lives of millions of men and women on several continents.

Among the critical influences on Wesley as he was groping for a direction to his life was some reading he wrote of thirteen years after it occurred:

> When I was about twenty-two, my father pressed me to enter holy orders. At the same time, the providence of God directing me to Kempis's Christian Pattern, I began to see, that true religion was seated in the heart, and that God's law extended to all our thoughts as well as words and actions. I was, however, very angry at Kempis for being too strict.... Yet I had frequently much sensible comfort in reading him, such as I was an utter stranger to before; and meeting likewise with a religious friend, which I never had till now, I began to alter the whole form of my conversation, and to set in

> earnest upon a new life. I set apart an hour or two a day for religious retirement. I communicated every week. I watched against all sin, whether in word or deed. I began to aim at, and pray for inward holiness. So that now, 'doing so much, and living so good a life,' I doubted not but I was a good Christian.[68]

Soon after his reading of Kempis, Wesley was elected Fellow of Lincoln College, and then another critical influence, his reading of Law's Christian Perfection and Serious Call, reinforced the inspiration of Kempis. He was convinced he should do some practical Christian work, so he began visiting the prisons, helping the poor and sick, "and doing what other good I could, by my presence or my little fortune, to bodies and souls of all men."[69] He had taken a first long step on a path that would lead him out of the Church of England and into the slums, streets, and fields to preach to crowds of working-class men and women, for whom the Established Church had been no more than a passive presence they were forced to support with taxes.

Although the reading of Kempis and Law had turned Wesley into a religious doer rather than a mere churchman, Martin Luther was responsible for his actual conversion. Like many young seekers for a secure faith, Wesley was often tormented by his "strange indifference, dullness and coldness and unusually frequent relapses into sin."[70] This was his sad state when, after having opened his Bible and read "Thou art not far from the kingdom of God."[71]

> In the evening [of May 24, 1738] I went very unwillingly to a society in Aldersgate Street, where one was reading Luther's preface to the Epistle to the Romans. About a quarter before nine, while he was describing the change which God works in the heart through faith in Christ, I felt my heart strangely warmed. I felt I did trust in Christ, Christ alone for salvation; and an assurance was given me that He had taken away <u>my</u> sins, even <u>mine</u>, and saved <u>me</u> from the law of sin and death.[72]

So it was the words of Luther on St. Paul that clinched the new faith of John Wesley and led him to found his own church. More than a hundred years later, young Sigmund Freud in Vienna underwent a conversion to medicine when he listened to a reading of a piece by Goethe on nature.

It was ironic that a few years after Wesley's conversion by way of Luther and St. Paul, he would be repelled by the book that had so crucially influenced John Bunyan--Luther's comment on the Epistle to the Galatians. He described his reaction:

> I was utterly ashamed. How could I have esteemed this book, only because I heard it so commended by others; or, at best, because I had read some excellent sentences occasionally quoted from it! But what shall I say? Now I judge for myself, now I see with my own eyes? Why, not only that the author makes nothing out, clears up not one considerable difficulty; that he is quite shallow in his remarks on many passages, and muddy and confused almost, on all; but that he is deeply tinctured with mysticism throughout, and hence often dangerously wrong.[73]

In this account by Wesley, we see that he kept his critical faculties in working order while he read. He was too rational to be taken in by the mysticism of Luther, who had brought him to trust in Christ. Wesley was a serious reader who made demands on authors.

Wesley, who knew the value of a liberal education and wide learning to a religious leader, urged his lay clergy, who usually were men of little learning, to read daily. Otherwise, he said, they could not become effective preachers or even thorough Christians. However, he wanted to prescribe their reading. Only devotional poetry, such as his brother Charles wrote, and religious books were recommended. He warned one disciple, "Beware you not be swallowed up in books! An ounce of love is worth a pound of knowledge."[74] It was ironic that Wesley, believing he had found the truth through print, squelched the impulse in others to read freely according to their own inclinations. What put him on the true path could lead others astray. His restraint on his flock was a left-handed tribute to the power of reading.

- JOSEPH SMITH, 1805-1844 -

Joseph Smith grew up in rural Vermont during a time of intense religious revivalism. Shouting preachers roamed the hinterland, threatening hellfire and damnation, working uneducated farmers and small-town people up to hysterical states at crowded camp meetings. While religious fever was in the air, basic education was hard to come by. As reported by Donna Hill in <u>Joseph Smith, the First Mormon</u> (1977), he wrote a labored letter about his own limited schooling:

> I hope you will excuse ... my inability in conveying my ideas in writing ... it required the exertions of all that were able to labor to render any assistance for the support of the Family therefore we were deprived of the bennifit of an education suffice it to say I was mearly instructed in reading writing and the ground rules of Arithmatic which constituted my whole literary acquirements.[75]

Because of his lack of learning, most of Smith's extensive output of writing--books, revelations, journals, and letters--was dictated to secretaries.

Joseph's mother said that while he was inclined to be meditative, he was not the reader the other children were, and "he was not much given to studying the Bible."[76] But he had been exposed to religion at home. The family prayed, read the Bible, and sang hymns together. Undoubtedly Joseph had heard revivalist preachers haranguing the country folk. So it was inevitable, in the absence of worldly distractions, that young Joseph, who was highly intelligent in spite of his scanty schooling, would do some serious thinking about holy matters. A brief autobiography gives an account of his early religious experiences:

> ... about the age of twelve years my mind became seriously imprest with regard to the all important concerns for the welfare of my immortal soul which led me to searching the Scriptures believeing as I was taught, that they contained the word of God ... from the age of twelve years to fifteen I pondered many things in my heart concerning the situation of the world of mankind the contentions and divions [sic] the wickedness and abominations ... my mind became excedingly [sic] distressed for I became convicted of my Sins...."[77]

Joseph continued to be troubled by the storm of conflicting religious opinions. Then he did some reading that put him right:

> In the midst of this war of words, and tumult of

opinion I often said to myself, what is to be done? Who of all these parties are right.... I was one day reading the Epistle of James, First Chapter, and fifth verse which reads, 'If any of you lack wisdom, let him ask of God....' I reflected on it again and again.... At length I came to the conclusion that I must either remain in the darkness and confusion or else I must do as James directs.... Immediately I was seized upon by some power which entirely overcame me as to bind my tongue so that I could not speak. Thick darkness gathered around me, and it seemed to me for the first time as if I were doomed to sudden destruction ... just at this moment I saw a pillar of light, above the brightness of the sun, which descended gradually until it fell on me.

It no sooner appeared than I found myself delivered from the enemy which held me bound. When the light rested upon me I saw two personages, whose brightness and glory defy all description, standing above me in the air. One of them spoke unto me calling me by name and said--pointing to the other--'This is my Beloved Son, hear him.'

My object in going to inquire of the Lord was to know which of the sects was right.... I was answered that I must join none of them, for they were all wrong, and the personage who addressed me said that all their creeds were an abomination in His sight; that those professors were all corrupt, that 'They draw near me with their lips but their hearts are far from me; they teach for doctrines the commandments of me: having the form of godliness but they deny the power thereof.'[78]

Those familiar with the Old Testament will recognize the similarity between the words of the "personage" and Isaiah 29:13:

Wherefore the Lord said, Forasmuch as this people draw near me with their mouth, and with their lips do honor me, but have removed their hearts from me.... [79]

After the divine visitation, during which Joseph said he was told other things he could not reveal, he came to, "lying on his back looking up into heaven."[80] Then he began to work out a true religion to replace the sects that were so abominable in the eyes of the "personage" who spoke to him.

There has been endless speculation over Joseph Smith's Book of Mormon and its origin. Was it written by Joseph himself? Some consider it a hodgepodge assembled from several sources. According to his first wife, however, it did not come from his reading of any manuscript. She wrote,

> No man could have dictated the writing of the manuscript unless he was inspired ... when returning after meals, or after interruptions, he would at once begin where he had left off, without seeing the manuscript or having any portion of it read to him. This was the usual thing for him to do. It would have been improbable that a learned man could do this; for one so ignorant and unlearned as he was, it was simply impossible.[81]

Joseph's own explanation, the mysterious "Urim and Thummin"[82] as the medium by which he was able to decipher the writing on the plates of gold, might have been suggested to him by the prophecy of Isaiah:

> And the vision of all is to become unto you as the words of a book that is sealed, which men deliver to one that is learned, saying, Read this, I pray you, and he saith, I cannot; for it is sealed.[83]

It seems likely that this passage from Isaiah influenced the following wording in the Book of Mormon:

> But behold it shall come to pass that the Lord God shall say unto him to whom he shall deliver the book; Take these words which are not sealed and deliver them to another, that he may show them to the learned, saying: Read this, I pray thee. And the learned shall say: Bring hither the book for it is sealed....[84]

After he had published the Book of Mormon, Joseph Smith is said to have studied Hebrew and Egyptian, difficult languages for anyone, especially one whose wife called him "unlearned." However that may be, it is clear that Joseph Smith was strongly influenced by reading the Bible. And as history has shown, Joseph Smith's writing--original, plagiarized, or a combination--shaped the lives of an army of pioneers who transformed an enormous expanse of wilderness into one of the most productive regions of the American West. Even today, the descendents of those pioneers flourish, increase, and enlarge the church based on Joseph Smith's writing in many communities thousands of miles from the Great Salt Lake.

- MARY BAKER EDDY, 1821-1910 -

It was not at all strange that Mary Baker Eddy, ailing from childhood, should have had a lifelong preoccupation with her health. But it was more than strange that she should have founded a flourishing church based on principles she said she discovered in the Bible. Her medical and spiritual trials and triumphs are recorded in her Retrospection and Introspection (1891) and by Robert Peel in Mary Baker Eddy (1966).

Her father, believing Mary's brain was too big for her body, kept her out of school. However, she was bright and learned from books:

> At ten years of age I was as familiar with Lindley Murray's Grammar as with the Westminster Catechism; and the latter I had to repeat every Sunday. My favorite studies were Natural Philosophy, Logic, and Moral Science. From my brother Albert I received lessons in the ancient tongues, Hebrew, Greek, and Latin. [85]

She claimed she did not retain this early learning: "After my discovery of Christian Science, most of the knowledge I had gleaned from schoolbooks vanished like a dream."[86] Still it seems that the writings of Michael Faraday, Charles Darwin, and Thomas Huxley, all of whom had stirred up the world of the intellect just before and during Mary Baker Eddy's time, would not actually fade from her retentive mind. And it is doubtful that she would have forgotten Jahr's New Manual of Homeopathic Practice, which she read almost as religiously as the Bible.

Here is her account of her discovery of the "Science of Divine Metaphysical Healing":

> The discovery came to pass in this way. During

> the twenty years prior to my discovery I had been trying to trace all physical affects to a mental cause; and in the latter part of 1866 I gained the Scientific certainty that all causation was Mind, and every effect a mental phenomena.
>
> My immediate recovery from the effects of an injury caused by an accident, an injury that neither medicine nor surgery could reach, was the falling apple that led me to the discovery how to be well myself, and how to make others so:
>
> Even to the Homeopathic physician who attended me, and rejoiced in my recovery, I could not then explain the <u>modus</u> of my relief. I could only assure him that the divine spirit had wrought a miracle which I later found to be in perfect Scientific accord with the divine law.
>
> I then withdrew from society about three years-- to ponder my mission, to search the Scriptures, to find the Science of Mind, that should take the things of God and show them to the creature, and reveal the great curative principle--Deity.
>
> The Bible was my text-book. It answered my questions as to how I was healed; but the Scriptures had to me a new meaning; a new tongue. The spiritual signification appeared; and I apprehended for the first time, in their spiritual meaning, Jesus' teaching and demonstration, and the Principle and rule of spiritual Science and Metaphysical healing,--in a word, Christian Science. [87]

In <u>The Christian Science Journal</u>, June, 1887, Mrs. Eddy gave a slightly different version of her healing. She was reading about the cure of the man with palsy in St. Matthew:

> It was to me a revelation of Truth. The lost chord of Truth (healing, as of old) I caught consciously from the Divine Harmony. [88]

She gave further insight into her healing by reading, in her <u>Miscellaneous Writings</u>:

> As I read, the healing Truth dawned upon my

sense.... That short experience included a glimpse of the great fact that I have since tried to make plain to others, namely Life is in and of the Spirit; this Life being the sole reality of existence. I learned that mortal thought evolves a subjective state which it names matter, thereby shutting out the true sense of spirit.[89]

Although Mary Baker Eddy's recollections of her discovery of Christian Science, recorded at intervals during her life, differ in some details, as is not unusual with events recalled after a lapse of time, they have a common element. Her reading of the Bible during sickness was the crucial factor in each version of the genesis of her church.

- EDITH STEIN, SISTER TERESA BENEDICTA OF THE CROSS, 1891-1942 -

Edith Stein's death in an Auschwitz gas chamber ended an active religious life that began with her conversion to the Roman Catholic Church after her reading of the autobiography of Saint Teresa of Avila. Her heroic life, which earned her the title of martyr, began in a wealthy Jewish family in Breslau.

In her teens Edith declared herself an atheist. She then studied philosophy at the University of Göttingen under Edmund Husserl, whose Phenomenology disavowed all belief in the unseen and rested on what was considered a scientific foundation. Edith went with Husserl to the University of Freiburg as his assistant. There she received her Ph.D. and established her reputation as the leading philosopher on the faculty.

The life of this remarkable woman, with pious emphasis on her spiritual qualities, was recorded by Sister Teresia de Spiritu Sancto in her book, Edith Stein (1952). According to Sister Teresia, "Edith Stein had only one love; knowledge. She had only one passion: books to deepen her knowledge."[90] Given these propensities, it was not surprising that Edith found her new faith in a book. It happened during a vacation. A friend invited her to select something to read:

I picked at random and took out a large volume. It bore the title The Life of St. Teresa of Avila, written by herself. I began to read, was at once captivated, and did not stop until I reached the end. As I closed the book, I said, 'That is the truth.'

Day was breaking. Edith hardly noticed it. God's hand was upon her and she did not turn from him. In the morning she went into the town to buy two things: a Catholic catechism and a missal. She studied them until she had mastered their contents. Then for the first time she went into a Catholic Church, the Parish Church at Bergzabern, to hear Mass. 'Nothing was strange to me,' said Edith later. 'Thanks to my previous study, I understood even the smallest ceremonies. The priest, a saintly-looking old man, went to the alter and offered the holy sacrifice reverently and devoutly. After Mass I waited till he had made his thanksgiving. I followed him to the presbytery and asked him without more ado for Baptism. He looked astonished and answered that one had to be prepared before being received into the Church. "How long have you been receiving instruction and who has been giving it?" The only reply I could make was, "Please, your Reverence, test my knowledge."' [91]

In a wide-ranging discussion of theology, Edith answered all questions with such thoroughness that the old priest was convinced of her readiness. She was baptized and began her life in the Church, taking the name of Teresa in grateful acknowledgement of her inspiration. Reborn, she was soon on her way to recognition for her writings and her speeches on various religious problems and, finally, to martyrdom at the brutal hands of the Nazis.

All that happened to her after she first picked up and looked into Saint Teresa's autobiography stemmed from her reading about the holy woman of Avila.

- MARTIN LUTHER KING, JR., 1929-1968 -

With his Christian name and family background in the ministry, Martin Luther King, Jr. came naturally to a life of religious activism. L. D. Reddick's Crusader Without Violence: A Biography of Martin Luther King, Jr. (1959) is a narration of his too-brief life.

As a gifted boy, Martin entered Morehouse College under a special program. After considering and dismissing law and medicine as professions, he decided to follow the family tradition and serve his fellow men and women in the church. After he completed his studies in Atlanta, he enrolled at Crozier Theological Seminary in Chester, Pennsylvania, from which he received his bachelor of divinity degree. Then he went to Boston University for his Ph.D.

An outstanding student all through his schooling, Martin was a heavy reader. Thoreau and Gandhi were important in preparing him for his historic civil rights victories and the Nobel Prize for Peace, which he won in 1964.

The leaders of the 1955 Montgomery bus boycott, of which King was elected leader, had taken Thoreau literally when he wrote, "Under a government which imprisons any unjustly, the true place for a just man is also in prison."[92] That statement and others by Thoreau had also struck home to a young Indian lawyer in South Africa when, around the turn of the century, he was working for the basic rights of exploited and ill-treated Indian workers who had been shipped over as a cheap labor force. When Gandhi found himself agreeing with the Concord man's words, "The only obligation which I have a right to assume is to do at any time what I think is right,"[93] his own resolve was strengthened. He then launched the epic campaign of passive disobedience. It didn't make much of an impact in South Africa. But under Gandhi's heroic leadership India won its freedom from the British imperialists and became a sovereign nation whose people controlled their own lives.

It was through another Morehouse man, Mordecai W. Johnson, that Gandhi's message reached King. Johnson, a pastor in Charleston, West Virginia, had faced a serious dilemma. He believed in brotherly love as taught in the Bible. But what he saw around him in the way of racial prejudice was discouraging. As he pondered what to do, he began to read Gandhi's writings. Then he visited India. He came back home "on fire with Gandhi's spirit."[94] It was during a talk by Johnson that King heard what Gandhi had done for his people. King, then a student at Crozier, was taken especially with the description of the "redemptive power of love as an instrument of nonviolent social reform."[95] King was inflamed by Johnson's enthusiasm:

He began to read all the books on Gandhi that he

could lay his hands on. The more he read and the more he talked with others about what he read, the deeper became his faith. Now, at last, he had found a philosophy that fitted in with his natural tendency as well as with his sense of social obligation. 96

So Martin Luther King, Jr. found the way to carry out his mission by reading Gandhi, who in his time had been inspired to lead his peaceful crusade by Henry Thoreau, the poor New England sage without portfolio. It is of interest that among the literary influences on Thoreau was the Bhagavad-Gita, the holy Hindu book that Gandhi also read devotedly. This long chain of reading is a classical example of the enduring power of print to change history by changing men.

- OBSERVATIONS -

It is hardly surprising that sixteen Christian leaders were profoundly influenced by The New Testament. But the force and durability of the influence is remarkable. Paul the Apostle made an especially powerful impact. For Augustine, Luther, and Wesley, Paul's Epistle to the Romans was crucial in confirming their faith. In The First Epistle of Paul to Timothy, Jonathan Edwards, doubtful about divine benevolence, found a loving God. When she read the story of the man cured of palsy in The Gospel According to St. Matthew, Mary Baker Eddy said she discovered the "healing Truth" of Christian Science.

Other crucial reading of the religious leaders included philosophy, the lives of holy men and women, and books promoting piety and good works. Aristotle cast such a spell on Aquinas that Catholic minds for centuries have been molded to follow the Greek philosopher's system of thought. Aristotle also played a part, along with Augustine, in shaping the thought of Wyclif. He, in turn, was revered by Hus, who absorbed and preached the fiercely independent ideas of the English reformer and died for his conviction. Augustine also swayed the thinking of Erasmus. Ignatius was weaned away from derring-do tales of armored knights to a missionary life by The Life of Christ and Flowers of the Saints. For Teresa of Avila, Augustine's Confessions and The Life of Christ by Ludolph were overwhelming. John Bunyan's "desires for Religion" were intensified by Dent's The Plaine Mans Path-way to Heaven, Bayly's The Practices of Piety, and Luther's comments on Galatians. Taylor's Rules for Holy Living persuaded Wesley to begin his Journal, and Law's Christian Perfection and Serious Call showed him the way to a life of service to humanity. When Edith Stein came upon the life of Teresa of Avila, she abandoned her atheism for Christian faith. And writings by and about Gandhi set Martin Luther King, Jr. to work on his human rights struggles.

Most of the sixteen, being intellectually curious, probably were bookish from their early years. But their childhood reading usually was only sketchily reported. By his own admission, Augustine "loved not study" as a boy. Both Spanish saints, Ignatius and Teresa, were addicted, in their youth, to tales of chivalrous deeds. As a stripling, Bunyan stuffed himself with chapbooks and adventure stories. The New Englangers, Edwards and Eddy, were nurtured in the intimate reading circles of their refined homes.

All but three of the sixteen had good or excellent educations. Some of them were among the most learned of their times, with graduate degrees from renowned universities. Of the less schooled, Mary Baker Eddy was largely self-taught. Bunyan enjoyed the skimpiest of schooling, while Joseph Smith, the least educated of the lot, was also the least literate. However, even he was said to have studied ancient languages as an adult.

It is unwise, of course, to be dogmatic in attributing an effect to a single cause when it is probably only one of many causes. The religious leaders certainly had many deeply moving experiences, aside from reading, that strongly influenced them. But they were without exception and beyond doubt highly susceptible to the influence of religious and inspirational books. Their decisive reading came usually during their early maturity, often at times of agonizing mental and physical stress. It was sometimes accompanied by mystical states. Then followed conviction of having discovered the ultimate truth.

In looking for cause and effect in the reading of the religious leaders, study uncovers sequences of events common to all. It begins as books are found to have changed their thinking and the direction of their lives and affected their writing. The examples of their lives and the impact of their writing made enduring and often drastic changes in the lives of uncountable readers of their own times and of distant generations. Reading is seen to be a time bomb planted in the nervous system. One never knows when it will be triggered and set off far-reaching explosions of ideas and actions. This sequence of events clearly demonstrates the power of books to shape lives and faiths, a power that is multiplied in unpredictable ways and incalculable force throughout the world wherever a reader picks up a book and opens it.

A most impressive fact that becomes clear in this review is the constancy of the power of print, through the centuries, over the minds of searchers for religious assurance. Fifteen hundred years passed between the day in medieval Milan when Augustine began reading the Bible after hearing a child chant, "Take up and read, take up and read," and Edith Stein's conversion by way of The Life of St. Teresa of Avila in twentieth-century Germany. Augustine lived before the printed book, in an age not yet disturbed by the distractions of technology. Edith Stein passed her brief years among all the noisy confusions and dangers of an industrial era, under the threat of bigotry, violence, and war. But both were carried away and radically changed by their responses to words on pages. And all of those between them, from Aquinas to Mary Baker Eddy, were likewise shaken and profoundly altered by their reading. What stronger evidence can there be of the enduring power of the written word to transform attitudes and actions and to exert a powerful influence over the course of history?

Chapter 5

THE DECISIVE READING OF SCIENTISTS

No learned discipline requires its practitioners to pay closer attention to cause and effect than science. Tracing the course of events they observe in nature or set in motion in experiments is basic to the work of scientists. If they are to make the accurate predictions essential in science, they must understand the relations between sequences of events. So it is not surprising to find in lives of scientists awareness of the crucial impact of reading on their activities.

- THE READING OF CHARLES DARWIN -

Since Darwin so decisively influenced his own time and ours, we are lucky to have abundant, well-documented evidence on the impact of his reading on his thinking and on his revolutionary discoveries. In his Autobiography (1892), he told much about the effect of reading on a mind struggling to bring new knowledge to light.

From nine to sixteen, Charles attended "Dr. Butler's great school in Shrewsbury." Although he called it "great," he wrote, "The school as a means of education was simply a blank." It was "strictly classical," with "only a little ancient geometry and history." He said, "Nothing could have been worse for the development of my mind." Darwin left the school convinced he was "considered by all my masters and my father as a very ordinary boy, rather below the common standard in intellect."[1] He was deeply mortified by his father's reproach: "You care for nothing but shooting, dogs, and rat-catching, and you will be a disgrace to yourself and all your family."[2]

As he looked back and inventoried himself in boyhood, he thought,

> the only qualities which at this period promised
> well for the future, were, that I had strong and
> diversified tastes, much zeal for whatever inter-
> ested me, and keen pleasure in understanding any
> complex problem or thing.[3]

He recalled sitting for hours reading Shakespeare's historical plays, Thomson's <u>Seasons</u>, and poems of Byron and Scott. He regretted that he later lost "all pleasure from poetry of any kind, including Shakespeare."[4]

The first reading solidly linked to Darwin's momentous lifework was in <u>Wonders of the World</u>. He spent many hours with it and argued the truth of the statements with other boys. The book, he believed, "first gave me a wish to travel in remote countries."[5] White's <u>Selborne</u> got him to watching birds and making notes on their habits. Chemistry also interested Charles, and he "read with care several books ... such as Henry and Parke's <u>Chemical Catechism</u>." This, he thought, "was the best part of my education at school, for it showed me practically the meaning of experimental science."[6] Dr. Butler had dismissed such reading as a waste of time.

In the face of the doubts of his teachers and his father, Darwin entered Cambridge University. During his last year there, he did some crucial reading. He recalled:

> I read with care and profound interest Humboldt's
> <u>Personal Narrative</u>. This work, with Sir J. Her-
> schel's <u>Introduction to the Study of Natural Philoso-
> phy</u>, stirred up in me a burning zeal to add even
> the most humble contribution to the noble structure
> of <u>Natural Science</u>. No one or a dozen books in-
> fluenced me nearly as much as these two. I copied
> out of Humboldt long passages about Teneriffe.[7]

Darwin's chance to follow in the path of Humboldt and other trailblazers of science came when he signed on the <u>Beagle</u> as a naturalist to observe and collect geological samples and specimens of flora and fauna. In his luggage was the first volume of Charles Lyell's <u>Principles of Geology</u>. In studying it he found the book to be "of the highest service ... in many ways." His experience in the first area he visited, the Cape Verde Islands, "Showed me clearly the wonderful superiority of Lyell's way of treating geology."[8]

Darwin came home loaded with study material from his five years sailing around the world on the Beagle. With his magnificent field experience behind him, and practiced in Lyell's system, he tackled the mammoth and exacting job of interpreting his material and publishing his findings. During this period he had what was probably his most momentous reading encounter:

> I happened to read for amusement Malthus on Population, and being well prepared to appreciate the struggle for existence which everywhere goes on from long-continued observations of the habits of animals and plants, it at once struck me that under these circumstances favourable variations would tend to be preserved and unfavourable ones to be destroyed. The result of this would be the formation of a new species. Here, then, I had at last got a theory by which to work....[9]

This was one of the most significant reading experiences in the history of science. A bright light had been kindled in the brain of an obscure young scientist. The tinder was a book in another field. Where can one find a clearer or more convincing illustration of the powerful impact of reading on intellectual progress?

Although he was quick to grasp the significance for his research of the reading he did in Malthus, Darwin wrote candidly in his Autobiography about his shortcomings as a reader. He claimed "no great quickness of apprehension or wit which is so remarkable in some clever men, for instance, Huxley."[10] He called himself a poor critic. At first reading, a book excited his admiration. He could find the weak points "only after considerable reflection." It was hard for him to "follow a long and purely abstract train of thought,"[11] so metaphysics and mathematics were beyond him. He depended upon a memory "extensive, yet hazy," to alert him to conclusions opposed to his own. And he could "after a time ... generally recollect where to search for my authority."[12] He had no memory for dates or for even a single line of poetry.

In his Reading Notebooks for 1838-1860, Darwin throws a different light on his involvement with books. Those years were his most productive period. He recorded a broad range of planned and actual reading. It included such disparate fare as poetry, even though he couldn't remember it or enjoy it, Burke's speeches, and a treatise on the quadrupeds of Paraguay. He noted that "Dr. Edwards on Influence of causes" had been "well skimmed," Lewis and Clark skimmed "half way through--probably nothing." Dublano's letters on Spain were "excellent," Scott's Life was "read aloud," Burgess on blushing had "nothing,"[13] Priestly Peru was "goodish," but F. A. A. Meyer's Naturegeschichte der Haustiere was "wretched."[14] This small sample of his reading, listed and evaluated in Darwin's quirky fashion, gives an idea of the rich and varied intellectual range of the reading of one of the most influential scientists who ever lived. It shows him to have been able to use his vast knowledge to make incisive judgments on books in many fields.

- READING THAT MOTIVATED ALFRED RUSSEL WALLACE -

Like Darwin and many other good Victorians, Wallace left an autobiography with an account of his reading, his thoughts, and his accomplishments. My Life: A Record of Events and Opinions (1905) points up some of the striking parallels in the early years of Darwin and Wallace. As boys, they both frolicked in rural England, getting a close look at plants and animals, raiding nests and burrows. Both were bookish. Wallace recalled listening to his mother telling stories of Jack the Giant-Killer and Little Red Riding Hood. But he said more realistic stories, such as Sandford and Merton, "perhaps impressed me more deeply than any."[15] And Aesop's fable of the thirsty fox and the almost empty pitcher led little Alfred to perform his first experiment. Like young Charles Darwin, Alfred was fascinated by narratives of exploration and adventure. His father's book club supplied the family with a stream of such books. Alfred remembered Mungo Park's travels in Africa and those of Denham and Clapperton. His father's reading of Defoe's "wonderful"[16] Journal of the Plague Year was a lasting memory. And "large dissected maps of England and Europe"[17] gave him a lifelong love of good maps and taught him about distant places, many of which he later visited.

When his father became librarian "to a fairly good proprietary town library,"[18] the boy was in his glory. He saturated himself in classics and novels of the day. Walton's The Compleat Angler was a favorite. Gradually Alfred concentrated on the subjects that would dominate his life. Practice in surveying and the use of a pocket-sextant led him to books on optics and mechanics. He felt in this way he laid the foundation for the interest "in physical science and acquaintance with its general principles which have remained with me throughout my life."[19] This foundation was strengthened when he came upon Loudon's Encyclopaedia of Plants. The catalogue of a Bristol nurseryman piqued his interest in orchids. This was deepened by an article in the Gardener's Chronicle on a flower show in London featuring delicate and exotic plants. Such reading served him well as he rambled and collected in his own neighborhood and later, when he, like Darwin, traveled to the far places to which he was drawn by his reading.

It was in Leicester, where he subscribed to "a very good library,"[20] that Wallace happened on the same book that set Darwin to dreaming of adventures abroad. This was Humboldt's description of his travels in South America, "which was, I think, the first book that gave me a desire to visit the tropics."[21] Wallace also credited Darwin's Journal with increasing his attraction to the hot countries. In the Leicester library, he wrote, "perhaps the most important book I read was Malthus's Principles of Population."[22] Wallace admired it for its "masterly summary of facts and logical induction to conclusions."[23] It was the first book he had read on any of "the problems of philosophical biology."[24] He retained its principles, "and twenty years later they gave me the long-sought clue to the effective agent in the evolution of organic species."[25]

It was an extraordinary double coincidence that Darwin and Wallace, each feeling his way toward the theory of evolution, came up with strikingly similar conclusions under the influence of a book in a different field than they were studying, a book with an opposing attitude to theirs--pessimism about man's future against optimism.

Although Humboldt and Darwin had intensified Wallace's determination to go into the tropics, it was W. H. Edwards' A Voyage up the Amazon (1847) that settled it for him. He was persuaded by the clear, bright writing and the beguiling descriptions of "the beauty and grandeur of tropical vegetation,"[26] by the account of the kind hospitality of the people, and, not least, by the cheapness of travel and living. He could not resist such attractions, and he sailed for Brazil. Most of the insects he collected were lost when his ship sank on the voyage home. But his experiences were set down in A Narrative of Travels on the Amazon and the Rio Negro (1853).

After his return from South America, books on social problems profoundly influenced Wallace. One was Herbert Spencer's Social Statistics. The ideas on the right use of land went deeply into Wallace's thought, "and, ultimately led to my becoming, almost against my will, President of the Land Nationalization Society."27 Wallace's The Malay Archipelago, the fruit of his Asian investigations, impressed John Stuart Mill, who was struck by Wallace's equating "civilization," as spread abroad by the British, with barbarism. Mill, who had been influenced by Henry George' Progress and Poverty, drew Wallace more deeply into social reform when he persuaded him to serve on the general committee of the Land Tenure Association.

By 1899, his reading had changed Wallace's views "once for all." He reached the conviction that not only was socialism "thoroughly practicable, but that it is the only form of society worthy of human beings."28 It alone promised "true happiness" for mankind, a way to bring about satisfaction of all "rational needs, desires, and aspirations."29 This radical transformation of the highly respected scientist was brought about by Edward Bellamy's novel, Looking Backward (1888), a world-wide best seller. Wallace found that

> Every sneer, every objection, every argument I had ever read against socialism was here met and shown to be absolutely trivial or altogether baseless.30

He read the book a second time, to "satisfy myself I had not overlooked a flaw in the reasoning."31 He found no such flaw.

We see in Wallace a creative scientist, widely traveled, courageous, dedicated to social justice, testifying to the decisive impact of reading on his work and his ideas. He was trained in careful evaluation of evidence. This makes the demonstration of the power of print on him especially impressive. As with many creative people, his reading went far beyond his own special field.

There has been some question about whether Wallace, rather than Darwin, deserved credit for the theory of evolution. Wallace unequivocally gave the credit to his great contemporary when he wrote in his autobiography,

> Mr. Darwin has given the world a new science,

and his name should, in my opinion, stand above that of every philosopher of ancient or modern times. The force of admiration can no further go!!!³²

- DARWIN'S IMPACT ON SOME OTHER DISTINGUISHED SCIENTISTS -

As from a mighty earthquake at sea surging tides race in all directions, to batter and rearrange distant shore lines, so the powerful ideas of Charles Darwin surged out to strike and change the minds of brilliant men in many lands, stimulating them to scientific achievements of a high order. Publication of these achievements has gone reverberating through the world of thought and action to further rearrange the intellectual landscape in surprising and often disturbing ways.

Among those changed by Darwin was his young cousin, Francis Galton. In <u>Memories of My Life</u> (1908) Galton described the Darwin shock:

> The publication of the <u>Origin of the Species</u> made a marked epoch in my own mental development, as it did in that of human thought generally. Its effect was to demolish a multitude of dogmatic barriers by a single stroke, and to arouse a spirit of rebellion against all ancient authorities whose positive and unauthenticated statements were contradicted by modern science....³³

The <u>Origin</u> did more than just shake up Galton. He said, "I was encouraged by the new views to pursue many inquiries which had long interested me."³⁴ It was heredity and the possibility of improving the human race that gripped Galton's interest. He wrote <u>Hereditary Genius</u> (1869), which, although recently questioned as to its thesis, became a landmark in genetics. It must have been more than cousinly courtesy that made Darwin sit down to write Galton that he had read only about fifty pages of his book, when "I must exhale myself, else something will go wrong with my inside."³⁵ Darwin praised the style, clarity, and originality of Galton's work. And he admitted to being converted in his thinking about genius when he wrote that before reading Galton, "I have always maintained that excepting fools, men do not differ much in intellect, only in zeal and hard work."³⁶

What ego satisfaction it was for Darwin to know that his writing had stimulated the gifted Galton to do such remarkable original work. And how proud Galton must have been to learn of his influence on his illustrious relative. Here is strong evidence of the reciprocal influence of two geniuses through their reading of each other.

If Galton was eager to applaud Darwin for the Origin, Thomas Huxley was not. He doubted the evidence was strong enough to sustain Darwin's theory. But chance took a hand in altering Huxley's opinion when The Times asked him to review the book. As he read he was bowled over and abashed: "How extremely stupid not to have thought of that."[37] This reading so persuaded him that he made a career of defending and promoting Darwinism. So persistent was his advocacy that he was nicknamed "Darwin's Bulldog."

One who quickly grasped and welcomed Darwin's exciting new ideas was a young German just getting started on a career that would make him one of the world's preeminent zoologists. This was Ernst Haeckel. Wilhelm Bölsche's Haeckel: His Life and Work (1906) told how, during his school days, like most young Germans of his time, Haeckel was enamored of Goethe. He had also been much taken with Humboldt's Aspects of Nature and Matthias Jakob Schleiden's The Plant and its Life.

But Darwin was to be the pivot of Haeckel's life. The evolutionist's theories had not yet taken hold in Germany. Schopenhauer had dismissed the Origin as the product of exact investigation, a method which, from a metaphysical viewpoint, he despised. On the other hand, among German zoologists and botanists Darwin was accused of unscientific "mystification," "metaphysics," and "philosophy in the worst sense of the word."[38] When Haeckel dug into the Origin in 1860, it was widely thought to be a dangerous book. But the young German found, "It profoundly moved me at the first reading."[39] It did more than that. It permeated his thinking. In his important book on radiolaria, he arranged the tiny marine protozoans as "a fairly continuous chain of related forms," on the basis of "the great theories of Charles Darwin ... which have opened out a new epoch for systematic biology...."[40] In 1866, Haeckel brought out what Huxley called "one of the greatest scientific books ever published."[41] It was The General Morphology of Organisms. The subtitle was General Elements of the Science of Organic Forms, Mechanically Grounded on the Theory of Descent as Reformed by Charles Darwin. This was a high tribute and a proud acknowledgement of one giant of science to the writing of another.

Luther Burbank was not exactly a giant of science. Peter Dreyer hit him off in the title of his book, A Gardener Touched with Genius (1975). Burbank was mostly self-taught. However, he had something in common with Haeckel. This was his debt to Darwin. As Burbank put it,

> When I was about nineteen, in 1868, probably the turning point of my career in fixing my life work was ... the reading of Darwin's 'Variations of Animals and Plants Under Domestication,' which I obtained from the library in Lancaster, Mass., my old home. Well do I remember ... that the whole world seemed placed on a new foundation. It was without question the most inspiring book I had ever read, and I had read widely from one of the best libraries in the state on similar scientific subjects. [42]

Burbank also acknowledged Humboldt and Thoreau as "decisive book influences."[43]

As a young man, he had made a little money from selling the rights to his Burbank potato. With that and some practical knowledge and inspiration from his reading, he left to seek his fortune in California, the paradise of gardeners. Based in Santa Rosa, he planted, grafted, cloned, and pollinated. He was enormously successful and won world fame and prosperity with his Shasta daisy, white blackberry, scented calla, stoneless plum, spineless cactus, and other botanical wonders.

Luther Burbank was one of the international army of peaceful experimenters who carried and applied in many fields the intellectual weaponry of Charles Darwin. In the process, he heightened the digestive and esthetic pleasures of his fellow citizens, while honoring himself and his great exemplar.

- THE IMPACT OF READING ON A GREAT LINE OF ASTRONOMERS AND PHYSICISTS -

While the discoveries of astronomers and physicists are based largely on their observations of natural phenomena, to put their findings in perspective and to assess their originality and importance they must rely on the writings of their forerunners. Those pioneers have provided what has been called the scientific grammar as a guideline from which to advance. When Newton wrote to Robert Hooke, "If I have seen further (than you and Descartes) it is by standing on the shoulders of giants,"[44] he was acknowledging his indebtedness to his reading.

In his dedication to Pope Paul III of On the Revolution of the Heavenly Bodies (1543), Copernicus wrote of what he owed to earlier writers. He knew he was on dangerous ground in reporting his observation that the earth actually moved. He needed support from the most impeccable authorities he could find. As he looked for evidence on whether any of them agreed with him, he was pleased and relieved to be able to cite from his reading of Cicero "that Nicetus thought the world moved."[45] And he found Plutarch reporting "that there were others of the same opinion."[46] Copernicus also demonstrated his careful and critical reading of Ptolemy, "who stands so far in front of all the others on account of his wonderful care and industry."[47] Having thus cleverly aligned himself with the one undisputed authority, Copernicus turned around and proved with his own primitive instruments that Ptolemy had made gross errors in placing the earth at the center of the universe. This is a fine example of the use of reading both as defense and attack.

Letters between Galileo and Johannes Kepler show that they both read Copernicus and accepted his findings on the relationship of the earth and the sun. This was basic, of course, in their approach to their own scientific work.

But it was some other reading that started Galileo on his astounding celestial discoveries. He told about it in The Starry Messenger (1610). He had heard of a "spy-glass" made by a "certain Fleming."[48] When he received confirmation of the invention in a letter from one of his students, he read with close attention and figured out how to make his own telescope. What he saw and reported on when he turned it toward the night sky--the mountains of the moon, the stars in the Milky Way, sun spots, and other marvels he was the first to see--made him an immortal of science. It also made him prey to the Holy Inquisition, whose bigoted judges believed neither what they plainly saw with their own eyes nor the proof written by their victim. His unorthodox revelations threatened their truly blind and despotic authority. He was tried by the

Church, found guilty of teaching Copernicanism, and punished by being placed in secluded house arrest. Now, after 350 years, the Church seems about to forgive Galileo, one of its most loyal sons, for having discovered one of the great scientific truths.

Kepler, Galileo's friendly correspondent, like Copernicus, paraded his debts to the books of ancient authorities. His Epitome of Copernician Astronomy (1618-21) leaned heavily on Aristotle. Book Four was intended to supplement Aristotle's On the Heavens. Kepler constantly referred to several of the ancient Greek's works, which he knew intimately. In asking his reader not to blame him for "seeking after novelty," he wanted to have his own "doctrines say whether there is truth" in him, because "most of the ones I hold have been taken from other writers."[49] Among those upon whom he built his "whole astronomy" were Copernicus, Tycho Brahe, and William Gilbert, whose "philosophy of magnetism"[50] he accepted. Kepler's deep knowledge made it possible for him to perform one of the most difficult and important feats in the history of astronomy, the correct calculation of the orbits of the planets. He used his reading to correct errors that had stood for two thousand years. All of his successors depended on his findings in their own work.

Had it not been for a fortuitous acquisition of a book, Sir Isaac Newton, the most prestigious English inheritor of the great truth-seeking tradition of Copernicus, Galileo, and Kepler, might have stayed on the family farm tinkering with machinery, building wind-up mills and water clocks, and carving wooden vessels. But when he was about fifteen, young Isaac bought "a book on Judicial Astronomy"[51] at the Stourbridge Fair. According to David Brewster's Memoirs of the Life, Writings, and Discoveries of Sir Isaac Newton (1885), Isaac, in perusing his new book, was puzzled by a picture of the heavens. His itch to resolve his puzzlement led him to buy "an English Euclid with an index of all the problems at the end of it."[52] He found the Euclid so simple that he threw it away "as a trifling book."[53] Next he tackled Descartes' La Géométrie. This was a challenge worthy of his intelligence. He struggled with it, laid it aside, and finally mastered it without help. He came to love geometry. He was also a close student of Kepler, whose works on optics and the movements of the planets were essential tools in his light experiments and his discovery of the law of gravitation. Other important reading influences on Newton were Pierre Gassendi on atomism, Robert Boyle on chemistry, and Henry More on the magical Hermetic tradition. All these writers played significant roles in Newton's monumental contributions to essential scientific knowledge. But it was finding that book on "Judicial Astronomy" at Stourbridge Fair that started him on the course that made him one of the supreme scientists of all time.

In contrast to Newton, Albert Einstein, two centuries later, was an intellectually undistinguished boy. When his father asked the headmaster of Albert's school what line of work his son should go into, the answer was, "It doesn't matter, he'll never make a success of anything."[54] Many years later, Einstein said he sometimes asked himself how it happened that he was the one to originate the theory of relativity. He concluded that "a normal adult never stops to think about problems of time and space."[55] Since his own mental development was slow, he felt he began to wonder about these problems only after he was an adult. He reasoned, "Naturally I could go deeper into the problem than a child with normal abilities."[56]

Actually, it was a pocket compass his father gave him when, at five, he was sick in bed, that first made him think about space. He believed the compass needle, always returning to north, must be acted on by something out in space. A few years later he read a book on Euclidian geometry. He was not sure just how the compass and the geometry book affected him.

But a family friend identified the immediate cause of Einstein's turn toward science. This man, Max Talmey, wrote that the boy "showed a particular inclination toward physics" and liked to talk about physical phenomena. Talmey gave him A. Bernstein's Popular Books on Physical Science and L. Büchner's Force and Matter, two books then popular in Germany. Albert took to these books immediately. The Bernstein book especially deepened his interest in physical science. When the boy began to show interest in mathematics, Talmey gave him Spieker's Lehrbuch der Ebenen Geometrie. Every week Albert would show his mentor the problems he had solved. Kant became his favorite philosopher after he read The Critique of Pure Reason at his benefactor's suggestion. He is also said to have read Darwin.

According to Ronald W. Clark's Albert Einstein: The Life and Times (1971), the scientist claimed that "through the reading of popular scientific books I soon reached the conviction that much of the stories in the Bible could not be true."57   So he became a religious skeptic and began to suspect all authority.   This suspicion of authority was reinforced when he was a student at Zurich by Ernst Mach's Science of Mechanics.   He found "Mach's greatness in his incorruptible skepticism and independence."58   The questioning attitude became ingrained.   It led him to disprove much that had been considered the absolute truth, including some of Newton's "laws."   From the evidence it is clear that much of the ammunition Einstein used to blow up false ideas came from his careful reading of a wide assortment of books.

- THE ASTOUNDING CONSEQUENCES OF THE MISTAKE YOUNG LOUIS PASTEUR FOUND IN HIS READING -

At the age of twenty-two, Louis Pasteur was asked to read "an account of a remarkably elegant experiment" by a celebrated German chemist, Eilhardt Mitscherlich, to the Academy of Science in Paris in 1844.   Jacques Nicholle, in Louis Pasteur: A Master of Scientific Inquiry (1961), told how Pasteur repeated the German chemist's experiment on paratartrate crystals and the polarization of light.   He spotted an "obvious contradiction"59 in Mitscherlich's work.   He found it impossible to believe that the molecular structure of two bodies could be the same when they reacted differently to polarized light.   Pasteur investigated the problem.   So began a train of events during which Pasteur saved from ruin the brewing, wine, and silk industries.   In the process, he made himself his country's most famous scientist and a national hero.

One of his other triumphs embroiled Pasteur in bitter controversy with established scientists who accepted "knowledge" from authorities without testing it.   In this case, once again it was Pasteur's sharp eye that detected an error in a scientific paper.   In a note on spontaneous generation by an academic named Pouchet, Pasteur came upon conclusions he could not accept.   In a series of experiments, Pasteur proved his case.   The simplicity, brilliance, and meticulousness of his methods set an example for all scientists.   Besides destroying a cherished but ridiculous myth, Pasteur opened the way to the discovery of pasteurization, which drastically reduced the devastation from germ-caused diseases.

Pasteur's effectiveness as a scientist and benefactor of mankind began when he read something by an "authority" carefully enough to find and correct a basic error.

- READING IN THE RACE TO SOLVE THE PROBLEMS OF THE GENES -

James D. Watson, twenty-four years old in the early 1950s, was knocking around the biological laboratories of the United States and Europe trying to figure out the structure of deoxyribonucleid acid, or DNA, the basic substance of life. In Copenhagen he came upon some writing by Linus Pauling. He read it and reread it. But he said, "Most of the language was above me." He could get only a general impression of Pauling's argument. He could not judge "whether it made sense." But he was sure "that it was written with style."60 One thing that caught his eye and stuck in his mind was Pauling's reference to something called an a-helix.

For Francis Crick, the Englishman with whom Watson worked on DNA, a crucial influence was his reading of What Is Life? by Erwin Schrödinger. This book, which introduced the idea that genes were essential parts of living cells, turned Crick from physics to biology and research at Cambridge University.

The Double Helix (1968) was unusually personal and uninhibited for a book on a scientific subject. In it Watson recalled the pell-mell search for the structure of DNA. His reading about the a-helix and Crick's reading on the genes as parts of living cells were basic in the search, in which they were joined by Maurice H. F. Wilkins. The three of them won the Nobel Prize in 1963 for their discovery, which had tremendous implications for future genetic research. The creation of new forms of life in the laboratory was brought closer by what they found.

Some years after the discovery of the double helix, reading again dramatically influenced critical genetic research. Dr. Hamilton O. Smith, at work in his Johns Hopkins laboratory in Baltimore, noticed something odd in the genes he was investigating. He was puzzled by the precise way in which they were being sliced. Then he remembered an article by Dr. Werner Arber of Basel, who had theorized the existence of powerful restriction enzymes. Such enzymes, unlike others, do not attack protein. They break the strands of DNA, however. Dr. Arber did not actually find the restriction enzymes. But recalling the article, Smith realized he had isolated what the Swiss scientist had written about. Dr. Daniel Nathans, a Johns Hopkins virologist, was on leave in Israel. When

Smith wrote to him about his findings and Arber's theory, he found a way to put the newly-identified enzymes to work breaking the genetic code. This brilliant international triple play further opened the way to the awesome possibilities of genetic engineering. It won the collaborators the Nobel Prize. Their work was described in the Baltimore Evening Sun (October 13, 1978), [61] by Jon Franklin and Michael J. Himowitz.

- POPULAR LITERATURE AND FICTION INSPIRE SCIENTISTS -

While practicing scientists constantly study professional literature, like Hamilton Smith, when he found the key to the genetic code, other geniuses of science have been stimulated by popular books and fiction in public libraries.

It was "in a far corner of the [Enoch] Pratt [Free] Library"[62] of Baltimore that Rachel Carson, the biologist, found Henry Williamson's Tarka the Otter and The Outermost House by Henry Beston. "Since then," she said, "I have read and reread them more times than I can count; they are among the books that I have loved best and have influenced me most."[63] Her reading of Albert Schweitzer's statement on his reverence for life also made a most powerful impact on her thinking. Gentle and peaceful though she was, this reading gave her a fierce determination to secure respect and protection for nature. She created a furor comparable to that aroused by Darwin when her Silent Spring came out in 1962. The book convulsed the leaders of the chemical industry. They attacked Rachel Carson most viciously. But she prevailed. The House of Life: Rachel Carson at Work ... (1972) by Paul Brooks tells how she stirred up and mobilized conservationists and concerned government officials, including Senator Ribicoff, Senator Robert Kennedy, and Stewart Udall, Secretary of the Interior. All of them read her book and were moved by it to enact laws protecting human, animal, and vegetable life from death by pesticides, and the earth, sky, and water from lethal pollution.

Robert Goddard, the pioneer of rocketry, like Rachel Carson, found that light reading stimulated his imagination and pushed him to action. He acquired much of his early education from the public library of Worcester, Massachussetts. His reading about carbon and diamonds was the inspiration for an experiment that almost blew up his attic "laboratory." Then H. G. Wells turned him to space. The War of the Worlds, which he read in the Boston Post, did the trick. On one of Wells' last birthdays, Goddard wrote to tell him he had read the story at sixteen, "and the new viewpoints of scientific application, as well as the compelling realism ... made a deep impression."[64] He decided, as a result, "that what might be called 'high altitude research' was the most fascinating problem in existence."[65] Goddard also recorded in his diary his reading of Jules Verne's Journey From the Earth to the Moon as a factor in his getting started with rockets.

Among Goddard's reading, as reported in Milton Lehman's This High Man: The Life of Robert H. Goddard (1963), was some technical material. This included Newton's Principia Mathematica, in which the Third Law on action and reaction caught his attention; articles on physics and chemistry in Cassell's Popular Educator; and Smithsonian Institution papers by Samuel P. Langley on his experiments with steam-powered aircraft.

This scientific reading was certainly useful to Goddard in his patient, long experimentation to develop effective rockets. But Goddard recognized the triggering effect of Wells' science fiction when he wrote,

> Wells' wonderfully true psychology made the whole thing very vivid, and possible ways and means of accomplishing the physical marvels kept me busy thinking.[66]

Like Goddard, young Isaac Rabi was fascinated by space. He spent much of his adult life in research and teaching in some of the world's most distinguished universities. These institutions boasted massive and comprehensive research libraries. But it was in the Brooklyn Public Library that Isaac's intellectual life began. In The New Yorker (October 13, 1975), Jeremy Bernstein reported on Rabi's first reading aside from textbooks, prayer books, and Yiddish Bible stories. He was a listless student at P. S. 22. But one day he saw a boy with a book that was "clearly not a schoolbook."[67] It aroused his curiosity. He found it had come from the neighborhood branch library. He made his way there and got a card after proving to a dubious librarian that he could read, even though he was undersized. He plunged right into the fairy tales in the children's section. He worked his way alphabetically through the fiction. Then he came to the science shelf:

> So I started with astronomy. That's where I first heard of the Copernican system and the explanation of the changes of the seasons, the phases of the moon, and the idea that the stars were suns, very distant suns ... for me it was a tremendous revelation. I was so impressed--the beauty of it all, and the simplicity. 68

Young Isaac did not read science exclusively. He kept looking into interesting books of fiction. Jack London's The Iron Heel made him think. Its précis of Marxist theory fascinated him. He read other leftist authors and was for a time involved with socialists. His reading in the field may have helped him understand Robert Oppenheimer when he was hounded out of the inner circle of atomic scientists for "disloyalty." Rabi had worked closely on the bomb with Oppenheimer. He was one of the few scientists who stood by his beleaguered colleague.

The Nobel Prize for Physics that was awarded to Rabi in 1944 for his atomic discoveries capped a brilliant career. The first step toward that career was taken when he showed up as a small boy at a branch of the Brooklyn Public Library and began going through the fairy tales, popular science, and fiction.

Carl Sagan, like Rabi, was a Brooklyn boy. He also found his branch library early and he was a regular customer. His first request was for books about the stars. After a contretemps with a librarian with Hollywood stars on her mind, he found the right books and began reading. Then, when he was a pupil at P.S. 101, he discovered the Edgar Rice Burroughs stories of John Carter's adventures on Mars:

> I simply devoured what seemed to me the riches of another planet's biology.... It was very exciting, and I loved those books. They were full of new ideas. I tried to imagine my way to Mars, the way Carter did: I would go into a vacant lot, spread my arms, and wish to be on Mars.... Suddenly, it dawned on me that this was fiction; maybe there was a better way to get to Mars. 69

Sagan found the better way, which was described in a profile in The New Yorker (June 21, 1976) by Henry S. F. Cooper, Jr. One stop along the way was the reading of a study for a multistage rocket by the British Interplanetary

Society. After study at the University of Chicago, seeing Mars for the first time through a telescope in Texas, and sessions at Berkeley, Stanford, and other famous centers of learning, he joined the faculty at Cornell University. He played a major role in planning the Viking rockets, the first man-made objects to leave the solar system.

In his Cornell office, Sagan kept on his wall a map of Burroughs' Mars, with marks showing where Carter had landed. This was his acknowledgement of his debt to fiction reading for his renowned space achievements.

- SOME UNPREDICTABLE RESULTS OF READING BY SCIENTISTS -

Among the many uncertainties of human experience are the consequences of reading. Some of the cases just cited show that one can never know what will result when a book is opened and read. Here are some more examples.

Around the middle of the eighteenth century, a poor boy in an out-of-the-way place was preparing himself, under the most unpromising circumstances, to make notable contributions in two demanding disciplines. He was Benjamin Banneker, a free black. He grew up on a farm at Ellicott Mills, a few miles from Baltimore. According to Henry E. Baker, in an article in the <u>Journal of Negro History</u> (April 1918) titled "Benjamin Banneker: The Negro Mathematician and Astronomer,"

> Young Benjamin's diligent reading of the books at his command served to develop his mental powers rapidly, giving him a retentive memory, correct forms of speech and a keen power of analysis.[70]

When his friend and neighbor, George Ellicott, lent him books, he was astonished that Benjamin needed no help with them. Like Isaac Newton, Banneker was endowed with remarkable native intelligence. He quickly mastered the abstruse astronomical information. Then he compiled his first ephemeris, a highly technical and intellectually demanding project. Several editions of Banneker's <u>Almanack and Ephemeris</u> were published in Baltimore during the 1790s. They are now rare collectors' items.

Banneker's part in the design of Washington, D.C.,

like his Almanack and Ephemeris, was extraordinary. He had mastered surveying and mathematics through reading and experience with the Ellicotts, who were involved with Pierre-Charles L'Enfant in designing a national capital on a malarial swamp. L'Enfant was temperamental and hard to get along with. President Washington fired him. The testy Frenchman left with most of the plans. The project was in limbo until Benjamin Banneker saved the day. His reading and his powers of observation and memory served him and the nation in good stead. He recreated L'Enfant's plans from memory, and the city took its characteristic shape, which, in its convolutions, was appropriate for pedestrians and slow-moving carriages. One must credit the reading of Benjamin Banneker for much of his brilliant achievement.

Another spate of reading with unexpected results was that of James B. Conant. He made his reputation as a chemist. Then in turn he took on the demanding presidency of Harvard University and the even more demanding job of High Commissioner in post-World War II Berlin. In My Several Lives: Memoirs of a Social Inventor (1970), Conant attested to the help he found in Burnet's History of His Own Time and Clarendon's History of the Rebellion. These works, along with other documents of the time, deepened his insight into human behavior. He found "The Puritan Rebellion furnished many examples of conduct under stress (including the conduct of scholars)."[71] He traced his "tendency to expect the worst when dealing with people" to "a prolonged self-inflicted dose of seventeenth-century history."[72] It is not exactly the outcome one would expect of this kind of reading.

But James B. Conant himself credited his reading of history with helping him, a scientist, learn to ride herd on an army of scholars and other independent-minded and often obstreperous characters.

Like Conant, B. F. Skinner, the behavioral psychologist, was influenced in an unexpected way by some reading. He became known for his skill in teaching pigeons to pilot bombs and play table tennis, for his controversial Skinner Box for infants, and for his even more controversial book, Walden Two, which proposed a socially-engineered Utopia. His reading, not unexpectedly, included the books of Bertrand Russell, John B. Watson, and Pavlov. But the clue to his scientific study of behavior, strangely, was found in a preface by Chesterton to Dickens' The Old Curiosity Shop. Skinner related the circumstances in Particulars of My Life (1976):

> There is an odd literary question which I wonder is not put more often in literature. How far can an author tell a truth without seeing it himself? I was once talking to a highly intelligent lady about Thackerary's Newcomes. We were speaking of the character of Mrs. Mackenzie, the Campaigner, and in the middle of the conversation, the lady leaned across to me and said in a low, hoarse, but emphatic voice, 'She drank. Thackerary didn't know it: but she drank.' ... How far can a writer thus indicate a truth of which he himself is ignorant?[73]

Skinner, after coming on this passage, wrote, "That was my cue. I was interested in human behavior, but I had been investigating it in the wrong way."[74] He had been trying to become a writer. A friend had told him that science was the art of the twentieth century. Skinner believed him. Since literature was dead as an art form, he would turn to science. And he did.

It is hard to understand just what it was in the passage quoted that made him do it. From what he wrote, his friend certainly had something to do with it. But Skinner held this bit of reading responsible for his switch from writing to science.

- OBSERVATIONS -

Since science is based on curiosity, it is not surprising that the youthful reading of the scientists covered a broad range of subject matter. Like infants, they reached out for whatever they could grab.

Having developed the reading habit, they usually concentrated on books about adventure and new discoveries, real or imagined. Factual or fanciful, the books they read helped shape their minds and their careers. Carl Sagan seems to have been as enduringly influenced by Edgar Rice Burrough's highly imaginary biology of Mars as was Newton by the fact-filled book on judicial astronomy. And The War of the Worlds, H. G. Wells' flamboyant fiction, made as momentous an impact on Robert Goddard as Darwin's soberly-reasoned Origin made on Ernst Haeckel.

One remarkable aspect of the reading of several of the scientists is the gap between the intentions of authors and the effect of their books on the readers. It is easy to see how books on adventure, discovery, and travel would have gotten Darwin, Wallace, Haeckel, Goddard, Rabi and Sagan to thinking seriously about the excitement of scientific exploration and of devoting their lives to it. And it is not an effort to visualize them and others aiming at careers in science being critically influenced by accounts of the wonderful advances of knowledge by pioneers of science. But when Malthus wrote his essay on population, it could not have been foreseen that both Charles Darwin and Alfred Russel Wallace would find clues to the theory of evolution in it. Who would have guessed that Louis Pasteur's finding of a mistake in a scientific paper he was asked to read would be the starting point for his succession of revolutionary discoveries? No one could have expected that the unguided, but careful reading, of poor black Benjamin Banneker, in astronomy and surveying, would enable him to compile his complicated Almanack and Ephemeris or to complete the confusing design of Washington, D.C. James B. Conant's application of knowledge garnered from seventeenth-century history in dealing effectively with complex twentieth-century administrative problems could not well have been anticipated. Nor could B. F. Skinner's decision to change from writing to science by reading about a strange conjecture in a Chesterton preface to a Dickens novel.

There is no doubt that many other influences played on the achievements of these scientists. It is risky to make arbitrary judgments on cause and effect when one has only a few bits of evidence. On the other hand, it seems beyond question that the reading reviewed, largely reported by the readers themselves, and credited by them with powerful influence, was indeed crucial in determining their lives and work.

There appears to be among scientists a special sensitivity to stimuli that others often do not respond to. They seem to have the ability, found among creative people, to see significant relationships that others miss. And they are able to put their perceptions to work in innovative ways. Karl Shapiro once called a library full of books "a platform for uninhibited leaps."[75] Most of the scientists have demonstrated the truth of Shapiro's statement as their reading has projected them to intellectual leaps of amazing heights and uninhibited originality.

Chapter 6

DECISIVE READING OF FIFTEEN PRACTITIONERS AND SCIENTISTS OF MEDICINE

The mountains of medical publications--journals, monographs, textbooks, histories of medicine, biographies and autobiographies of outstanding men and women doctors and investigators--show how basic reading is for those who work in the many medical fields. Following is a series of brief reviews of the reading of fifteen medical practitioners and scientists whose contributions have advanced knowledge and relieved human suffering. Identifying the crucial reading and the circumstances under which it occurred should help us to a better understanding of the role of reading in the careers of these creative men and women of medicine.

- AMBROISE PARÉ, 1510-1590 -

Paré, often called the father of modern surgery, gained much of his superb skill in treating gunshot wounds as an army surgeon. He came on one of his most important discoveries, the use of a soothing mixture for wounds instead of the standard agonizing application of boiling oil, when he ran out of the searing oil and improvised with a blend of egg yolk, rose oil, and turpentine. He was more conservative than most of his slashing contemporaries, cutting only when no other treatment seemed possible. But he was also an enlightened innovator. He abandoned castration in hernia operations, implanted teeth, fashioned artifical limbs and eyes, and was among the first to observe that syphilis caused the swelling of blood vessels.

Like most sixteenth-century surgeons, Paré learned much by observing and assisting in operations. He also attended lectures at the Paris Hôtel Dieu, adding to his knowledge by systematic reading. J. Malgaigne, in <u>Surgery and Ambroise Paré</u> (1956), lists the hundreds of authorities cited by Paré. These include the Bible, church fathers, ancient wise men, Arab doctors, medieval savants, and his Renaissance contemporaries. He was most indebted to Galen, Hippocrates, Aëtius, Pliny, Avicenna, and Giovanni da Vigo. So heavy was his borrowing over almost fifty years that his biographer called him a plagiarizer, while forgiving him because everybody in his day did it.

In Briefve Collection de l'Administration Anatomique ... Paré wrote of his debt to Galen:

> My friends, who are newly dedicated to surgery. Considering that knowledge of anatomy is like the foundation upon which all your other precepts pertaining to surgical perfection must be supported: in your behalf I am encouraged to write and to put in brief Galen's teachings concerning the said anatomy, as he was the one whose doctrine is sound and to whom is owed almost all we have in this area of medicine and surgery. I do not want to imply that I have read Galen in Greek or Latin, for it did not please God to give me the grace in my youth to be taught either language. Likewise, I would not conceal the fact I got the said document of Galen from the French translation of Master Jehan Canape, Regent Doctor in the Faculté de Médécine, living at Lyons.[1]

This is at once a refreshing acknowledgement of his debt to Galen and his lack of Latin and Greek, two languages so important in Renaissance scholarship.

Paré explained and justified his borrowing when he wrote:

> If some want to compare me to the crow embellished by the plumes of the parrot and other birds, then left bare when each recognized and took back his feathers, I reply that, despite the foregoing admission, there is nothing in this little book which I have not got by my own labor and which I have not done by myself. So that these great worthy personages from whom I have enriched myself cannot accuse me of doing them any more wrong than a candle does to her sister from whom she takes the light, I wish to inform you that I did not undertake this book until after having worked for a long

time at the Hôtel Dieu in Paris, in the wars, and in other places.[2]

Paré went even further in admitting his borrowing in the following "Author's Sonnet" which introduced his complete works:

> This Book, which now first sees the light of day,
>   Heir of my art, does all the secrets hold
>   Left by the Arabs and the Greeks of old
>   In lengthy writings of our fathers gray.
> 'Tis filled with precepts various, as gay
>   As meadows dotted with blooms thousandfold
>   When they feel the warmth of the rays of gold
>   Of the Sun above on his vernal way.
> Now up and away, my child so dear,
>   For forty years my constant care to read
>   Go and beg all kindly to emulate
> Lysippus, who Apelles gently chid:
>   But you, the envious, avaunt! I bid
>   My work, despite you, have long life as fate.[3]

In Paré we have the perfect example of the reader who, by reading to enrich his writing, has placed all his successors in his debt. As he lighted his candle from the books of his predecessors, so successor surgeons have lighted theirs at the works of Paré.

- ANDREAS VESALIUS, 1514-1564 -

Like many young men of the Renaissance with the means and will to acquire a broad education under the most distinguished teachers, Andreas Vesalius traveled across Europe to prepare himself for the practice of medicine. After his elementary schooling in his native Brussels, he studied at the University of Louvain, the medical school of the University of Paris, and the University of Padua where he received his M.D. degree. His education gave him a generous humanistic outlook and a knowledge of Latin and Greek. He also picked up some Arab learning and medicine, at Louvain having made a paraphrase of the writings of the famous Persian physician, Rhazes.

Books, of course, were a constant part of his education. As he was quoted in <u>Andreas Vesalius of Brussels</u> ... (1964) by C. D. O'Malley,

> I recall clearly that when I was at the Castle School of the University of Louvain ... I devoted myself to philosophy. In such commentaries on Aristotle's De Anima as were read to us by our teacher, a theologian by profession and therefore, like our other instructors ... ready to introduce his own pious views into those philosophers, the brain was said to have three ventricles.[4]

Vesalius was to discover for himself the true structure of the brain by dissecting many cadavers. And in his own great work, The Seven Books on the Structure of the Human Body, often called the Fabrica, he reflected his comprehensive training and his detailed knowledge of anatomy from careful and close study of tissue.

Galen was the supreme authority on anatomy. His writings were almost sacred. But Vesalius, who lectured at Padua, unlike many others did not suspend his common sense as he read. Nor did he ignore the evidence before his eyes. His critical reading of Galen was a splendid example of the use of literature to correct long-standing errors. He pointed out that he had lectured three times on Galen's On Bones "before I dared call attention to his mistakes."[5] Light is thrown by O'Malley on the thoughtful use Vesalius made of his reading:

> We may ... visualize Vesalius between the years 1539-1540 and 1542 reading the works of earlier writers on anatomy, pondering, carrying on his investigations and teaching, noting discrepancies from his own observations and additions to the body of anatomical knowledge, even perhaps writing chapters of his book and essaying them as lectures to his students. Nor could it be overlooked that at the outset of this period he had already revised three of Galen's works, especially the Anatomical procedures.... Such close study of Galen's text must have helped assure him that he was on the right track and that Galen had followed the wrong one.[6]

Vesalius' studies of the human body put him on slippery ground on the question of the location of the soul. He knew all too well that he took grave risks if he disagreed with ancient authorities and the church hierarchy. In the Fabrica he tried to protect himself:

> Lest I come into collision here with some scandalmonger or some sort of censor of heresy, I shall wholly abstain from considerations of the divisions of the soul and their locations, since today, and especially among our people, you will find a great many censors of our very holy and true religion. If they hear someone murmur anything about the opinions of Plato, Aristotle or his interpreters, or of Galen, regarding the soul, even in the conduct of anatomy where these matters especially ought to be examined, immediately they judge him to be suspect in his faith and somewhat doubtful regarding the immortality of the soul.
>
> They do not understand that this is a necessity for physicians if they desire to engage properly in their art, to apply remedies correctly to any ailing member, to give consideration to those faculties that guide us, their number, what each is individually, and in what member of the being it is located.... As if one were unable to propose any error in the decisions of those grave authors, or to corroborate their reasons by something new, or to oppose the superficial arguments of others; as if the most holy faith by which we gain salvation through pious works, and by which the souls of men achieve eternal felicity, must be questioned and discussed only according to the teachings of those authors and according to opinions supplied by weak human reason.[7]

The dilemma of the Renaissance medical investigator was nicely exemplified when Vesalius appealed to the Emperor

> to permit this youthful work of mine [he was twenty-eight] to come into the hands of men--to whom for many reasons it is obnoxious--for a short time, under your splendid patronage, until through experience, judgment, and erudition that come with age I may render it more worthy of so great a prince and I may offer another acceptable gift on some other subject taken from our art.[8]

The custom of the time made him grovel in this ceremonial style to spread a truth that contradicted the dogmas of Galen. His critical reading of the ancient medico made it possible for Vesalius to advance the science of anatomy. His writing influenced all future anatomists and surgeons. He set an example to others as he learned and added to essential knowledge by reading to stimulate thought, maintaining a healthy skepticism of "authorities," using his own reason and experience as corrective guides.

- WILLIAM HARVEY, 1578-1657 -

Like Vesalius, Harvey topped off his medical training at Padua. He took with him a sound basic English education in religion, Latin, the classics, philosophy, and rhetoric. He had been introduced to medicine at Gonville Hall and Caius College, Cambridge.

When, according to Geoffrey Keynes, in The Life of William Harvey (1966), Robert Boyle, the famous chemist and founding member of the Royal Society, asked Harvey how he came to discover the circulation of the blood, his answer suggested that Fabricius, who taught at Padua, was an important source. De Venarum Ostiolis, a treatise on the valves of the veins, published at Padua, was one of Fabricius' major contributions to medical knowledge. In his De Motu Cordis, Harvey referred to Fabricius' findings, but pointed out that Fabricius did not understand the function of the veins. Even so, his reading of the book on the valves was crucial. It started him toward his own revolutionary discovery. In addition to the evidence of this careful reading, Harvey's writing shows his familiarity with dozens of ancient and contemporary writers. He knew Galen's works thoroughly and was well up on Aristotle.

Aristotle had written that "Those who run naked in the summer have a healthier colour than those who wear garments."[9] After reading this, Harvey advised his readers:

> The shape of the skin is the shape of the body, wherefore the best fashion to leap, to run, to do anything [is to] strip to the skin. Fashion is but excess of covering fantastically arranged.[10]

Harvey paid the philosopher a high tribute when he wrote that he "prized Aristotle's judgement so highly that I would never recede from his Oracles without premeditation."[11] He showed he was a most discriminating reader, using the giants of the mind respectfully and diligently, garnering what he could from their wisdom, but, like Vesalius, always thinking for himself, and, if necessary, improving on them.

- JOHN HUNTER, 1728-1793 -

John Kobler, in The Reluctant Surgeon: A Biography of John Hunter (1960), wrote:

> Since his death ... John Hunter has been variously described by his fellow scientists as 'the Shakespeare of medicine,' 'A philosopher whose mental grasp embraced the whole range of nature's works,' and 'one of the greatest men the English nation has produced.'[12]

This genius, however, was anything but a willing student at grammar school, where he was subjected to

> a little reading and writing ... a great deal of spelling and figures; geography which never got beyond the dullest statistics, and a little philosophy, and chemistry dry as sawdust and as valuable for deadening purposes.[13]

Young John Hunter was also sentenced to Latin, and "from the age of nine" the pupils were required to speak it exclusively in class and in conversation. He hated it.

It is not surprising that with this attitude, coupled with his chronic skipping of classes, he was put down "as an idle, surly dullard, irredeemable by punishment or reward."[14] What his teachers did not know was that John found knowledge in nature, where he studied on his own. His mother gave up on him and took him out of school when he was thirteen. All he carried with him was "a permanent distaste for the halls of academe"[15] and the ability to write barely coherent English.

He took this antipathy for reading to the University of Glasgow, where he received no degree. This lack did not keep him from establishing and carrying on a large practice in obstetrics, nor did it prevent him from founding pathological anatomy in England. It is remarkable that in spite of his distaste for reading he wrote several major books on the circulation of the blood, the skeleton, and reproduction. The Anatomy of the Human Gravid Uterus, Exhibited in Figures was a landmark anatomical book. Hunter relied mainly on his own observations and on the mammoth collection of anatomical specimens he collected in his research. But it was said that his limited reading caused him needless effort, and that "He might spend weeks struggling with a problem unaware that it had been solved by other investigators."[16]

John Hunter is an exception to the rule that reading makes the full medical man. However, his books were essential to his successors.

- EDWARD JENNER, 1749-1823 -

Edward Jenner was well prepared to get along with John Hunter, under whom he studied surgery in London. Like his master, he had a taste for natural history and had collected nests and fossils around Cirencester as a boy. His great career was described by F. Dawtrey Brewitt in The Life of Edward Jenner, M.D., F.R.S.: Naturalist and Discoverer of Vaccination (1931).

Although his formal education was scant, Jenner knew how to put information to work. He heard a milkmaid say she could not catch smallpox because she had had cowpox. This led to his discovery of an effective vaccine, the first step in a two-hundred-year campaign against one of the most devastating scourges ever suffered by the human race.

While Jenner admitted small indebtedness to reading, his own writing spread knowledge of his discovery around the world. In 1800, his pamphlet, An Inquiry into the Causes and Effects of Variolae Vacciniae, reached the United States. It was read by Dr. Benjamin Waterhouse of Massachusetts. He secured some lymph and, starting with his own children, launched a vaccination program that immunized many Americans, including the family of President Thomas Jefferson. Jenner's work was translated into French and went through three editions in seven months. Guided by Jenner's writing, the doctors of the world have finally wiped out the terrible disease.

The only reading that made a strong impact on Jenner, of which I could find a record, was not related to medicine. He was called upon the testify before the House of Lords on a challenge to the legitimacy of his country neighbors, the Berkeley family. He dreaded this ordeal and was afraid it would bring on a nervous breakdown. He compared his feelings to those of "Cooper the poet, when his intellect at last gave way to his fears about the execution of his office in the House of Lords."[17] He said, "It was reading 'Cooper's life,' I believe, which saved my own senses, by putting me fully in view of my danger."[18] Luckily for Jenner, Parliament was dissolved and he was spared the agony of testifying, for which his reading of the life of the poet had prepared him.

- FLORENCE NIGHTINGALE, 1820-1910 -

The English lady whose dreams, struggles and achievements were chronicled by Cecil Woodham-Smith in <u>Florence Nightingale</u> (1951) could easily have lived a comfortable, even a luxurious life. She came from a well-placed family where, under the tutelage of her gifted father, she received an excellent education in the classics and languages. She was attractive enough to have made a rich marriage. But Florence had other fish to fry. Reform was in the air during her impressionable years, and she was stimulated by the new ideas on social betterment. She felt God was calling her to a life of service to humanity. She tried a number of times to break out of her sheltered cocoon. However, she was frustrated by her family and the obstacles faced by middle-class nineteenth-century women who wanted to use their talents and brains.

Nursing attracted her, but it was considered a low calling. Nurses were often disreputable women. Florence began studying Parliamentary reports on public health and made herself an expert in the field. It was the reading of a document sent by a friend that led to the realization of her dream:

> In October [1846] Chevalier Bunsen sent her the Year Book of the Institution of Deaconesses at Kaiserswerth ... with overwhelming joy she realized that Kaiserwerth was what she had been seeking. There she could have training in nursing, and objections raised against British hospitals did not apply. The religious atmosphere, the ascetic discipline placed the nurses above suspicion. On October 7 she wrote ... 'There is my home, there are my brothers and sisters at work. There my heart is and there, I trust, will one day be my body.'
>
> The Year Book became her treasure, but she did not dare mention Kaiserwerth to her mother. Fanny was more successful than ever, and Embley [the family home] was filled for autumn parties; and so, she wrote ... whenever she wanted 'refreshment in the midst of this table d'hote of people ...' she went upstairs and secretly read the Year Book. [19]

Finally, she overcame all obstacles and went to Germany. She completed the four-year course, came back to London, and was appointed superintendent of the Institution for the Care of Sick Gentlewomen, where she was a successful administrator. But she wanted a greater challenge. It came with the Crimean War. There she took the first steps toward immortality for her heroic work, against odds and official foot-dragging, in introducing cleanliness, system, and human concern for soldiers wounded in combat. Her alleviation of human suffering through her skillful and caring management of nursing service made her famous around the world. Among the fruits of her work were a Sanitation Department in the Indian Office, a school for nurses in England, and an army medical school.

She was the first woman to receive the Order of Merit. At her death, the nation offered a national funeral and burial in Westminster Abbey. By her wish, these honors were declined.

In her later years, Florence Nightingale was attracted by the writings of medieval mystics. Old age brought blindness and a clouded mind. But her life of merciful service to the suffering lighted up a dark part of human existence. And it all started with her loving reading of the Kaiserwerth Year Book.

- ELIZABETH BLACKWELL, 1821-1910 -

Like her contemporary, Florence Nightingale, Elizabeth Blackwell struggled long, through many discouragements, to reach her goal. As indicated by the title of her biography, <u>Lone Woman: The Story of Elizabeth Blackwell, the First Woman Doctor</u> (1970), by Dorothy Clarke Wilson, this English-born, American-raised woman fought her way to a medical degree against odds that seemed insuperable, especially for a woman of her time. But Elizabeth was a woman of great courage and tenacity.

The Blackwell family was large and well off when Elizabeth was born into it at Bristol, where her father was a sugar refiner. They read together or listened to the father read from Cowper or another poet. They sailed through poets, essayists, historians, and other serious writers. It was a sticky wicket when the girls of the family discovered Sir

Walter Scott's novels. Would their father approve? He did, after his own reading, and with enthusiasm.

Bad days were ahead for the Blackwells. The sugar refinery burned down. So the family moved to New York to start over. But after initial success they were ruined by another fire. Then they tried to get back on their feet in Cincinnati. However, the father died, leaving the then impoverished family to shift for themselves. Through their pluck and unwillingness to give up, they stayed together and survived precariously.

Elizabeth had continued the education begun at home. She studied French, history, and physiology. The last she found unpleasant. She was disgusted at the thought of studying the human body, and the exposure in the classroom of a bullfrog's eye turned her stomach. How, then, did this delicate woman ever get started on the road to distinction as the first doctor of her sex, surgeon, gynecologist, and founder and administrator of hospitals and nurses training schools?

An early push came from some reading she did in her teens. As she put it in her journal:

> February 14 [1836]. Read [John] Foster's essay on decision of character. How I do long for some end to act for, some end to be obtained in this life, for though that most glorious end 'to serve God and enjoy him forever' is before me and trust I am laboring toward that end, yet God has given us talents to be used in earthly pursuits; and to go on every day in much the same jogtrot manner without an object is wearisome.[20]

But it was not reading that made her decide to become a doctor. It was a heart-wrenching experience with a friend dying of cancer, whose suffering was increased because she had to be treated by a man. She pleaded with Elizabeth to go into medicine so she could care for sick women. Elizabeth had never thought of such an unlikely calling. But she promised to think about it.

Her reading of the New England writers, Emerson, Thoreau, Theodore Parker, Bronson Alcott, and Margaret Fuller, had intensified her desire to work for the public good. She regularly followed the literature of several socialistic communities then getting started in the country. Her study of reformers like Cousin and Fourier strengthened her resolve to become an agent of useful change. Reading Swedenborg, with his emphasis on the reality and the presence of heaven and hell, made her "accutely conscious of the heavens and hells all around her."[21] Teaching in Kentucky and South Carolina showed her close up the evils of slavery and poverty.

A friend in Cincinnati had lent her Elizabeth Jackson's Memoirs, a book containing information on French medical education. This raised her hopes. But she had to earn her living, and to get into any medical school anywhere seemed beyond her. However, when she was teaching in Charleston and living in the home of a doctor who was also a professor in the local medical school, her hopes revived. She read the doctor's medical books, picked up some medical nomenclature, and identified the bones in the office skeleton.

What stimulated her most, though, were books that showed her the respected place held in medicine by women back to ancient times. Healing, frequently in history, had been the recognized province of women. Hebrew midwives mentioned in the Bible "might very well have been trained in the Temple of Sais, where gynecology and obstetrics were taught by women."[22] In Greco-Roman history she found the names of many women who were medical students and doctors as well as midwives. Elizabeth was excited to read about "Aspasia, such a specialist in obstetrics that she was quoted in Greek and Latin medical works for over a thousand years."[23] She learned that three early Roman Christian women, Fabiola, Marcella, and Paula, "devoted themselves to healing the sick, establishing hospitals which became models for institutions spreading all over Europe."[24] Think of the thrill Elizabeth felt when she read about Trotula in the Middle Ages,

> who served on the faculty of the first medical school in Europe, at Salerno, at the height of its fame in the eleventh century, and whose books on gynecology were studied for five hundred years. Like many physician's wives, she had acquired knowledge as an assistant to her husband in an era when medicine was largely a family occupation. And at Salerno, center of European science, there were not only women professors on the faculty but in time the whole department for women's diseases was handed over entirely to women! In the eighteenth century at the University of Bologna ... Anna Morandi Manzolini ... assisted her husband and, after his death succeeded to his chair as professor of anatomy.[25]

Elizabeth's excitement at finding that so many women had actually blazed the trail was intensified when she found she would not be the first doctor of her name. Elizabeth Blackwell, a Scotswoman, a century earlier had studied medicine with her husband and continued his practice when he was jailed for debt. Her namesake had also published a book on herbs that became a classic in medical libraries. This discovery of the earlier Elizabeth Blackwell was the clincher. She wrote to her sister, "My mind is fully made up. I am quite fully resolved to go through with the study of medicine."26

And she did. After being turned away from a number of schools, finally she was admitted to the Geneva Medical College, a small institution in upstate New York, when the senior class voted--in jest, they thought--to permit a woman to study among them. She went through the course with flying colors. With her degree in hand, she practiced in New York City, studied in France, and went on to an illustrious career.

She organized hospitals and medical schools for women in New York and London, and generally reflected great credit upon herself, proving that a determined woman, even a tiny one, such as she was, without influence or position, could distinguish herself in a profession that made heavy demands, intellectually and physically, on its practitioners.

Her brilliant success in the work through which she benefited so many humans and set an example that was followed by other courageous women, was due in large part to the stimulation of the provocative and practical books she read.

- RUDOLF VIRCHOW, 1821-1902 -

While Nightingale and Blackwell were breaking new ground for women in medicine, a German genius was working in obscurity on his idea that cells are the basic units of life. His findings, which were described in Erwin H. Ackerknecht's _Rudolf Virchow: Doctor, Statesman, Anthropologist_ (1953), set medicine on a new course in which cellular pathology became the most vital field of investigation. Virchow was not only a giant of medicine, he was also respected as an anthropologist, and admired as a statesman.

He studied medicine at the Berlin Friedrich-Wilhelm Institute as a poor government-subsidized student, agreeing to serve as an army doctor. His radical political ideas raised questions about him. But he was an outstanding student, mastering eight languages. This gave him access to much of the world's knowledge in its original form, a big factor in his success.

Virchow's extensive reading included the works of the most articulate reformers of the time--Friedrich Engels, Pierre-Joseph Proudhon, Louis Blanc, and Julius Froebel. From the writing of Gustave von Struve he took the slogan, "Education, Freedom, and Prosperity for All."[27] That he knew Goethe's books intimately is shown by the small volume he wrote, an early study of Goethe's anticipation of the importance of the new science of biology.

Probably the most decisive reading Virchow did on cells was in the writings of John Goodsir, anatomist of Edinburgh, and Robert Remak, German neuroanatomist and embryologist. From Goodsir, in Virchow's words, "one of the earliest and most acute observers of cell life,"[28] he gained basic information on the cell's role in nutrition. Remak's work gave him new insight into the multiplication of cells through their division.

Other reading that made an impact on Virchow dealt with hospital procedures during the American Civil War. Committed to the cause of the common people, he praised "the democratic spirit of initiative ... and the excellence of American methods...."[29] His work in building military hospitals and using hospital trains in the wars of 1866 and 1870 undoubtedly owed much to his study of the American reports.

Clearly, his reading was a major factor in Virchow's illustrious career, during which he pushed medical science ahead with his pioneering of the concept of pathological processes, by applying the cell theory to explain some basic facts about disease. His reading also influenced his reform of medical education.

- JOSEPH LISTER, 1827-1912 -

Joseph Lister, born a Quaker, grew up in a home where piety, humility, and learning were all valued. Each child read for the father while he dressed in the morning.

When he was six, Joseph wrote to his mother from school:

> Again I must tell thee that I have got to the
> Death of Henry the seconed [sic] in English history.
> I remain thy affectionate son, Joseph. 30

At eight he asked his sister for permission to use her large Latin dictionary because he had found "John's little Dictionary inadequate for the exercises he was doing."31

In Quaker schools Joseph studied Latin, French, mathematics, and science. Because of his faith, Oxford and Cambridge were closed to him. So he entered University College in London to study medicine. He graduated with high honors, became a fellow of the Royal College of Surgeons, and served as house surgeon at University College Hospital. Then he went to Scotland to win distinction as a surgeon and teacher at Glasgow University, where he developed the revolutionary antiseptic measures that dramatically cut deaths from infections and made his name a household word around the world.

It was in Glasgow, according to Richard B. Fisher's <u>Joseph Lister: 1827-1912</u> (1977), that some reading led to his historic demonstration of the efficacy of antisepsis in surgery. Walking home with a colleague, Thomas Anderson, the professor of chemistry,

> They discussed putrefaction, what it is and what causes it, and Anderson suggested that Lister should read certain papers on fermentation by the French chemist Louis Pasteur. In particular Anderson recommended 'Mémoires sur les corpuscles organisés qui existent dans l'atmosphère, Examin de la doctrine des générations spontanées' ... The other paper mentioned by Anderson was 'Examin du rôle attribué au gaz oxygène dans la destruction des matières animales et végétales après la morte' ... Lister obtained the papers immediately. 32

Pasteur showed Lister the relationship between putrefaction and germs. He acted upon this knowledge by using carbolic acid to protect surgical wounds from bacteria. He had learned about carbolic acid from a newspaper article on its successful use in treating the sewage of Carlisle and ridding cattle of parasites.

Lister's monumental victory was the defeat of the

germs that Pasteur had discovered were the cause of infectious disease. When Pasteur's seventieth birthday was celebrated with great ceremony at the Sorbonne in 1889, Lister spoke. In the presence of the immortal Frenchman, he proclaimed his debt:

> 'Thanks to you, Surgery has undergone a complete revolution which has deprived it of its terrors and enlarged almost without limitations its power for good.' When Lister had finished, Pasteur rose from his seat on the platform to embrace him, according to the official record of the occasion, 'like the living picture of the brotherhood of science in the relief of humanity.'[33]

This was one of the most touching scenes in the history of science, showing the overflowing generosity of the true scientific spirit. And the power of print to improve the human condition was a determining factor.

- WILLIAM OSLER, 1849-1919 -

In Dr. Osler, one of the most distinguished and admired physicians of his time, the love of medicine was joined to the love of books. Harvey Cushing's The Life of Sir William Osler (1925) deals comprehensively and devotedly with these two inseparable loves. Cushing showed that Osler's bookishness began early and never flagged. On his bedside table when he died was his favorite copy of Sir Thomas Browne's Religio Medici, which he said "should be in the hands--in the hearts too--of every medical student."[34]

As the youngest of nine children of an Anglican minister in western Ontario, William was part of a household where usefulness and learning were valued. His early reading of Religio Medici

> was one of the strong influences which turned my thoughts toward medicine as a profession, and my most treasured copy--the second book I ever bought --has been a constant companion for thirty-one years--comes viae vitaeque.[35]

While he was a medical student at McGill University, from which he received his M.D. degree, he came under the influence of Carlyle. He was worried about the future. Then,

> I picked up a volume of Carlyle ... and in it I read the familiar sentence, 'Our main business is not to see what lies dimly at a distance but to do what lies closely at hand.'[36]

He gave credit to this advice for starting him in the habit of using "to the full the single talent with which he often said he had been entrusted."[37]

Among Osler's many statements on the importance of books, this was one the strongest:

> Books are tools, doctors are craftsmen, and so truly as one can measure the development of any particular handicraft by the variety and complexity of its tools, so we have no better means of judging the intelligence of a profession than by its general collection of books. A physician who does not use books and journals, who does not need a library, who does not read one or two of the best weeklies and monthlies, soon sinks to the level of the cross-counter prescriber, and not alone in practice, but in those mercenary feelings and habits which characterize a trade....[38]

Dr. Osler followed his own prescription. In addition to the extensive professional reading he did as a matter of course, his lifelong habit was to read in bed every night before turning out his light.

After a sixteen-year tenure as professor of medicine at The Johns Hopkins University in Baltimore, which his teaching and writing helped make one of the world's most respected medical institutions, he was appointed to the prestigious Regius Chair of Medicine at Oxford University, where he also served as curator of the Bodleian Library. During his early Oxford years, he wrote the following on his proposed College of the Book:

> There should be a college where men could learn everything relating to the Book, from the preparation of manuscript & the whole mystery of authorship, to the art of binding; everything from the manufacture of paper to the type with which the book is printed; everything relating to the press & to the mart; everything about the history of printing from Gutenberg to Hoe; everything about the pre-

cursors of the printed book: the papyrus, the rolls, the parchment & the vellum, even about the old writing on the burnt books of Ninevah; everything about the care of books; how to catalogue, how to distribute them; how to make them vital units in a community; everything that the student should know about the use of books, his skilled tools in the building of his mind....[39]

Osler's proposed College of the Book was never established at Oxford as he hoped. But the best professional library schools have been trying for years to live up to his high standards. And the medical libraries in Baltimore, Oxford, and McGill, to which he left his own collection, are evidence of the strength of his commitment to reading as an essential in the practice of medicine.

One man's reading of Osler's great textbook, The Principle and Practice of Medicine, which he wrote while he was at Hopkins, demonstrated in a spectacular way the power of books to shape developments of the utmost significance to the welfare of humanity. The reader was the Reverend Frederick T. Gates, an adviser on philanthropy to John D. Rockefeller. Here is his account of his momentous reading:

> In the early summer of 1897 my interest in medicine was awakened by a ... Minneapolis boy who in his loneliness in New York used to spend his week-ends with us in Montclair.... I determined as a result of my talks with this enthusiastic young student to make myself more intelligent on the whole subject of medicine, and at his suggestion I bought a copy of Dr. Osler's 'Principles and Practice of Medicine' ... I read the whole book without skipping any of it. I speak of this not to commemorate my industry or intelligence but to testify to Osler's charm, for it is one of the very few scientific books that are possessed of high literary quality. There was a fascination about the style itself that led me on, and having once started I found a hook in my nose that pulled me from page to page, and chapter to chapter, until the whole of about a thousand large and closely printed pages brought me to the end.
>
> But there were other things besides its style that attracted and intensified my interest.... To

the layman student, like me, demanding cures, and
specifics, he had no word of comfort whatever. In
fact, I saw clearly from the work of this thoroughly
enlightened, able and honest man, perhaps the foremost practitioner in the world, that medicine had--
with ... few exceptions ...--no cures, and about
all that medicine up to 1897 could do was to suggest
some measure of relief, how to nurse the sick, and
to alleviate in some degree the suffering. Beyond
this, medicine as a cure had not progressed. I
found further that a large number of the most common diseases, especially of the young and middle-
aged, were infectious or contagious, caused by in-
finitesimal germs that are breathed in with the atmosphere, or are imparted by contact or are taken
in with the good or drink or communicated by the
incision of insects in the skin. I learned that of
these germs, only a very few had been identified
and isolated. I made a list--and it was a very long
one at that time, much longer than it is now--of
those germs which we might reasonably hope to discover but which at yet had never been, with cer-
tainty, identified; and I made a longer list of the
infectious or contagious diseases for which there
had been as yet no cure at all discovered.

When I laid down this book I had begun to realize how woefully neglected in all civilized countries
and perhaps most of all in this country, had been
the scientific study of medicine.... It became clear
to me that medicine could hardly hope to become a
science until it should be endowed, and qualified
men could give themselves to uninterrupted study
and investigation, on ample salary, entirely independent of practice.... Here was an opportunity
for Mr. Rockefeller to become a pioneer. This
idea took possession of me. The more I thought
of it the more interested I became. [40]

His new knowledge gained from Osler's inspired writing
moved Gates to quick action. He sent Rockefeller a memorandum outlining the problems of medicine and suggesting how
an institute along the lines of the Koch Institute in Paris might
make a broad attack on disease. The ideas "took root in the
mind of Mr. Rockefeller and, later, of his son."[41] Eminent
doctors were consulted, plans were drawn, and the Rockefeller
Institute for Medical Research was founded. This was fol-

lowed by Rockefeller grants for medical education, a hygiene and public health school at Hopkins, and campaigns against diseases in many regions of the world. The Rockefeller grants radically changed medicine. They paid for time-consuming research into basic problems, modernized the teaching of doctors, and were responsible for some of the spectacular victories over human suffering that made the twentieth century as notable for humanitarianism as for war and all its horrors.

And it all came about because of a remarkable chain of reading that began with young William Osler's reading of Sir Thomas Browne and Carlyle. The stimulation of these writers was a strong force that drove him to excel in teaching and practice. The series of crucial reading encounters was climaxed when one of the few men in a position to get action on some of the urgent problems Osler described, read his book and moved John D. Rockefeller to launch powerful assaults on plagues and scourges that had been tormenting and killing humans from time immemorial. Seldom has the power of print been so persuasively recorded.

- WILLIAM HENRY WELCH, 1850-1934 -

The man who recruited Dr. Osler for The Johns Hopkins University School of Medicine, William Henry Welch, was, like him, one of the movers and shakers of modern medicine. He came from a family of doctors in Norfolk, Connecticut. He was not at first a good student, preferring to catch rabbits to his school work. But he soon became serious about following the family profession. After completing the course at the New York College of Physicians and Surgeons, he put in some years in Europe with excellent teachers and researchers who were breaking new ground and adding to scientific knowledge. Returned home, inspired by the progress he had seen abroad, he became professor of pathology at New York's Belleville Hospital Medical College. Then he went to Baltimore to help organize the new medical school. There he set up the first effective American department of pathology. Welch's career and work are the subjects of <u>William Welch and the Heroic Age of American Medicine</u> (1941) by Simon and Thomas Flexner.

They gave a good idea of his bookishness:

Welch was, of course, an omnivorous reader.

> Sitting up in bed till dawn, he enjoyed everything from books on ancient Greece and Rome, from the history and literature of the Middle Ages, to modern novels and detective stories. Factual books were his great delight. Visitors to the University Club are still shown with reverence a battered set of the Encyclopaedia Britannica which Welch is said to have worn out almost singlehanded; he is reputed to have read it through several times. And the members of the Maryland Club, refusing to be outdone, also ascribe their battered Encyclopaedia to Welch, adding proudly that he also wore out their Dictionary of National Biography. [42]

Welch was among the foremost medical scientists and teachers of his time. It was not surprising that he became one of the most trusted advisers to the Rockefellers as they distributed many millions of dollars to various medical projects, after having been motivated by Gates, who had been overwhelmed by reading Osler. Welch involved himself in public health programs all over the world. One of the many heroes of public health he taught and encouraged was Dr. Walter Reed, the conqueror of yellow fever.

After his long years in the classroom and research laboratory, consulting, and directing The Johns Hopkins School of Hygiene and Public Health, he was ready for retirement. But then he was called upon to tackle his last big assignment as the first professor of the history of medicine in the United States. It was fitting that things took this turn. Dr. Welch had urged the establishment of an adequate medical library and the creation of a professorship of the history of medicine. The chair was endowed by the General Education Board, a Rockefeller-supported body. Funds were included for books. So Welch traveled once more to Europe, this time to buy for the library. The collection reflected his concept of the broad scope of medical studies. He was interested, for example, in the public health aspects of ancient aqueducts and sewers. The Hebrew sanitary code and religious sanctions were significant for him. He went back

> to the beginnings of rational medicine with Hippocrates, the Alexandrian school, Galen, the notions of miasm.... In his lectures he stressed the 'well-known fact that there are no social, no industrial, no economic problems which are not related to problems of health.' He emphasized the importance

of the 'humanitarian movement' during the nineteenth century. [43]

Osler, as we have seen, was an avid and wide-ranging reader who loved rare volumes. Welch, on the other hand, "searched not for rare books but for useful ones; he was planning a working library for scholars." As he put it,

> This is of course something quite different from a bibliophilic collection like Osler's--I am not going in for that at all, though it would be nice if someone presented the library with such treasures. [44]

Through Welch's honored medical career runs the unbroken thread of his own reading. As a student at the College of Physicians and Surgeons, he had lamented when his subscription to the Nation expired, "I feel quite in the woods without my weekly pabulum."[45] In New York he had taken full advantage of his easy access to the library of the New York Hospital, then the second largest medical library in the country. He wrote:

> I had a key to the library and could go there night and day, whether it was open or closed. That was an extraordinary privilege, and I would stay after twelve o'clock at night.... When we consider what the opportunities were, listening to the didactic lectures and attending not very interesting clinics, that library was an education in itself, because you cannot read up on a subject like that without getting interested in all kinds of sidelines, and the English and French journals were very interesting at the time. It was comparatively easy for me to look up a subject after that. I regard that experience as a very valuable part of my education. [46]

In this passage Welch showed himself to have the incurable addiction to books that marks those superior humans whose mastery of their fields rests on thorough knowledge of the basic literature.

- DANIEL HALE WILLIAMS, 1855-1931 -

Dr. Daniel Hale Williams pioneered in heart surgery. His story was told by Helen Buckler in Daniel Hale Williams: Negro Surgeon (1968).

As a boy Dan worked at barbering in Janesville, Wisconsin. He was full of intellectual curiosity, and he quickly read through the library of the Young Men's Association. Then he borrowed histories and biographies from a friendly customer. A lecture by Robert Ingersoll made a deep impression on him:

> Dan came away from Ingersoll's lecture excited and elated. The man's words sparkled in his consciousness like an invasion of meteors from another planet: 'When people read they begin to reason, and when they reason, they progress.' He was reading, so perhaps he was progressing after all. What else had Ingersoll said? 'Every library is an arsenal, filled with the weapons and ammunition of Progress, and every fact is a Monitor with sides of iron and a turret of steel ... the life of a lie is simply a question of time. Nothing but truth is immortal.' That gave you hope. 47

Dan's hope led him to study law. He put in a winter "turning the dusty pages of Littleton and Blackstone."48 But this dry experience convinced him that the law was not his destiny. Then he read in the newspaper about the work, mostly treating victims of accidents, of the town's leading doctor. That appealed to him. The doctor took him on as an apprentice. Such apprenticeship was then a common way of getting into medicine. Dan was ambitious. While he learned valuable lessons by watching the doctor, it was not enough. He drove himself:

> And fortunately he had the dictionary habit. He buckled down to learn the strange new vocabulary. His Latin was a help, and his German. Soon he was turning the dogeared pages of ... Gray's Anatomy and The National Dispensatory--with twice the avidity he had employed in reading Littleton's Tenures or Blackstone's Commentaries. 49

He followed his apprenticeship with study at the Chicago Medical College, which awarded him the M.D. degree in 1883. Some reading there opened the way to his daring surgery on the heart. A doctor in Danzig had demonstrated that the thoracic cavities of dogs and rabbits could be opened and the pericardium incised and repaired in a few minutes. A Philadelphia experimenter named Roberts, learning of the Danzig findings, predicted that heart wounds "will be treated by pericardial incision to allow extraction of clots and perhaps to suture the heart muscle."⁵⁰ Dr. Williams was keeping up on new developments.

In 1895 he was called upon to use his information and skill when a man was brought to the hospital with a stab wound that had torn the pericardium. The surgeon thought of the article on Roberts' prediction. But he remembered too "that Roberts had not fulfilled his own prophecy, nor had anyone else so far as he had ever read."⁵¹ Dr. Williams knew that Theodor Billroth, a German surgeon, whose textbook he had studied, warned that he "who would attempt to suture a wound of the heart is not worthy of the serious consideration of his colleagues."⁵² However, faced with the emergency before him--a man sure to die if nothing were done for him--Dr. Williams, balancing the evidence, the experiments with animals he had read about, and the warning of Dr. Billroth, made his decision. He

> Successfully opened the chest ... sutured the pericardium which had been cut, tied off a bleeding blood vessel, and, after opening the chest again to drain off fluid in the pleural cavity, helped the patient get well and return to an active life.⁵³

The evidence of the decisive influence of reading on the gifted and courageous Dr. Daniel Hale Williams is strong and clear.

- HAVELOCK ELLIS, 1859-1939 -

Havelock Ellis--writer, doctor, sexologist--was a reader whose wide-ranging interests took him into many fields of literature. His own writings are full of illusions to ancient, medieval, and modern books that influenced his life. However, as he told in his Dance of Life (1929), it was something he read when he was nineteen that determined his destiny. He reported:

> I was still interested in religious and philosophical questions, and it so chanced that at this time I read the 'Life in Nature' of James Hinton, who had already attracted my attention as a genuine man of science with yet an original and personal grasp of religion. I had read the book six months before and it had not greatly impressed me. Now, I no

> longer know why, I read it again, and the effect
> was very different. Evidently by this time my
> mind had reached a stage of saturated solution
> which needed but the shock of the right contact to
> recrystallise in forms that were a revelation to
> me. Here evidently the right contact was applied.
> Hinton in his book showed himself a scientific biol-
> ogist who carried the mechanistic explanation of
> life even further than was the usual. But he was
> a man of highly passionate type of intellect, and
> what might otherwise be formal and abstract was
> for him soaked in emotion. 54

Ellis was taken especially with Hinton's view of the world "as an orderly mechanism." But although it was mechanical,

> it was vital, with all the glow and warmth and
> beauty of life; it was, therefore, something which
> not only the intellect might accept, but the heart
> might cling to. 55

Ellis described his response to Hinton's book in some of the most vivid passages on the impact of reading. For example:

> The bearing of this conception on my state of mind
> is obvious. It acted with the swiftness of an elec-
> tric current; the dull aching tension was removed;
> the two opposing psychic tendencies were fused in
> delicious harmony, and my whole attitude toward
> the universe was changed. It was no longer an
> attitude of hostility and dread, but of confidence
> and love. My self was one with the Non-Self, my
> will with the universal will. I seemed to walk in
> light; my feet scarcely touched the ground; I had
> entered a new world. 56

Upon a youth searching for guidance among many ideas, even the force of such an overpowering impact might have faded quickly. The young soon replace one enthusiasm with another. But Ellis was hooked for good: "The effect of that swift revolution was permanent." After "a moment or two of wavering," his

> primary exaltation subsided into an attitude of calm
> serenity towards all those questions that had once
> seemed so torturing. In regard to all these matters

> I had become permanently satisfied and at rest, yet absolutely unfettered and free. I was not troubled about the origin of the 'soul' or about its destiny: I was entirely prepared to accept any analysis of the 'soul' which might commend itself as reasonable. Neither was I troubled about the existence of any superior being or beings, and I was ready to see all the words and forms by which men try to picture spiritual realities are mere metaphors and images of an inward experience. There was not a single clause in my religious creed because I held no creed. I had found that dogmas were--not as I had once imagined, true, not, as I had afterward supposed false--but the mere empty shadows of intimate personal experience.... I had sacrificed what I held dearest at the call of what seemed to be Truth, and now I was repaid a thousand-fold. Henceforth I would face life with confidence and joy, for my heart was one with the world and whatever might prove to be in harmony with the world could not be out of harmony with me. [57]

During his long life, Havelock Ellis was not always in harmony with the universe and vice versa. He was sexually frustrated, sometimes embattled, and called a dirty old man. But his reading of Hinton certainly was a critical turning point in his life. Having, as he said, "become indifferent to shadows, for I held the substance,"[58] he persisted stubbornly as he promoted open discussion of sex problems and championed women's rights long before these causes were considered respectable. It is clear that the reading of Havelock Ellis played a fundamental part in one of the most significant social movements of history.

- MARIE STOPES, 1880-1958 -

Marie Stopes' painful education in the facts of life, and her struggle for self-fulfillment for herself and other women were detailed in Ruth Hall's <u>Passionate Crusader: The Life of Marie Stopes</u> (1977). She was one of the women for whom Havelock Ellis' writings were especially designed. In her he hit his target dead center, according to her biographer:

> Possibly the most formative influence on her

> thinking at this time ... was Havelock Ellis. In
> <u>Man and Woman</u>, published in 1894, and <u>Studies in
> the Psychology of Sex</u> ... Ellis ... stressed the
> ills that befell sexually deprived women. Men must
> stop regarding women as a cross between 'an angel
> and an idiot,' overcome their ignorance, and exer-
> cise some imagination and sensitivity. 'We have to
> imagine a lock,' he wrote, 'that not only requires
> a key to fit it, but should be only entered at the
> right moment and, under the best conditions, can
> only become adjusted to the key by considerable
> use.... The grossest brutality may be and not
> infrequently is, exercised in all innocence by an
> ignorant husband who simply believes that he is
> performing his "marital duties."' Perhaps of
> greater importance to Marie were Ellis' major pre-
> occupations. Impotent for most of his life, Ellis
> was married to a Lesbian and suffered, in addition,
> from urologia. His own problems gave him enor-
> mous sympathy with sexual abnormalities and, not
> unnaturally, he concentrated on them in his writings.
> This aspect of Ellis disgusted Marie--reading the
> <u>Studies</u> ... was 'like breathing a bag of soot; it
> made me feel choked and dirty for three months.'
> The experience reinforced her feeling that what the
> world needed was sexual guidance for the relatively
> normal, like herself. [59]

It is no wonder that Ellis' writing came home to her. She was still a virgin after two years of marriage, and deeply frustrated.

Marie had grown up in a repressed family which was going broke. Social life was limited--no dancing at home. Still, she secured a good education, winning a doctorate in botany from the University of Munich, after attending a London school for girls. It was in Hampstead, near her school that, for the first time, she had access to a large lending library:

> She read voraciously and secretly--comparative
> theology, Swedenborg, Kant, Confucius and the
> whole of Darwin. Her reading of Darwin brought
> about Marie's first conflict with religious bigotry.
> One of her Scottish aunts, a highly religious woman,
> expressed horror at [her father] Henry's even men-
> tioning the name of Darwin in front of his daughters.

Naturally Marie championed her father and confessed that she herself read Darwin, whereupon her aunt whisked her off to the study, demanding immediate repentance and recantation. Marie refused and was formally committed to hell. The experience contributed to her growing independence of judgment. She rejected the idea of a vengeful God and replaced her mother's rather narrow, formalised religion with the more direct approach to the Deity implicit in Henry's Quaker leanings.[60]

But the austere Friends did not come up to her concept of what charity should be, and she drifted away. She found relief from repression as

> She read Browning and Swinburne and, ignoring [her mother] Charlotte's advice, found 'the real Shakespeare' not in the plays but in the Sonnets and Venus and Adonis. Her great expectations of sexual experience appear to have been derived from these, from novels, and from the only book on sex she had read before her marriage.[61]

That book was Edward Carpenter's Love's Coming of Age, published in 1896. She referred to it often in letters and although she rejected Carpenter's Marxism,

> Marie's romantic nature responded ecstatically to his vision of true lovers, whose glances 'penetrate far beyond the surfaces, ages down into each other, waking a myriad antenatal dreams.'[62]

Carpenter argued that sex was not just for making babies, but "union, the physical union as the allegory and expression of the real union" was "the prime object of sex."[63] It is not at all strange that this steamy writing, so daring in those Victorian years, would work Marie up and make her search for a satisfying sex life.

Ruth Hall pointed out that,

> Like most great propagandists, Marie was a product of other people's ideas, a link between their originality and her own awareness that others might need such knowledge.[64]

Among other writers who influenced Marie Stopes were

Francis Galton and H. G. Wells. Galton looked for an improved race conceived by genetically superior parents. Wells foresaw

> a world state which would favour the procreation of: 'what is fine and efficient and beautiful in humanity--beautiful and strong bodies and powerful minds, and a growing body of knowledge to check the procreation of base and servile types, of fear-driven and cowardly souls, of all that is mean and ugly and bestial in the souls, bodies and habits of men.'65

It was from reading the most advanced thinkers of the age that Marie Stopes drew her radical, but sensible, ideas for her Married Love (1918), a landmark on the road to human enlightenment. Her reading encouraged her to expose to public scrutiny thoughts and ideas that had been hushed up for a hundred years in the name of a false respectability that had darkened one of the saddest periods in the long struggle for lives lived in harmony with nature.

- KAREN HORNEY, 1885-1952 -

Karen Horney's active life and two-continent career is set forth in Jack L. Rubins' Karen Horney: Gentle Rebel of Psychoanalysis (1978).

Karen found reading hard at first. But having learned, she soon developed a heavy addiction that lasted all her life:

> Her favorite reading those early years were the popular novels of Karl May, the German Zane Grey. He described the adventures of a young German lad wandering in the Indian Southwest among the Indians, prospectors, cowboys and cavalrymen during the mid-eighteen hundreds. Of the Indian chiefs the hero met, Winnetou, Chief of the Apaches, was the greatest. The two became tribal brothers by exchanging blood, according to tribal custom. These books achieved a tremendous popularity and thrilled millions of German children for five generations, even though the author never left Germany. They pictured the downtrodden Indians sympathetically with dignity. Karen used to play out the various roles with her closest girlfriend, Tutti, usually

taking the part of Winnetou herself. She would invent props for their adventures, such as the little flag sewed for the leader that was found in her box of childhood treasures after her death. Indeed, she later recalled with how much pleasure she and Tutti had gone through a highly dramatized ritual ceremony of blood sisterhood, each pricking her finger and mixing the drops--as Winnetou had done. 66

Following elementary school, Karen went to a Hamburg parochial school. It emphasized religious studies, philosophy, literature, history, mathematics, German, French, and English. Only elementary science was taught. Human biology was excluded.

After completing her medical studies at Göttingen, Dr. Horney took psychoanalytical training under Karl Abraham, a close associate of Freud. Then she entered private practice and taught at the Berlin Psychoanalytic Institute. Questioning some of Freud's basic ideas, she veered from orthodox Freudianism. In 1932 she came to the United States to teach, practice, and develop a separate branch of psychiatric thought.

Her reading strongly influenced her direction. She knew the works of Kierkegaard and some Oriental philosophers. But it was Albert Schweitzer who probably made the greatest impression on her. The second part of <u>Philosophy of Civilization</u> spoke to her. In it, Schweitzer

considered humanistic religious ethics and morality: some of his ideas are similar to those Karen was to apply to the individual in her later theory. For instance, he discussed the will to live as the highest form of knowledge. This is contrasted with cognitive knowledge, which is 'from the outside and forever remains incomplete,' whereas 'the knowledge derived from my will to live is direct and takes me back to the mysterious movement of life as it is in itself.... The essential nature of the will to live is the determination to live itself to the full. It carries the impulse to realize itself in the highest possible perfection ... an imaginative force determined by ideals.' This is the life force which had freed Karen from her inner dungeon when she was eighteen, which she made the highest goal of her medical studies and which she was now positing as

> a basic tendency in every human being--in contrast to Freud's death instinct. For Schweitzer, 'everything ... which can be brought under a description of material and spiritual maintenance or promotion of human life' is moral and good. Everything in human relations that leads to 'material or spiritual destruction of human life' and development, is bad and immoral. In modified form, this was to become Karen's philosophy, embodied in her evolutionary theory of morality. 67

Besides Schweitzer's work, the books of two other men impressed her strongly. The writers were Paul Tillich and Aldous Huxley. From Tillich's The Courage to Be, she took stimulating ideas that reinforced Schweitzer's thought on the "courage to affirm oneself" in the face of the awareness of the threat of death, and

> these ideas of his excited and stirred Karen deeply, stimulating the vague thoughts then swirling around in her mind, which were to emerge later in her theory in a more psychological context. 68

Huxley's The Perennial Philosophy, lent by a friend, deepened her knowledge of the thoughts of great mystics and prophets of East and West. In Huxley's words, they dealt with

> the metaphysics that recognizes a divine Reality, substantial to the world of things and lives and minds; the psychology that finds in the soul something similar to divine Reality; the ethic that places man's final end in the knowledge of the immanent and transcendental Ground of all being. 69

So it appears that Karen Horney, like others closely involved with people in their mental and religious concerns, was from her youth a sensitive and absorptive reader, drawing constantly on the writings of the foremost intellects of the ages. And that reading made a big difference in what she was able to do for her patients, her students, and for a caring kind of mental medicine.

- OBSERVATIONS -

Most of the fifteen practitioners, health workers, and

medical scientists first read at home. In several cases, the family read together. Nine were from homes that were literate, if not bookish. One, Karen Horney, had trouble learning to read.

Eleven read across a broad range of subjects. The education of the three who lived before the eighteenth century --Paré, Vesalius, and Harvey--was based on classical authorities who were held as almost sacrosanct. The ten of the nineteenth century and later--when the old authorities were challenged and often disproved--followed the literature of reform in addition to their professional reading. Especially keen on the most advanced social and scientific thinkers of their times were Elizabeth Blackwell, Rudolf Virchow, Havelock Ellis, Marie Stopes, and Karen Horney. One might speculate on the possible connection between their extra-professional reading interests and their commitment to causes outside their own fields.

When one looks at the actual impact of reading on the fifteen, it is clear that except for two--Hunter and Jenner-- the impact was unmistakable.

Although reading was not responsible for Paré's discovery of a painless alternative to boiling oil in amputations and other major military surgery, in his contributions to the alleviation of human suffering he proclaimed his debt to Galen and other ancient writers. And he wryly compared his heavy borrowing from others to lighting one candle from another with no loss to the first. His "Author's Sonnet" cheerfully and even proudly acknowledged what he owed to the secrets of "the Arabs and the Greeks of old."

Like Paré, Vesalius leaned heavily on Galen. But he used his critical skills to improve on his authority. The result was his matchless work on the human body that added immeasurably to essential knowledge.

It was Harvey's reading of Fabricius' book on the valves of the veins that gave him a push toward his proof that the blood circulates, one of the most momentous discoveries in the history of medicine, a finding basic to every doctor who followed Harvey.

John Hunter and Edward Jenner were curious deviations in this luminous line of medical men and women who were dedicated readers and critically influenced by their reading.

It may be I have not looked hard enough for evidence. But books by and about them show that Hunter and Jenner relied mainly on their powers of observation and their experimentation in their discoveries. As close students of nature in their youth, they both plundered nests and burrows, collecting eggs and other specimens in preference to studying books. Neither was well schooled. No formal curriculum required them to follow a rigorous reading program. They learned their work as apprentices in bloody operating rooms. A clue to their disinclination to open books very often was the advice Hunter is said to have given his young pupil Jenner: "Why think--why not try the experiment?" Both men undoubtedly could have made their work easier by reading. However, their secure places in the pantheon of medical immortals were achieved through their own powers, native and acquired in practice. They appear to be sports among their bookish species.

What on the surface appeared to be a mundane document was decisive in the glorious career of Florence Nightingale. But it is clear that her study of the Year Book of the Deaconesses at Kaiserwerth clinched her resolve to take the nursing training that was the first big step in her historic work of mercy and reform.

Although Elizabeth Blackwell read a great deal, it was not from books that she received the critical stimulus to go into medicine. That came from the appeal of a dying friend. However, her resolve to fight her way into and through medical school was crystallized when she read of the honored place in medicine earned over the centuries by remarkable women.

Like Elizabeth Blackwell, Rudolf Virchow was given to reading books by radicals and reformers. They strengthened his determination to lead a life of service. But what enabled him to find the answer to one of nature's most obscure secrets in demonstrating the role of the cell in diseases of organs and tissues, was his reading of the works of John Goodsir and Robert Remak. This reading led Virchow to make one of the most basic contributions to medical science.

Louis Pasteur, that giant among scientists, was directly responsible for Joseph Lister's history-making creation of aseptic surgery. Pasteur's reports on germs and his brilliant proof that spontaneous generation is a myth enabled Lister to understand the relationship between bacteria and putrefaction. Understanding that basic fact, he demonstrated how patients could be protected from infection, the deadliest danger in surgery. The idea of using carbolic acid as an antiseptic came from a newspaper article Lister read about sewage treatment in the city of Carlisle.

William Osler was one of the most convincing witnesses to the power of reading. He told how Sir Thomas Browne's Religio Medici turned him toward a career in medicine and persuaded him that "No one should approach the temple of science with the soul of a money-changer." And Osler recalled how, as a medical student, he read Carlyle's advice: "Our main business is not to see what lies dimly at a distance but to do what lies clearly at hand." This advice, he said, gave him a practical guide for his day-to-day work and made it possible for him to accomplish what he did "with just an ordinary stock of brains."

Dr. Osler's textbook, The Principle and Practice of Medicine, provides one of the strongest proofs of the momentous consequences of reading. It was fortuitous that the reader in this case enjoyed the confidence of the richest man in the world, who was just then ready to give away big chunks of his fortune. The motivation for this reading--to understand more about medicine because of being thrown into company with a young medical student--had nothing to do with the result. However, the Reverend Frederick T. Gates' reading of Osler's book triggered a whole chain of historic events when, as adviser on philanthropy to John D. Rockefeller, Gates showed the tycoon how some of his money could do a lot of good. Mr. Rockefeller liked the idea, and many of his millions began flowing into projects designed to make basic improvements in medical science. Researchers working in endowed institutions or out in the field across the world made discoveries and devised procedures and methods that dramatically reduced or wiped out diseases that had brought mass misery and death to the people of entire regions. The Rockefeller grants underwrote a new kind of medical education, using the newest basic findings in pathology, biology, and bacteriology. Doctors were turned out armed with the precise weapons of science in place of the crude tools of the old guess-and-hope-for-the-best practitioners. Worldwide revolutionary improvements in public health were conceived and carried out by teachers and students of the Rockefeller-supported School of Public Health and Hygiene at The Johns Hopkins University. The benefits of this medical research and its application are beyond calculation.

Who knows what would have happened in medicine had Gates not read Osler at the propitious time in 1897, when medicine needed the stimulus of vast investments for facilities and equipment, and when a brilliant group of medical scientists was prepared to make the most productive use of the support? The Rockefeller millions might have gone to other worthy causes. Someone else might have raised medicine from an uncertain art practiced in the absence of basic information, to a science of increasing effectiveness in the relief of human suffering. But the fact remains that Gates did read Osler's textbook. He was stunned by Osler's stark view of the state of medicine. He persuaded Rockefeller to pitch in, and history was made. This example shows the absolutely unpredictable results reading can bring about. A book can contain the power to shape spectacularly the course of human events.

Like his friend and colleague Osler, William Henry Welch was a man of books and a great doctor. He also excelled as a planner and administrator. His lifelong reading was extremely varied. Encyclopedias and reference books were his meat. Welch knew his way around libraries from the time he was a medical student, and he made full use of them. His record does not show the overwhelming influence of a single book. But as he skillfully guided the Rockefellers in the application of the money Osler's book had broken loose, he had constantly in mind the printed record of the history of medicine and ready knowledge of the newest developments as reported in journals. This comprehensive grasp of the field, gained through wide reading over many years, made it possible for Dr. Welch to direct the use of the Rockefeller research and education funds as effectively as any man alive at the time.

The pioneering surgery Dr. Daniel Hale Williams so brilliantly performed on the pericardium of a stab victim was made possible by Dr. Williams' reading as well as by his courage and skill. He was supported by the information he had gathered in journals, as he applied his scalpel and tied his sutures in his epic-making operation.

The crucial reading of Havelock Ellis is of special interest on at least two counts. In the first place, it was a <u>second</u> reading of <u>Life in Nature</u> by James Hinton that made the decisive impact on Ellis. Six months earlier he had not been "greatly impressed." The second matter of special interest in Ellis' reading of Hinton was the apocalyptic effect on him. The book "acted with the swiftness of an electric current." He "seemed to walk in light; my feet scarcely touched the ground; I had entered a new world." Now he had "become indifferent to shadows, for I held the substance." One must look at the spell Goethe cast on Flaubert, who said the German's "poetry overcame him like wine," or the powerful effect on young Henry Mencken of Mark Twain, who opened a "new world of gorgeous wonders," to find such an intense response to reading. Ellis had something to say about the impact of his reading that will be useful in the concluding observations.

For Marie Stopes, a most responsive reader, two crucial influences were Havelock Ellis and Edward Carpenter. After her great expectations of sex had been heightened by Browning and Swinburne, and the works of "the real Shakespeare," the Sonnets and Venus and Adonis, Ellis' Man and Woman and Studies in the Psychology of Sex and Carpenter's Love's Coming of Age were strong and obvious influences on her monumental Married Love. It was a book that shocked and enlightened millions whose natural sexual inclinations had made them feel guilty and sinful.

Among reading that covered many fields, Karen Horney found in Albert Schweitzer's Philosophy of Civilization a guiding principle that led her to reject Freud's idea of the death instinct and to adopt an affirmation of life. This positive philosophy, strengthened by Paul Tillich's "courage to affirm oneself" and Huxley's selection of thoughts and ideas of great mystics, became an effective instrument in Karen Horney's sensitive treatment of patients and in her teaching, both of which have influenced many psychiatrists and the practice of psychiatry.

It is clear from this brief review of the reading of fifteen leaders in medicine that, for all but two, reading was indeed a decisive influence in their achievements, which have been shining landmarks in human progress. It would be difficult to think of influences other than their reading that were as crucial in their magnificent contributions to the well-being of their fellow humans.

Chapter 7

DECISIVE READING OF FREUD AND JUNG, PROBERS OF THE UNCONSCIOUS

Both Sigmund Freud and Carl Gustav Jung left significant accounts of reading that affected their trailblazing contributions to the understanding of the unconscious. So their involvement with books is worth examining for light on the circumstances under which they read, the reading that influenced them, and the nature of its influence.

- SIGMUND FREUD, 1856-1939 -

In <u>An Autobiographical Study</u> (1952), Freud wrote:

> My early familiarity with the Bible story (at a time almost before I had learnt the art of reading) had, as I recognized much later, an enduring effect upon the direction of my interest.

I have not come upon any specific evidence of the "enduring effect" of Freud's early Bible reading. However, like many well-educated men, he probably drew on the Bible often, without thinking about it.

Freud once thought of studying law. But Darwin's revolutionary theories just then were challenging long-standing scientific and religious beliefs and agitating the world's intellectuals. Darwin's ideas held a strong attraction for Sigmund because, as he said, "they held out hopes of an extraordinary advance in our understanding of the world."[1]

However, the appeal of Darwin was countered by the influence of Goethe. Freud recalled:

> ... it was hearing Goethe's beautiful essay on Nature read aloud by Professor Carl Brühl just before

I left school that decided me to become a medical student.[2]

Goethe's Fragment upon Nature, written in 1782, about a hundred years before Freud heard it, is homage to the magnificence of nature:

> Nature! We are surrounded by her, embraced by her--impossible to release ourselves from her and impossible to enter more deeply into her. Without our asking and without warning she drags us into the circle of her dance and carries us along until exhausted we drop from her arm.
>
> She creates ever new forms; what exists has never existed before; what has existed returns not again--everything is new and yet always old.
>
> * * *
>
> She has set me within. She will lead me without. I commit myself to her. She may command me.[3]

Goethe's poetic essay is full of such romantic glorifications of nature. Why did it move Freud to go to medical school? Fritz Wittels, one of Freud's first biographers, in Freud and His Time (1931), assumed "the meaning and the beauty which Goethe injected into nature"[4] captivated the young student. Freud's response to Goethe shows the undoubted, but unexpected, influence of literature in the making of a major decision.

It was not unexpected, however, that a young man as bookish as Freud discussed novels with his bride and that they would recite poetry to each other. In his letters to her, he quoted Burns, Byron, Scott, and Milton. He also expressed his liking for Fielding, Dickens, George Eliot, and Thackerary. Two books that moved him deeply were Don Quixote and The Temptations of Saint Anthony. Freud's sensitive reaction to Cervantes' immortal novel was shown when he wrote to his young wife:

> Don't you find it very touching to read how a great person, himself an idealist, makes fun of his ideals? Before we were so fortunate as to apprehend the deep truths of our love we were all noble knights passing through the world caught in a dream, mis-

> interpreting the simplest things, magnifying commonplaces into something noble and rare, and thereby cutting a sad figure. Therefore we men always read with respect about what we once were and in part still remain.[5]

Of the <u>Temptations of Saint Anthony</u>, Freud wrote how Flaubert's novel,

> in the most condensed fashion and with unsurpassable vividness throws at one's head the whole trashy world: for it calls up not only the great problems of knowledge, but the real riddles of life, all the conflicts of feelings and impulses; and it confirms the awareness of our perplexity in the mysteriousness that reigns everywhere. These questions, it is true, are always there, and one should always be thinking of them. What one does, however, is to confine oneself to a narrow aim every hour and every day and get used to the idea that to concern oneself with these enigmas is the task of a special hour, in the belief that they exist only in those special hours. Then they suddenly assail one in the morning and rob one of one's composure and one's spirits.[6]

These responses to Cervantes and Flaubert are telling examples of Freud's imaginative power to take from fiction ideas that would become central to his work.

In addition to his devotion to the writings of the best novelists, Freud was interested in books about the forbidden. He found the literary sources of his <u>Totem and Tabu</u> (1913) mainly in Sir James Frazer's <u>Totemism and Exogamy</u> and <u>The Golden Bough</u>.

Freud was also attracted to writings on demoniac possession, which he went into in connection with his studies of hysteria. He found <u>Malleus Maleficarum</u> especially suggestive. This guide to <u>catching and killing witches</u> was a best-seller over the centuries, having gone through many editions since its publication in 1486. It was useful to the Holy Inquisition in deciding about the sexual activities of those unfortunate enough to be brought before its judges. The sexual activities described in the <u>Malleus Maleficarum</u> were the same as those his patients told <u>Freud about as they</u> recalled their childhoods, and the book made a strong impression on him.

In partial explanation of himself, Freud wrote in 1900:

> ... I am not really a man of science, not an observer, not an experimenter, and not a thinker. I am nothing but by temperament a conquistador-- an adventurer, if you want to translate the word-- with the curiosity, the boldness, and the tenacity that belong to that type of being.[7]

That fits Freud quite well, especially in connection with his reading. Like a buccaneer, he plundered all kinds of books to enrich his store of knowledge and to gain insights. He was indeed heavily in debt to his reading for many of his discoveries, which revolutionized the treatment of mental illness.

- CARL GUSTAV JUNG, 1875-1961 -

In his Memories, Dreams, Reflections (1973) Jung told of Freud's delayed, but profound, influence upon him:

> As early as 1900 I had read Freud's The Interpretation of Dreams. I had laid the book aside, at the time, because I could not grasp it. At the age of twenty-five I lacked the experience to appreciate Freud's theories. Such experience did not come until later. In 1903 I once more took up The Interpretation of Dreams and discovered how it all linked up with my own ideas. What chiefly interested me was the application to dreams of the concept of the repression mechanism, which was derived from the psychology of the neurosis. This was important to me because I had frequently encountered repressions in my experiments with word associations; in response to certain words the patient either had no associative answer or was unduly slow in his reaction time.[8]

Placing his own observations alongside of Freud's interpretations, Jung was able to "corroborate Freud's line of argument."[9] But he was unable to accept Freud's ideas on sexual trauma and repression. At first it was hard for him " to assign Freud the proper place in my life, or to take the right attitude toward him."[10] However, he wrote a paper defending Freud's theory of neurosis and, in spite of the disapproval of conservative German professors, joined the followers of Freud, "because he had opened up a new path of investigation, and the shocked outcries against him ... seemed absurd."[11]

Before Jung started school, his father had already taught him some Latin. Even before he could read, he had "pestered" his mother to read to him

> out of the Orbis Pictus, an old, richly illustrated children's book, which contained an account of exotic religions, especially that of the Hindus. There were illustrations of Brahma, Vishnu, and Shiva which I found an inexhaustible source of interest. My mother later told me that I always returned to these pictures.[12]

The pictures gave him "an obscure feeling of their affinity with my "original revelation"--which I never spoke of to anyone."[13] That "original revelation," to one of the two personalities he believed he possessed, was a phallic dream that haunted him for many years.

As he began to think for himself, young Carl felt "cut off from the Church and my father's and everyone else's faith." His father was a clergyman with whom his talks about religion had been inconclusive. Feeling he was an "outsider," he was "filled with sadness." In this plight,

> I began looking ... for books that would tell me what was known about God.... At last I hit upon Biedermann's Christliche Dogmatik.... Here, apparently, was a man who thought for himself, who worked out his own views. I learned from him that religion was 'a spiritual act consisting in man's establishing his own relationship to God.' I disagreed with that, for I understood religion as something that God did to me; it was an act on His part to which I must simply yield, for He was the stronger.[14]

Pondering Biedermann's ideas on the nature of God and the "reasons for suffering, imperfection, and evil,"[15] he found nothing to satisfy him. So, "That finished it for me. This weighty tome on dogmatics was nothing but fancy drivel."[16] Carl considered the book "a fraud or a specimen of uncommon stupidity whose whole aim was to obscure the truth."[17] It left him disillusioned and even indignant.

While he squirmed in this painful dilemma, at his mother's suggestion he read Faust:

> It poured into my soul like a miraculous balm. 'Here at last,' I thought, 'is someone who takes the devil seriously and even concludes a blood pact with him--with the adversary who has the power to frustrate God's plan to make a perfect world.'[18]

Although Jung had some reservations about the trickery Goethe had used in Faust and was disturbed "that Goethe too had fallen for those cunning devices by which evil is rendered innocuous," he had discovered that "Faust had been a philosopher of sorts."[19] So he tried to fill the void in his own knowledge of philosophy through Krug's General Dictionary of the Philosophical Sciences. But he found it hard to come to grips with philosophers who seemed to "know God only by hearsay."[20]

While his No. 2 personality was searching in secret frustration through his father's library for enlightenment on religious and philosophical questions, his No. 1 personality, during intervals,

> openly read all the novels of Gerstäcker, and German translations of the classic English novels. I also began reading German literature, concentrating on those classics which school, with its needlessly laborious explanations of the obvious, had not spoiled for me. I read vastly and planlessly, drama, poetry, history, and later natural science. Reading was not only interesting but provided a welcome and beneficial distraction from the preoccupations of personality No. 2, which in increasing measure were leading me to depressions. For everywhere in the realm of religious questions I encountered only locked doors, and if ever one door should chance to open I was disappointed by what lay behind it.... More than ever I wanted someone to talk with, but nowhere did I find a point of contact.... Why has no one had experiences similar to mine? I wondered. Why is there nothing about it in scholarly books? Am I the only one who has ever had such experiences? Why should I be the only one? It never occurred to me that I might be crazy, for the light and darkness of God seemed to me facts that could be understood even though they oppressed my feelings.[21]

Jung wrote, "Between my sixteenth and nineteenth years the fog of my dilemma slowly lifted."[22] His No. 1 personality emerged. In systematic reading he found the ideas of Pythagoras, Heraclitus, Empedocles, and Plato "beautiful and academic, like pictures in a gallery, but somewhat remote."[23] He felt the breath of life only in Meister Eckhart, "not that I understood him."[24] The Schoolmen left him cold,

> and the Aristotelian intellectualism of St. Thomas appeared to me more lifeless than a desert. I thought, 'They all want to force something to come out by tricks of logic, something they have not been granted and do not really know about....'[25]

After being parched in the intellectual desert, he came upon a strange oasis, Schopenhauer:

> He was the first to speak of the suffering of the world, which visibly and glaringly surrounds us, and of confusion, passion, evil--all the things which the others hardly seem to notice and always tried to resolve into an all-embracing harmony and comprehendability. Here at last was a philosopher who had the courage to see that all was not for the best in the fundaments of the universe. He spoke neither of the all-good and all-wise providence of a Creator, nor of the harmony of the cosmos, but stated bluntly that a fundamental flaw underlay the sorrowful course of human history and the cruelty of nature: the blindness of the world-creating Will. This was confirmed not only by the early observations I had made of diseased and dying fishes, of mangy foxes, frozen or starved birds, of the pitiless tragedies concealed in a flowery meadow; earthworms tormented to death by ants, insects that tore each other apart piece by piece, and so on. My experience with human beings, too, had taught me anything rather than a belief in man's original goodness and decency. I knew myself well enough to know that I was only gradually, as it were, distinguishing myself from an animal.[26]

From Schopenhauer, Jung went to Kant's _Critique of Pure Reason_, which put him "to some hard thinking." In Kant he found "the fundamental flaw ... in Schopenhauer's system."[27] Jung thought Schopenhauer

had committed the deadly sin of hypostatizing a
metaphysical assertion, and of endowing a mere
noumenon, a <u>Dich an sich</u>, with special qualities.
I got this from Kant's theory of knowledge, and it
afforded me an even greater illumination, if that
were possible, than Schopenhauer's 'pessimistic'
view of the world.[28]

This reading in philosophy, Jung said, made a big
change in him. From "shy, timid, mistrustful, pallid, thin,
and apparently unstable in health," he became "assertive and
more communicative."[29] It is true he was maturing physically at this time, and that undoubtedly had much to do with
the change. But he credited his reading with turning his life
around. With the turning, his No. 1 personality took over.
He entered the University of Basel, aiming at a career in
medicine. But his No. 2 personality was aroused again when
he read Nietzsche's <u>Thoughts out of Reason</u> and <u>Thus Spake
Zarathustra</u>. About this time, he was attracted to spiritualism
by a book from the library of a classmate's father. Jung became convinced of the authenticity of the material on spiritualism. While he was experiencing this welter of influences
and enthusiasms, Jung had just about decided to specialize in
internal medicine when a book persuaded him to take another
direction. As he told it:

> In preparing myself for the state examination ...
> the textbook on psychiatry was the last I attacked.
> I expected nothing from it, and still I remember
> that as I opened the book ... the thought came to
> me, 'Well, now let's see what a psychiatrist has to
> say for himself.' The lectures and clinical demonstrations had not made the slightest impression on
> me. I could not remember a single one of the
> cases, but only my boredom and disgust.

* * *

> Beginning with the preface, I read: 'It is probably due to the peculiarity of the subject and to its
> incomplete state of development that psychiatric textbooks are stamped with a more or less subjective
> character.' A few lines further on, the author
> called the psychoses 'diseases of the personality.'
> My heart suddenly began to pound. I had to stand
> up and draw a deep breath. My excitement was intense, for it had become clear to me, in a flash of

> illumination, that for me the only possible goal was psychiatry. Here alone the two currents of my interest could flow together and in a united stream dig their own bed. Here was the empirical field common to biological and spiritual facts, which I had everywhere sought and nowhere found. Here at last was a place where the collision of nature and spirit became a reality.
>
> My violent reaction set in when Krafft-Ebing spoke of the 'subjective character' of psychiatric textbooks. So, I thought, the textbook is in part the subjective confession of the author. With his specific prejudice, with the totality of his being, he stands behind the objectivity of his experience and responds to the 'disease of the personality' with the whole of his own personality. Never had I heard anything of this sort from my teacher at the clinic. In spite of the fact that Krafft-Ebing's textbook did not differ essentially from other textbooks of the kind, these few hints cast such a transfiguring light on psychiatry that I was irretrievably drawn under its spell.30

Yielding to the spell of Krafft-Ebing's <u>Lehrbuch der Psychiatrie</u>, Jung joined the staff of a psychiatric hospital in Zurich. One of the great careers in psychiatry was launched as Jung settled in at the hospital, went on to teach and developed a large practice.

During this period, Jung began seeing flaws in some of Freud's basic ideas. In Freud's view, Jung's disavowal of the central importance of sexuality made him a heretic. Jung, on his side, could not accept what he considered Freud's unscientific dogmatism. They went their separate ways, each attracting followers and establishing his own branch of psychoanalysis.

In spite of their grave disagreements, Freud and Jung both believed in the importance of the unconscious. They also shared a common interest in the esoteric. Over the years, Jung's interest deepened. A dream revived his fascination with archaeology and myths. He wrote:

> ... I took up a book on Babylonian excavations, and read various works on myths. In the course of this reading I came across Friedrich Creuzer's <u>Symbolik</u>

und Mythologie der Alten Völker--and that fired me! I read like mad, and worked with feverish interest through a mountain of mythological material, then through the Gnostic writers, and ended in total confusion. I found myself in a state of perplexity similar to the one I had experienced at the clinic when I tried to understand the meaning of psychotic states of mind. It was as if I were in an imaginary madhouse and were beginning to treat all the centaurs, nymphs, gods, and goddesses in Creuzer's book as though they were my patients. While thus occupied I could not help but discover the close relationship between the ancient mythology and the psychology of primitives, and this led me to an intensive study of the latter.

In the midst of these studies I came on the fantasies of a young American altogether unknown to me, Miss Miller. The material had been published by my revered and fatherly friend, Théodore Flournoy, in the Archives de Psychologie (Geneva). I was immediately struck by the mythological character of the fantasies. They operated like a catalyst upon the stored-up and still disorderly ideas within me. Gradually, there formed out of them, and out of the myths I had acquired, my book Wandlungen und Symbole der Libido.[31]

During his middle years, Jung was tortured by uncertainties and the difficulty of confronting his own unconscious, which was surfacing in his dreams. In this state, he began exploring the ideas of the alchemists. He had originally thought of alchemy as "something off the beaten track and rather silly."[32] Then, he wrote,

Light on the nature of alchemy began to come to me only after I had read the text of the Golden Flower, that specimen of Chinese alchemy which Richard Wilhelm sent to me in 1928. I was stirred by a desire to become more closely associated with the alchemical texts. I commissioned a Munich bookseller to notify me of any alchemical books that might fall into his hands. Soon afterward I received the first of them, the Artis Auriferae Volumino Duo (1593), a comprehensive collection of Latin treatises among which are a number of the 'classics' of alchemy.

> I let this book lie almost untouched for nearly two years. Occasionally I would look at the pictures, and each time I would think, 'Good Lord, what nonsense! This stuff is impossible to understand.' But it persistently intrigued me, and I made up my mind to go into it more thoroughly. The next winter I began, and soon found it provocative and exciting. To be sure the texts still seemed to me to be blatant nonsense, but here and there would be passages that seemed significant to me, and occasionally I even found a few sentences which i could understand. Finally I realized that the old alchemists were talking in symbols--those old acquaintances of mine. 'Why this is fantastic,' I thought. 'I simply must learn to decipher all this.' By now I was completely fascinated, and buried myself in the texts as often as I had the time. One night while I was studying them, I suddenly recalled a dream that I was caught in the seventeenth century. At last I grasped its meaning. 'So that's it! Now I am condemned to study alchemy from the very beginning.'[33]

After some time, Jung was able to puzzle out the meaning of the cryptic writing. He saw that "analytical psychology coincided in a most curious way with alchemy."[34] Then,

> everything fell into place; the fantasy-images, the empirical material I had gathered in my practice, and the conclusions I had drawn from it. I now began to understand what these psychic contents mean when seen in a historical perspective. My understanding of their typical character, which had already begun with my investigation of myths, was deepened. The primordial images and the nature of the archetype took a central place in my researches, and it became clear to me that without history there can be no psychology, and certainly no psychology of the unconscious. A psychology of consciousness can, to be sure, content itself with material drawn from personal life, but as soon as we wish to explain a neurosis we require an anamnesis which reaches deeper than the knowledge of consciousness. And when in the course of treatment unusual decisions are called for, dreams occur that need more than personal memories for their interpretation.[35]

As Jung went deeper and deeper into the occult, he believed he was getting closer to his objective. As he put it:

> My life has been permeated and held together by one ideal and one goal; namely, to penetrate into the secret of personality. Everything can be explained from this central point, and all my works relate to this one theme. 36

As the long passages just quoted show, Jung was most strongly influenced in matters central to his life work by his reading of strange works that, on the surface, seemed far afield, but on closer study turned out to have been essential for his investigations.

- OBSERVATIONS -

Freud and Jung were readers from their early years with lifelong devotion to books. Their written works are cluttered with references to their reading.

Each had at least one encounter with literature that determined his life work. Freud, listening to the reading of Goethe's <u>Fragment upon Nature,</u> decided to study medicine. This is one of many instances of the awesome power of literature to exert overwhelming influence in a succeeding age and in a way far from the intent of the author. With Jung, the motivation came from Krafft-Ebing's <u>Lehrbuch der Psychiatrie,</u> which he read reluctantly in preparation for his state examination. There are not many instances I have seen recorded in which a textbook, usually dull required reading, made such a powerful impact. Jung's reading of Freud's classic on dreams, some years later, a reading that took him into Freud's camp, was one of the most momentous events in the history of psychoanalysis.

Freud and Jung were both young men with good basic educations and at points of important decision-making when they found in literature the answers to their most significant problems concerning a choice of careers.

Both men canvassed a wide range of human knowledge and speculation. They were at home in German literature and well grounded in the ancient classics, and they knew the great works of fiction from other cultures. They were, of course, heavy consumers of the professional literature in their own and related fields. And both had a taste for out-of-the-way books, especially those that probed strange phenomena of human nature.

They gained penetrating insights from their reading, being quick to relate ideas in apparently unrelated books to their own central interests. It could hardly have been anticipated that from <u>Malleus Malificarum</u>, with its lurid descriptions of the sexual proclivities of suspected witches, Freud would deepen his understanding of the childhood experiences related by his patients. Jung's gaining of confidence and the assurance that he was not alone in his youthful personal anguish after doses of Schopenhauer and Kant was not exactly what one would have expected. Nor was it predictable that Jung, going more deeply into the occult than Freud, would bring to bear on the problems of his patients and his own intellectual concerns the speculations and mystifications of the alchemists, whose writings gave him so much trouble in the unraveling.

Extreme sensitivity and openness to their reading were common to the two. Jung, however, although he generally admired the writing and accepted many of the ideas of Goethe, Schopenhauer, Kant, and others, was often more critical than Freud. Both responded imaginatively to their reading as they related what they learned in their exotic sources to their personal and professional problems. Their ability to see relationships between apparently unrelated phenomena and to use those relationships in fruitful ways is characteristic of highly creative individuals.

Freud and Jung, then, were men of books, who took their reading seriously and were deeply and lastingly influenced by what they read. They set an example for the generations of psychiatrists who followed them in going to the broad and varied world of books, including the esoteric, to enrich the discipline and make it one of the most interesting and controversial of medical specialties. Many of the men and women in psychiatry seem, more than those in other professions, to use arcane books creatively. This is possibly the most valuable long-term influence of the omnivorous reading of Freud and Jung.

Chapter 8

BOOKS AS ARMOR AND WEAPONS: THE READING OF MILITARY LEADERS

The path to successful military leadership is not commonly looked for in books. In his classic, On War, Carl von Clausewitz wrote that

> Only those activities emptying themselves directly into the sea of War have to be studied by him who is to conduct its operations. [1]

He said this explained "the rapid growth of great generals, and why a general is not a man of learning." Clausewitz pointed out,

> as a rule, the most distinguished Generals have never risen from the very learned or really erudite class of officers, but have been mostly men who, from the circumstances of their position, could not have attained any great amount of knowledge. On that account those who have considered it necessary or even beneficial to commence the education of a future General by instruction in all details have always been ridiculed as absurd pedants. [2]

Then, having set up his straw man, Clausewitz showed the fallacy of the argument:

> It would be easy to show the injurious tendency of such a course, because the human mind is trained by the knowledge imparted to it and the direction given to its ideas. Only what is great can make it great; the little can only make it little, if the mind itself does not reject it as something repugnant. [3]

Although information on the reading of military leaders understandably has seemed to their biographers and to themselves, if they wrote their own lives, less important than the stories of their victories, there is evidence that some of the most distinguished captains of history were strongly influenced by their reading.

- ALEXANDER THE GREAT, 356-323 B.C. -

As the son of a king, Alexander had all the advantages to be enjoyed in his time and place. A. R. Burn's <u>Alexander the Great and the Hellenistic World</u> (1947), showed a boy who was "serious-minded, untiring, passionately keen to succeed in any difficult task, and yet more keen the more difficult it was." Burn wrote:

> He was a great reader, too. He had been early caught by the glamour of the Tale of Troy, like most Greek boys; and he never grew weary of it. As far as the Oxus and the Indus, he carried with him his personal copy of the Iliad, called the Casket Iliad from its richly wrought travelling case. At nights it lay, with his dagger, under his pillow. Moreover he ... described it as 'a handbook of military conduct'; and as Agamemnon and Nestor had certainly nothing to teach him on tactics, it is clear that what he means is that it taught the lessons of courage and companionship and the importance of personal leadership in battle.[4]

When, according to Plutarch's <u>Alexander</u>, he was campaigning in distant Asia, "destitute of books,"[5] he asked a friend to send him something to read, he was sent Philistus' <u>History</u> [of Sicily], the plays of Euripides, Sophocles, and Aeschylus; and two volumes of modern poetry, the dithyrambic odes of Telestes and Philoxenos.

To give Alexander the best possible tutelage for kingship, his father had called in Aristotle to teach him philosophy and rhetoric, subjects for which Aristotle's own writings were the texts. Alexander had been taught since babyhood to seek glory for himself. This ambition was strengthened by Aristotle in his <u>Ethics</u> and <u>Politics</u>, which held that "the really great man was more or less a law unto himself."[6] Alexander was deeply attached to his teacher and stayed in touch with him even during his campaigns far from Greece. He used to say that he loved him no less than his father-- "the one had given him life, but the Philosopher had shown him how to live well."[7]

Certainly Alexander gave himself a comprehensive practical education as he conquered much of the known world. He lived among many peoples with widely differing cultures. But he took Greek ways with him wherever he went and they dominated the colonies he planted so profusely in remote Asia. Homer and Aristotle's instruction gave him an abiding knowledge and love of Greek literature and art. The result, in spite of the brevity of his life, was an almost worldwide diffusion of Greek civilization.

- JULIUS CAESAR, 100-44 B. C. -

We do not know enough about Caesar's reading to be able to pinpoint its influence. Plutarch, in a possibly fictional story, had Caesar reading about Alexander while he was governing in Spain. After the reading,

> he sat a great while very thoughtful, and at last burst out into tears. His friends were surprised, and asked him the reason of it. 'Do you think,' said he, 'I have not just cause to weep, when I consider that Alexander at my age had conquered so many nations, and I have all this time done nothing that is memorable?'[8]

If that story is true, reading about Alexander spurred Caesar to the great deeds that, like those of the Greek conqueror, changed the course of history.

Walter Gérard, in Caesar: A Biography (1952), reviewed what he assumed was young Julius' education. At ten, after a boyhood in a house of women, he was turned over to a grammaticus. The boy was put through Latin, Greek, and rhetoric, learning "to read and think from Homer, first in Latin translation ... then in the original text."[9] Some modern literature also was covered. Since oratory was essential in the public career for which he was preparing, pronunciation and mastery of style were required. He studied poetics, the history of literature, general history, philosophy, and morality. Much of the material had to be committed to memory.

After this strict basic regimen, Caesar broke away and got into whatever radical and licentious books he could lay his hands on. One influence of this reading was his writing of some risqué verses that his successor, Augustus, withdrew from circulation. This is a loss of sorts. We know that, in spite of having studied morality, Caesar was sexually promiscuous. It would have been interesting to compare his accounts of his bedroom adventures with his narration of his victories on the field of battle.

The rest of what we know about Caesar's connection with bookish matters has to do with libraries. He was, it seems, responsible for the destruction of the great library in Alexandria when he commanded the Egyptian fleet in the harbor be set on fire. The fire, spreading to the famous library, is said to have consumed it. But he made at least minor amends, according to one version of his good works, with the public libraries he had set up in Rome.

- NAPOLEON BONAPARTE, 1769-1821 -

The Mind of Napoleon (1955), a selection of his writings and conversations, shows the French emperor to have been better read and more intellectually curious than one would expect of a man so constantly busy bloodying his enemies on so many foreign battlefields. He had about eight years of schooling in the Brienne military college and the Paris military academy, where he finished forty-first in a class of fifty-one.

Although it is not possible, from what Napoleon wrote, to pick out a writer who influenced him above all others, Voltaire was one of his favorites when he was young. Years later, he said that he had read "everything that is published,"[10] and lamented:

> The things now published are wretched--I am disgusted. What a difference between today's writing and Voltaire! The more I read Voltaire the better I like him. That man is always reasonable, not a charlatan, not a fanatic.... I even like his historical writings a great deal, although they are much criticized.[11]

As a young Jacobin, Napoleon had been taken by Rousseau:

> Until I was sixteen, I would have fought to the death for Rousseau against all the friends of Voltaire. Today it is the other way around. I am especially disgusted with Rousseau since I have seen the Orient. Savage man is a dog.[12]

Marshal Foch, the hero of World War I, recalled advice Napoleon gave his officers that shows how he valued military literature. He told them to "read and reread the campaigns of the Great Captains from Alexander to Frederick."[13] He also showed that he had read Machiavelli with perception:

> Machiavelli is right: one must always live with one's friends with the idea that they may turn into one's enemies. He should also have said, with anybody.[14]

In observations on a proposal for a special school for literature and history in the Collège de France, Napoleon demonstrated not only great interest but much insight into the values of history and its teaching. Judgments about good and bad history were essential: "The way history should be read, is in itself, a real science."[15] He observed that much is chewed over and repetitious:

> Thus acquaintance with the choice of good historians, reliable memoirs, of true contemporary chronicles form a useful and real branch of knowledge.[16]

Emphasizing the need for accurate information, he wrote:

> If in a great capital like Paris there were a specialized school of history, beginning with a course in bibliography, a young man instead of wasting months getting lost in inadequate or unreliable literature would be guided toward the best works and would acquire sounder knowledge by an easier and shorter road.[17]

He saw a special task for professors of history. It was to bridge the gap between the mass of information about the distant past and the lack of sound information about recent times. He said,

> It is easier for your young people to learn about the Punic Wars than to know something of the American Revolution, which took place in 1783.[18]

His own son, he believed, "should read much history and meditate upon it: it is the only true philosophy."[19]

During his last dismal exile, Napoleon felt nostalgia for his lost capital city: "There is nothing that surpasses Paris, with its public parks and libraries."[20] Although he once wrote,

> The statistics of my armies are, as far as I am concerned, the most enjoyable works in my library and those I read with the most pleasure in my moments of relaxation,[21]

he was, as he showed in his responses to Voltaire and Rousseau, a man who valued good reading for itself and felt its beneficent influence.

- ARTHUR WELLESLEY, DUKE OF WELLINGTON, 1769-1852 -

The conqueror of Napoleon, when he was still known by his original name, Arthur Wesley, was thought by his mother to be a dull, unpromising boy. His first formal schooling, after he was transplanted at an early age from Ireland to England, was at the undistinguished Brown's Seminary. At twelve, he was sent to Eton. He studied "Upper Greek," and

> toyed with Ovid, Terence, and the Vulgate. By the next Easter ... although Ovid still predominated, there were nutritious extras in the way of Caesar, Aesop, and the Greek Testament.[22]

As for the Eton experience, at the end of which he stood fifty-third in a class of seventy-nine:

> Its effects remain slightly mysterious. For the classical attainments with which Eton equipped her sons for public life, were not for him. He once described his rules for public speaking ... 'I never speak about what I know nothing, and ... I never quote Latin.'--a wise abstention, since his qualities were always uncertain.[23]

These aspects of the Duke of Wellington's life and the rest of his glamorous, spotty career were documented in two substantial biographies, The Great Duke (1972) by Arthur Bryant and Wellington (1931) by Philip Guedalla.

Following the two years of unproductive drudgery at

Eton, Arthur and his mother spent a year in Brussels. His mother, concluding he was "good for powder and nothing more,"24 placed him in a French military school. There, for two years, he learned riding, ballroom deportment, dining room manners, and fluent French. This was time well spent, even though his seat on a horse was considered not stylish, only secure.

Next came the business of buying Arthur an army commission. First he served in a number of units in England, and then he had a tour back in Ireland as aide-de-camp to the viceroy. There, in addition to his slight military duties, he tended to the family estate business and sat in the Irish parliament.

His big chance came when he was assigned to India, where there was plenty of action. To prepare himself, he bought a carefully selected lot of books in Bond street. There were a couple of dozen volumes on Indian history, culture, and military campaigns. Some were on Egypt, Greece, and Persia. With him to India went Caesar's Commentaries, Plutarch's Lives, Smith's Wealth of Nations, and works by Locke, Blackstone, Bolingbroke, and Swift. His seriousness about languages was shown by grammars in German, Persian, and Arabic. He also carried a number of dictionaries. This was surely not a selection by an intellectual lightweight.

Lighter reading which traveled in the young officer's baggage to India included Rousseau's Nouvelle Héloise, six volumes of Woman of Pleasure, the "interminable" Aventures du Chevalier de Faublas, and Leonora, "the latest German romance"25 in translation.

He spent over fifty-eight pounds for the books, a good sum, especially for a man deeply in debt. In addition, he took many other books, already in his possession, to read on his long voyage to India. It was reported,

> His programme of reading was severe, but salutary. For nearly half his acquisitions were palpably designed to equip him for the East with a substantial grasp of its history, language, and administration. His purchases were strong upon the late wars with Tippoo; excepting Caesar, all his new military books were purely Indian; nor was current controversy disdained. It was clear from these elaborate researches that Colonel Wesley

destined himself for a long stay in India, since officers in quest of quick promotion and the first voyage home scarcely require such full documentation.26

Arthur Wesley won his first great military victories in India. He turned out to be a competent commander of men, and an effective combat officer, decisive, well organized, and attentive to the needs of his men. He also found time to read. In Bombay he augmented his library. His love of the theater was shown by the 19-volume Bell's <u>Shakespeare</u> and the <u>British Theatre</u> in 34 volumes. Other purchases suggested he was looking ahead to his return to England. They were Gentz's <u>The State of Europe Before and After the French Revolution</u> and <u>Summary Account and Military Character of the Several European Armies That Have Been Engaged During the Late War</u>. He lightened and varied his fare with <u>Sporting Magazine</u>, <u>Universal Magazine</u>, and Priestley's <u>Socrates and Jesus Compared</u>.

Bound for home, now Major-General Sir Arthur Wellesley, he indulged in some relaxing reading as shown by these additions to his library: <u>Love at First Sight</u> in five volumes, <u>Illicit Love</u>, <u>Lessons for Lovers</u>, <u>Filial Indiscretion, or the Female Chevalier</u>, and like steamy stuff. He had bought 26 volumes. He even found time to read Crébillon's <u>Letters of Madame de Pompadour</u>.

It appears then that the future Duke of Wellington, although indifferently schooled, turned out to be a formidable reader with a taste for both the grave and the gamy. It is possible to trace the relationship of some of his reading to certain actions. He is said to have studied the memoirs of Frederick the Great, which were rich in lessons in military strategy. But Major-General Lloyd's <u>Reflections on the General Principles of War</u> seems to have made the strongest impact on his thinking. Lloyd had recommended a radical change in battle deployment by increasing the light infantry to one-fifth of each battalion and making them more effective than heavy infantry. As Guedalla wrote:

> Here, in his little library of 1796, was the germ that may have led an officer in 1809 to attach a rifle company to each brigade of his command on the Peninsula, to form Portuguese brigades with one battalion to every five--Lloyd's exact proportion --trained and equipped as <u>Caçadores</u>, and to put out

Military Leaders / 155

a line of skirmishers whose fire could invariably hold the French <u>voltigeurs</u>. So perhaps his country's debt was greater than it ever knew to Major-General Lloyd....27

For his spectacular success in driving the French out of Spain, Wellesley was rewarded with the title of Duke of Wellington. After an unfortunate lapse into politics and service as prime minister, where his performance was as sorry as his battlefield achievements were superlative, he again took command of the British army. His victory over Napoleon at Waterloo made him a superhero, and he died idolized by the people.

The Duke of Wellington's discriminating reading, among the fluffy fare he consumed, was helpful to him throughout his brilliant military career. And his careful study and application of the recommendation on the use of light infantry in Lloyd's book was the key to his Spanish triumphs, which prepared him for Waterloo and immortality.

- CARL VON CLAUSEWITZ, 1780-1831 -

The man who literally "wrote the book" on modern war and was the mentor of Lenin and Mao Tse-tung and all the generals since his time, went on his first campaign at twelve, "after a very mediocre education."28 His life and career were recorded by Roger Parkinson in <u>Clausewitz: A Biography</u> (1971).

His brief time in combat against the French in the Rhineland was followed by some years of garrison duty. He used his time during the peaceful years to improve his chances of promotion by studying mathematics, history, and French. He also made a close study of the career of Frederick the Great. During this period, Clausewitz wrote:

> By sheer chance I obtained some political and religious tracts and other books about the perfectability of man. There, with one stroke, the vanity of the young soldier became a great philosophical ambition. I was then, at that time and moment, so close to the inspiration as the nature of the spirit will allow. If this glow had been better maintained in me and had been used better, I might have become a much more worthwhile person than I am.29

156 / Caught in the Act

Whether the reading of the tracts on politics and religion and the books on the perfectability of man had any influence or not, at the War College in Berlin Clausewitz studied the unmilitary subjects of philosophy and literature. To his study of Kant he credited his success in his own writing and his "dialectical sharpness."[30] He enjoyed the political philosophers Voltaire, Montesquieu, and Machiavelli. "No reading," he said, "is more necessary than the writing of Machiavelli." He considered "those who pretend to be revolted by his principles are nothing but dandies who take on humanistic airs."[31] In addition to this serious reading, so basic to his military education, he enjoyed books on travel and people. In a lighter vein, he was fond of Sterne's Tristram Shandy.

After some years of campaigning, during which he was a prisoner of war and served with the Russian general staff, he was appointed administrative head of the War College where he served for twelve years. Most of his important writing, including the incomplete On War, was done during those years. It was an irony that as influential as his masterpiece was for the military leaders of all the well-armed nations, his main dictum that "War is a continuation of policy by other means," and not an end in itself, was lost sight of. His book was the pretext for power-hungry generals to push civil governments aside and take over when the fighting started, then to govern themselves, backed by their armies, instead of turning the reins over to the elected rulers. It is a process that is worldwide and still going on. This is a good example of the unhappy outcome of a general misreading of a classic.

- ROBERT E. LEE, 1807-1870 -

Like most young Southerners of old, established families, Robert E. Lee, when young, had a go at the classics. Douglas S. Freeman, in R. E. Lee: A Biography (1934), pointed out that in three years at the Alexandria Academy,

> He read Homer and Longinus in Greek. From Tacitus and Cicero he became so well-grounded in Latin that he never quite forgot the language, although he did not study it after he was seventeen.[32]

At West Point, Lee concentrated on engineering, his main military interest. His texts were Newton's Principia, Gregory's Treatise on Mechanics, and Enfield's Institutes of

Natural History. He mastered French well enough to read Rousseau's Confessions, and he studied Spanish. He steered clear of fiction as "an intellectual narcotic,"[33] but he enjoyed and remembered poetry. Apparently the newspapers were his main everyday reading.

As a dedicated cadet, serious about his calling, Lee read military material with care. "Light Horse Harry" Lee, his father, had written Memoirs of the War in the Southern Department, which helped Robert understand the fight for independence. He learned about the campaigns of Caesar and Hannibal from his reading. Napoleon's battles, as reported by Antoine-Henri Jomini, received his thorough consideration. Military subjects led the way among the 52 books he borrowed from the Military Academy library. Machiavelli's Art of War, the works of Alexander Hamilton, and Atkinson's Navigation--borrowed seven times--were among the most significant reading.

As superintendent of the Military Academy, he continued to take books and magazines from the library, some of them for his wife and daughters. He was also building up a small library of his own, mostly French treatises on military design and construction.

Lee's most crucial reading seems to have been in French: Jomini's Traité des Grandes Opérations Militaires and Napoleon's Considérations sur l'Art de la Guerre. Napoleon had recommended that in defending a capital the commander should not allow his forces to be pinned down. He should

> manoeuvre incessantly, without submitting to be driven back to the capital ... or shut up in an entrenched camp in the rear.[34]

There is a parallel between what Napoleon advised and Lee's operations between the Rapidan and the James in 1864.

- ULYSSES S. GRANT, 1822-1885 -

Although General Lee was forced to surrender to Grant, it is generally agreed that he was ahead of his younger conqueror by a country mile in education and intellect. In Meet General Grant (1928), W. E. Woodward pointed out there were no free schools out where Grant grew up in rural Ohio. A subscription school ran three months a year and scattered some crumbs of "reading, writing, and nothing else" among the pupils. Even this "meant nothing to Ulysses, whose intellectual hunger was easily satisfied."[35] He "was slow at answers, and his negligent appearance seemed to invite physical correction."

One of his Military Academy roommates recalled that Grant "took small interest in his studies ... seldom read a lesson more than once ... and spent his time in idleness or in poring over romances."[36] In his <u>Memoirs</u> (1885-86), Grant recalled:

> I could not sit in my room doing nothing. There is a fine library connected with the Academy from which cadets can get books to read in their quarters. I devoted more time to these than to the course of studies. Much of the time, I am sorry to say, was devoted to novels, but not those of a trashy sort. I read all of Bulwer's then published, Cooper's, Marryat's, Scott's, Washington Irving's work, Lever's, and many others I do not remember.[37]

Woodward wrote, "It is certain that Grant was never familiar with any of the classic campaigns of Napoleon or Frederick the Great." A close friend said "that he never read a book on strategy."[38] When the city of Boston gave him a gift of books after the war, "An inquiry to avoid duplication showed that he did not own a military book of any kind."[39] Grant's explanation of his success in war went like this:

> Some of our generals failed because they worked out everything by rule.... They were always thinking about what Napoleon would do. Unfortunately for their plans, the rebels would be thinking of something else. I don't underrate the value of military knowledge, but if men make war in slavish observation of the rules, they will fail. No rules will apply to conditions of war as different as those that exist in Europe and America. Consequently, while our generals were working out problems that would have looked well on a blackboard, practical facts were neglected. To that extent I consider remembrances of old campaigns a disadvantage.[40]

Unless he got some unknown inspiration from the stacks of novels he spent his time on at West Point, Grant's reading does not seem to have contributed to his achievements. He was a farmer at heart, good with horses, persistent, too trustful of his friends, and he hated war. He is a paradox among the great captains of history.

- FERDINAND FOCH, 1851-1929 -

As a boy, Foch read and pondered the campaigns of Napoleon. Cyril Falls, in Marshal Foch (1939), reviewed his education, beginning at the lycée of Tarbes, his birthplace in the Pyrénées. Then he studied at the seminary of Polignon and the Jesuit college at Saint Etienne. His study of Louis-Adolfe Thier's The Consulate and the Empire, massive volumes, was such that, according to B. H. Liddell Hart in Foch: The Man of Orleans (1932), he used to say, "At eleven I knew the battles of Marengo and Trafalgar off by heart."[41]

After his elementary schooling, Foch prepared in the Jesuit school of Saint Clément at Metz for the elite Ecole Polytechnique admission examination. The Franco-Prussian War interrupted his studies and he enlisted in the army. After the fighting was over, he attended the Polytechnique and then the artillery training school. Most of the next several decades were spent in active service and study of the military arts and sciences. The lives of great men and the problems of leadership were his main interests. He had a long tenure at the war college, studying and teaching. When World War I broke out in 1914, he was due for retirement. But his knowledge and experience were too valuable to lose in a time of national peril. Under his leadership as supreme commander of the allied forces, the German army was crushed. He was honored by appointment as a Marshal of France and world-wide recognition as a war leader of genius.

During the years before his climactic service, he had plenty of time for reading. Among his favorite authors were Corneille, Racine, La Bruyère, and Shakespeare in translation. The writers who attracted his professional attention were Jomini, von der Goltz, Bernhardi, Hoenig, Bonnal, and, above all, Clausewitz.

Although in teaching Foch looked to Clausewitz for the

elements of war, he found the German's writing "ponderous." Reading him called for "critical power and a wide knowledge of history ... for producing the juices to counteract the Clausewitzian fermentation."[42] But Foch struggled with the complexities of the philosopher of war and taught his principles the best he could. Traces of Clausewitz can be detected in Foch's own Des Principles de la Guerre.

Foch was one of the most discriminating readers among military leaders. And his reading was a big factor in his success in saving France.

- ALFRED T. MAHAN, 1840-1914 -

If it is true that the pen is mightier than the sword, Alfred T. Mahan furnished the proof. He was strongly influenced by his reading. In turn, he was a decisive influence on several generations of military and government leaders from Germany to Japan.

As the son of a scholarly professor at the Military Academy, Alfred was raised in a setting favorable to learning. He studied and absorbed the spell-binding sea stories of James Fenimore Cooper and Marryat. He had a good lesson in the power of books when, at twelve, his father, whose sympathies were with the South, took away a copy of Uncle Tom's Cabin he had received as a gift.

With the stimulus of the sea tales by which he had been so fascinated, Alfred was well prepared for the salty atmosphere of the Naval Academy when he entered. He studied hard and made a good record at Annapolis.

Mahan continued studying during his active naval service. According to Charles C. Taylor in The Life of Admiral Mahan (1920), the first book to make a big impact on his strategic thinking was Sir William Napier's History of the War in the Peninsula. He recalled:

> During my last tour of shore duty I had read carefully Napier's Peninsular War, and had found myself in a new world of thought, keenly interested and appreciative, less of the brilliant narrative--though that few can fail to enjoy--than of the military sequences of cause and effect. The influence of Sir John Moore's famous march to Sahagun--

less famous than it deserves to be--on Napoleon's campaign in Spain, revealed to me by Napier like the sun breaking through a cloud, aroused an emotion as joyful as the luminary himself to a navigator doubtful of his position.[43]

Taylor wrote, "From this time onward, military ideas seem to have taken possession of his mind."[44]

An even more powerful impulse came to Mahan when he read Mommsen's History of Rome while he was ashore in Lima, Peru. It

> opened his eyes to the advantages lost by Hannibal through his inability to use the sea effectively in his great campaigns against the Romans.[45]

Mahan described the effect of this reading:

> While my problem was still wrestling with my brain there dawned on me one of those concrete perceptions which turn darkness into light--give substance to shadow. He who seeks finds, if he does not lose heart; and to me, continuously seeking, came from within the suggestion that control of the sea was an historic factor which had never been systematically appreciated and expounded. Once formulated consciously, this thought became the nucleus of all my writing for twenty years to come.[46]

Mahan kept on with his intensive exploration of all available works by masters of strategy. The writings of Napoleon, Jomini, and Hanley were full of provocative ideas. Henri Martin's History of France awakened him to the realization of the importance of commercial and maritime policy to a nation, especially under the guidance of a man like Colbert, the famous French foreign minister. He was encouraged by reading Jomini "to make a critical analysis of the great naval campaigns and conclusive battles of the world."[47] And,

> From Napoleon and Jomini he had learned the living principles of strategy and the close relation in warfare between the Statesman and the General; and upon those foundations he set himself to prove to the world how stupendous an influence upon the

destinies of nations had been, for centuries, the military and commercial control of the sea.[48]

One practical result of the greatest importance for the country's military future stemmed from the reading of Mahan's Influence of Sea Power upon the French Revolution and Empire by the Secretary of the Navy, who had proposed closing the Naval War College. But after reading Mahan's book, which was written at the College, the Secretary said the College was "worth all the money that was being spent on"[49] it.

When The Influence of Sea Power upon History came out in 1890, it was immediately recognized as a seminal work. One of its first American enthusiasts was Theodore Roosevelt, then a Civil Service Commissioner in Washington. He wrote to Mahan:

> During the last two days I have spent half my time, busy as I am, in reading your book. That I found it interesting is shown by the fact that after having taken it up, I have gone straight through and finished it.
>
> I can say with perfect sincerity that I think it much the clearest and most instructive general work of the kind with which I am acquainted. It is a very good book--admirable; and I am greatly in error if it does not become a classic.[50]

Roosevelt was exactly right. The book quickly became a classic. It was translated into many languages. In all the naval and potential naval powers it was accepted as a bible of maritime strategy. It spurred the beefing up of the great navies of the world. The British learned from Mahan "the priceless lesson of the paramount necessity of an adequate margin of Naval strength."[51] A high Japanese official was so impressed he announced:

> My desire is that my fellow-countrymen should read this book in such a spirit, and put forth an effort to make their country a great sea power in the Pacific Ocean.[52]

The impact upon Wilhelm II of Germany was electric. After reading it, he declared, "Our future lies upon the water.... The trident must be in our fist."[53]

It is apparent from these examples of the effect of Mahan's ideas, although they are only a few of those that could be cited, that they strongly influenced the cataclysmic events that devastated much of Europe during World War I. And Mahan's ideas came from his intensive reading.

- BILLY MITCHELL, 1879-1936 -

Mitchell did for air power what Mahan had done for powerful navies. But it is not as easy to pinpoint the influence of specific reading as with Mahan.

Billy Mitchell's background--he was born in Nice to a wealthy American family--was unusual for a man who would become the most vociferous pleader for a strong air force. His U.S. army service began in the infantry, from which he was transferred to the signal corps. One idea obsessed him. That idea was that the airplane was destined to become the deadliest weapon of war.

The books of Jules Verne were very popular when Mitchell was growing up. He may very well have read <u>From the Earth to the Moon</u>. As Isaac Don Levine reports in <u>Mitchell, Pioneer of Air Power</u> (1943), he was a reader. During the early years of his service, as he advanced from private to captain in assignments in Cuba, the Philippines, and Alaska, he read whatever he could find on the new subject of aviation. As a member of the signal corps, he was under the command of a general who was convinced of the future of flying. When he was studying for his promotion, Mitchell concentrated on balloons--their construction and use --and on the gliding experiments of Lilienthal and Chanute and Professor Langley's attempts at heavier-than-air flights.

During World War I, as a reward for his study and commitment, he was promoted to the rank of brigadier-general. He commanded the largest air armada assembled up to that time, using up to 200 planes in mass bombing attacks.

Mitchell's aggressiveness in arguing the cause of airplanes for combat got him in trouble with the old guard. They couldn't be budged from their exclusive commitment to land and sea warfare fought with the weapons of past wars. He was court-martialed and left the service, a disruptive intransigent to some and a hero to others. He was honored, only posthumously, by Congress, for the ideas he so vigorously advanced before the tradition-bound military leadership was ready for them. Those ideas were undoubtedly reinforced, if not generated, by his early reading on flight.

- DOUGLAS MacARTHUR, 1880-1964 -

One of the most brilliant and egotistical of American generals, Douglas MacArthur was a mama's boy and a man of books as well as an officer of commanding presence. In <u>American Caesar: Douglas MacArthur, 1880-1964</u> (1978), William Manchester wrote:

> He never went to church, but he read the Bible every day and regarded himself as one of the world's two great defenders of Christendom (The other was the Pope). [54]

As the son of a famous general, it was natural for Douglas to head for the army. His record at the Military Academy, from which he graduated in 1904, was the highest in his class.

Although he is commonly thought of as a great combat commander and a master of strategy, opinion divides on other aspects of the man. One of his friends said that MacArthur's mind, "a beautiful piece of machinery,"[55] had to be

> stimulated almost exclusively by reading because he never had the benefit of daily rubbing elbows with his intellectual equals--let alone his superiors. [56]

In MacArthur's <u>Reminiscenses</u> (1964), he recalled his initiation into the world of the intellect while he was a student at the West Texas Military Academy:

> There came a desire to know, a seeking of the reason why, a search for the truth. Abstruse mathematics began to appear a challenge to analysis, dull Latin and Greek seemed a gateway to the moving words of the leaders of the past, laborious historical data led to the nerve-tingling battlefields of the great captains, Biblical lessons began to open the spiritual portals of a growing faith, literature to bare the souls of men. My studies enveloped me, my marks went higher, and many of the school

medals came my way. But I also learned how little such honors mean after one wins them. [57]

MacArthur, usually so dead serious about everything pertaining to himself, as can be seen from this sample, poked fun at himself at least once. He was in a West Point classroom,

> when the first section was studying the time-space relationship later formulated by Einstein as his Theory of Relativity. The text was complex and, being unable to comprehend it, I committed the pages to memory. When called upon to recite, I solemnly reeled off almost word for word what the book said. Our instructor ... looked at me somewhat quizzically and asked, 'Do you understand this theory?' It was a bad moment for me, but I did not hesitate in replying, 'No sir.' You could have heard a pin drop. I braced myself and waited. And then the slow words of the professor, 'Neither do I, Mr. MacArthur. Section dismissed.' I still do not understand the theory. [58]

From his father, MacArthur inherited over 4,000 books, a collection rich in British and American history and Chinese culture. These books gave him "a remarkable vocabulary, a mastery of Victorian prose, a love of neo-Augustan rhetoric, and a ready grasp of theory."[59]

MacArthur's second wife, a Southerner, plied him with biographies of Confederate generals--Lee, Stonewall Jackson, Nathan Bedford Forrest, and others. MacArthur tore through them at the rate of three a day, and he kept up with the newspapers at the same time. He was probably the most avid reader of all our generals.

While planning his campaign to return to the Philippines and conquer Japan by way of New Guinea and the string of South Pacific Islands, he occupied a bungalow whose earlier tenant had assembled a fine library in several languages. And,

> Unless he was preoccupied with battle reports, the General would pace the room, reading of Papuan aborigines, native lore, and anthropology, or, if he was in the mood for European literature, the works of Zola, Shaw, Ibsen, and others. Phrases

> from this cultural smorgasbord would find their way into the aureate communiques he dictated ... each morning.[60]

It was said that in dealing with a single idea he could quote Shakespeare, the Bible, Mark Twain, Napoleon, and Lincoln. To add color to his reports, he drew on such varied sources as melodramas he had seen in New York 25 years earlier, Plato, and the Bible. He had a razzle-dazzle style in writing to match his personal flamboyance.

Manchester believed MacArthur especially enjoyed Dostoevski's <u>Crime and Punishment</u>, where

> the key tension lies between Profiry, the police inspector, and Raskolnikov's mind, and in the end that is the criminal's undoing. Similarly, MacArthur was trying to make a mental leap over the towering green hell of the Owen Stanley Range, to the coconut-fringed village of three houses called Buna. There the Japanese commander was poring over the same Papuan maps MacArthur was studying and like him, was issuing orders to feverish troops in the jungly mountains.[61]

Even though this picture of the general under the influence of Dostoevski may be a fancy of Manchester in his attempt to get inside MacArthur's mind, it is obvious that the books he read sank in and stayed with him. He certainly used his reading and reflected its influence in his leadership.

- DWIGHT EISENHOWER, 1890-1969 -

In background and personality, Eisenhower was vastly different from MacArthur. He came from poor, unlearned parents in a Kansas backwater from which he progressed slowly as a conscientious plodder. But he shared with MacArthur a love of reading. Kenneth S. Davis reported in <u>Soldier of Democracy: A Biography of Dwight Eisenhower</u> (1945) that Ike and his brothers satisfied their need for books when,

> With whatever pocket money they managed to earn they bought paper-backed Western novels, devouring their contents with greedy eyes. They played out all the stories they read. Abilene became the

wildest of cow towns and Wild Bill was cleaning it up again with his smoking guns. Edgar could remember a favorite story about Wild Bill killing six men in a saloon brawl when he first became town marshal, and about the burial of those six men in the Abilene cemetary. The boys could never find those graves, but the story they accepted as 'gospel truth.'62

Ike did not limit his interest to bad men and marshals. He told a friend, "I like to read what is going on outside of Kansas. Makes me realize that Kansas isn't all the world."63 He broadened his horizons largely through reading newspapers. But he also took an interest in history and biography:

> One volume which seems to have had a tremendous influence on him was a Life of Hannibal--author unknown [probably Theodore Ayrault Dodge]--in which the campaigns of the Second Punic War were described in detail. Other boys had looked at that book and had even tried to read it, attracted by the prospect of exciting war stories, but all of them abandoned it after a few pages, complaining that it was 'too deep' for them. Dwight read it with evident pleasure, and ever afterward Hannibal--whose strategical and tactical brilliance had been so tragically frustrated by unsound logistics--was among his heroes.64

After graduating from the Military Academy in 1915, ranking 61st academically out of a class of 104, Eisenhower did the normal rookie work of a career officer. He had a tour in San Antonio, Texas, and during World War I he trained tank battalions at several bases in the United States. A big change came for him when he served in the Panama Canal Zone under Brigadier General Fox Connor, who convinced him that another war was coming in which he would be called upon to take a commanding role. With the general guiding his reading, he began preparing himself, putting up maps in his quarters and hitting the books. He got into Napoleon's campaigns and strategy by way of the memoirs and commentaries by Jomini and Clausewitz. Prominent in his course of study were Ardant du Picq's Battle Studies and Foch's The Principles of War. Even more prominent was the pragmatic writing of Denis Hart Mahan, father of the naval expert. In Outpost, Mahan had written:

> How different is almost every military problem, except in the bare mechanism of tactics. In almost every case the data upon which a solution depends are lacking.... Too often the general has only conjectures to go on, and these based on false premises.... What is true now, at the next moment may have no existence or exist in the contrary sense.... These considerations explain why history produces ... so few famous generals.[65]

Mahan also gave the classical advice of fast movement against a disorganized and demoralized force, a lesson applied with smashing success during the final routing of the German army during World War II by Eisenhower.

While Eisenhower did not flaunt his erudition as MacArthur did, he showed in his greatest victories, in which he commanded the biggest armies ever assembled, that he had learned from his reading some of the basic lessons taught by the most distinguished writers on the art of war.

- SHORTER SKETCHES OF THE READING OF SOME OTHER MILITARY LEADERS -

It will be noticed that I have omitted the names of some of history's greatest military leaders. This is because I found only scanty evidence. However, reading significantly influenced each one of those whose most critical encounters with books will now be sketched.

Although GUSTAVUS ADOLPHUS, 1594-1632, is known mainly as a fighting Swede who spent much of his brief life leading his armies in bloody battles across Europe, he was also a man who valued books. C. R. L. Fletcher, in Gustavus Adolphus and the Struggle of Protestantism for Existence (1897), pointed out that the Swedish king was fluent in five languages and knew several others. Being able to read Xenophon in the original Greek enabled him to study the military art as it was known to one of the ancient experts who had fought in many campaigns, including some of the epic conquests of Cyrus the Great, one of the most brilliant of commanders. Wherever he went, Gustavus is said to have carried a copy of Grotius' De Jure Belli ac Pacis, which laid the basis for international law.

Since his father thought he was stupid and even forbade

him to learn Latin, the boy who became FREDERICK THE GREAT, 1712-1786, educated himself. This he accomplished, according to Walther Hubatsch's Frederick the Great of Prussia ... (1975), largely by covert reading. He shared proscribed books with his sister. One book that made a strong impression on him was Fénelon's Télémark, the story of "the ideal prince as a virtuous, just, and peaceful shepherd of his people."66 Voltaire's writing and personal conversation when he was a guest at court had a lasting influence on Frederick. And it was said that he gave careful study to Tacitus, Sallust, and Cornelius Nepos, useful authors for a soldier-king. Reading and writing were a diversion for Frederick, even during his rough days in the field. The value he placed on general access to good books was shown when he opened the Royal Library in Berlin to the public.

GIUSEPPE GARIBALDI, 1817-1882, soldier and nation-builder, rose from poverty, although never very far above it, and to fame, almost entirely on his own initiative. Books were his schooling. Resisting formal education, he taught himself what he needed to know to become a ship's master out of books on mathematics, astronomy, geography, and commercial law. According to Jasper Ridley's Garibaldi (1974), he had come under the influence of Mazzini, who was writing and working for a democratic and unified Italy. Whenever he went ashore, he looked in bookshops for information about martyrs and their radical causes. Claude Saint-Simon was an especially strong influence through his Le Nouveau Christianisme, which paid tribute to the cosmopolitan who adopts a struggling country as his own "and offers his sword and blood to all peoples who are struggling against tyranny." Such a man "is more than a soldier; he is a hero."67 That is what Garibaldi was, a hero fighting for the freedom of men and women in South America and Europe from oppression. His reading influenced him in the stormy course he followed.

The story of the most decisive reading of our most famous World War I general is soon told. In his youth, JOHN J. PERSHING, 1860-1948, was addicted to dime novels. He also read some of the classics of English literature. But he found his destiny in a newspaper. After teaching in a Missouri school for Negroes, studying at a teacher-training school, and dipping into Blackstone and Kent while toying with the idea of following the law as a profession, he came upon this item in a weekly paper:

170 / Caught in the Act

> Notice is hereby given that there will be a competitive examination held at Trenton, Missouri ... for the purpose of selecting one Cadet for the Military Academy at West Point.[68]

Pershing took the examination, passed and became the "one Cadet" to go to West Point. He did well there and then started out on the diverse tours of duty of the career army officer. First he fought Indians. Then he led troops in combat against the fierce Moros in the Philippines. Next he chased Pancho Villa around Mexico for a while. And finally, after commanding the American expeditionary force in Europe, he came home a national hero. And it all happened because he read that newspaper notice of a West Point examination out there in Missouri.

There is an irony in the decisive reading of ERWIN ROMMEL, 1891-1944. Desmond Young, in Rommel, the Desert Fox (1950), told of finding "a well-thumbed ... German translation of ... Der Feldherr ..."[69] in Rommel's library. This pamphlet on the art of generalship was by the very man whose army was routed by Rommel's Afrika Corps in the North African sands. It is reasonable to assume that much of what he knew and used to beat Sir Archibald Wavell came from Wavell's manual for generals.

VO NGUYEN GIAP, 1912-   , was already a committed nationalist and rebel against the French rulers of Vietnam when he read Ho Chi Minh's Colonialism on Trial. He found the book a revelation and said, "To read a book denouncing colonialism for the first time inspired and thrilled us."[70] Giap kept reading Ho's inflammatory writings, and when they met they were immediately friends. Ho's fervent messages calling on the people to join together and free themselves were in Giap's thoughts as he became a master of guerrilla warfare and led his army in its spectacular victories over the French and then the United States forces. The influence of Ho's writing on Giap and Giap's triumphs in throwing off the yoke of the imperialists were reported in "Giap--The Victor of Dien Bien Phu" in The [London] Sunday Times Magazine, Nov. 5, 1972.

- OBSERVATIONS -

It was to be expected from the nature of the occupation that the great military leaders were, mostly, less bookish than writers and scientists. As Clausewitz pointed out, usually they were not from the most erudite class. And academic education, which calls for heavy attacks on books, was thought in Clausewitz's time to be unnecessary for leadership in the armed forces.

But even though the great commanders do not measure up to the learned professions academically, they were generally pretty well educated. Most had graduated from military schools. Some had studied on their own, and several had taken advantage of peacetime lulls to read to improve their minds and skills, as well as to relax with books.

About half of them came from homes with some books, but only Mahan and MacArthur came from what might be called bookish homes. I found little precise information on the ages at which the future commanders began reading. Most seemed to have done some reading as boys.

Reading about history and the military exploits of famous commanders strongly influenced about half of those who would themselves make history. Caesar's depression at reading how much more Alexander the Great had accomplished at the same age possibly goaded him in his desperate struggle to get to the top of the heap. Machiavelli was crucial for Clausewitz, Frederick the Great, Foch, and possibly others. The Duke of Wellington found the idea on the use of light infantry that made him victorious in Spain in Lloyd's book on the general principles of war. Mommsen's History of Rome opened Mahan's eyes to the essential role of naval strength in large land operations. Hannibal was a hero to young Dwight Eisenhower who, like the Carthaginian general, commanded enormous forces operating over vast spaces. It seems that Rommel's reading of Wavell helped him understand and anticipate the man he defeated. And Giap was stimulated in his monumental feats of arms by the writings of Ho Chi Minh.

The one entirely fortuitous reading encounter seems to have been young John Pershing's chancing upon the notice of the West Point examination in a weekly newspaper.

The scope of the reading of the military leaders was fairly wide. A few of them were stirred by such philosophic thinkers as Aristotle, Voltaire, Kant, and Rousseau. Some, especially the Europeans, were familiar with Latin and Greek classics. Gustavus Adolphus was at home in several ancient and modern languages. Among the most scholarly were Clausewitz, Foch, Mahan, and MacArthur.

The military men, when they read, were purposeful. Books for some of them, made an important impact on their lives and their achievements on the field of battle or in their contributions to military thinking. At least one, Alfred T. Mahan, under the influence of his reading, changed the course of history. It is clear then, that among their other manifold uses, books have indeed served as weapons and armor in many wars over many centuries.

Chapter 9

OBSERVATIONS, A SUGGESTION, AND CONCLUDING THOUGHTS ON THE IMPACTS OF READING, MOVIES, AND TV

Observations:

1. Catching the reader in the act and following up on the consequences show that reading had changed profoundly the lives of some of the world's most renowned leaders, and, through them, often it has changed history.

2. Most of the readers came from homes where books were available and read.

3. Most of them had a good education.

4. Most were lifelong readers who read widely.

5. Most of the decisive reading came during adult years.

6. Most of the decisive reading was purposeful, but some chance reading had extraordinary consequences.

7. The decisive impact usually came with the first reading, although for a few a second reading was decisive.

8. The decisive reading, especially of religious leaders, was often an overwhelming revelation, with striking immediate impact and long-lasting influence on attitudes and behavior.

9. Movies and TV change lives also and seem to make their greatest impact on the young.

Suggestion: A study should be made, as objective evidence accumulates on the newer media, to find out if there are significant differences in the long-range influence of the various media. The study should focus on the individual and, like the Terman study of gifted children, should cover a generation or more. The findings could be helpful in using each medium most effectively in the intellectual preparation of oncoming generations.

Although there is much less recorded material on the impact of the newer media on the individual than on reading, which makes comparisons risky, here, against the background of Barth's statement quoted in the Introduction, are some concluding thoughts on reading, the movies, and TV.

Barth claimed that "literature can shake lives to the core." We have seen that happen. However, he contradicted himself and went against the evidence when he also said, "literature is our greatest limitation" and "doesn't appeal directly to any of the physical senses." Now recall the effects of some of the reading we have reviewed.

Think of the "soft ravishment" of Melville by Hawthorne's Mosses from an Old Manse as it "spun him around in a web of dreams." Goethe's poems were wine to Flaubert, making his head swim and his eyes blur. And Rousseau's Confessions thundered like an earthquake through Tolstoy's brain. Consider what Paul's Letter to the Romans did to Augustine: "instantly ... by a light as it were of serenity infused into my soul, all the doubt of darkness vanished away." Teresa of Avila "remained for a long time dissolved in tears" upon reading Augustine. The erotic Song of Solomon so heated Jonathan Edwards that he admitted to "a sweet burning in my heart." After the first fifty pages of Galton's Hereditary Genius, Darwin exclaimed, "I must exhale myself, else something will go wrong with my inside." Havelock Ellis' second reading of Hinton's Life in Nature "acted with the swiftness of an electric current; the dull tension was removed," and his "feet scarcely touched the ground." But for Marie Stopes, reading Ellis' Studies in the Psychology of Sex was "like breathing a bag of soot." She felt "choked and dirty for three months." Jung recalled his response to Krafft-Ebing on the psychoses: "My heart suddenly started to pound. I had to sit up and take a deep breath. My excitement was intense." And for Mahan, Napier's Peninsular War "aroused an emotion as joyful" as that of a lost navigator when the sun breaks through and he finds his position.

These reactions were probably heightened in the telling. But they show that each of the readers was touched in some physical sense. Clearly, Barth underestimated the sensual power of print.

Further, evidence does not show that literature is alone in possessing certain other powers he claimed for it. Barth contended that "Words written on a page are our greatest source of stimulation" and "literature remains the only medium that gets inside to our interior life." The meaning of "interior life," of course, is hard to define with precision. However, when young Jack Smith felt "a call as powerful as the call of the cloth to an altar boy" when he saw the movie, The Front Page, and gave up music for journalism, his "interior life" seems to have been reached. And Donald Bowie, writing that TV "was becoming in my life what a dog was supposed to be to a boy," showed how the medium had gotten through to his "interior life." It may be that Jack Smith and Donald Bowie lack the kind of interior lives Barth had in mind. But they, and the others who imitated TV models, acted as if they had been stimulated and touched deeply within themselves.

When Barth said, "We may go to a movie [or see one on TV] and weep like a child and still despise the film," he did not prove that we may not have been affected in some lasting way. It is as mistaken to deny that the other media can change people as it is to claim exclusive powers of penetration for print.

With all its competition, what are the chances for the book? My own experience bears on this question. When I began work as a librarian in 1936, print was preeminent. Since then, the other carriers of information and ideas have flooded into library collections. I have evaluated and acquired materials in all the media and supervised their use. Each of them--recordings, radio, movies, computerized information banks, and TV--serves a useful purpose. And their potential has barely been scratched. But I am convinced that certain characteristics of the book make it unreplaceable.

The compactness and easy portability of the book served Teresa of Avila as she stole away with The Life of Christ by Ludolph of Saxony and, in a quiet place, blissfully united with God as she read. That compactness and portability still enables a reader quietly to absorb an author's message far from electric outlets and batteries. Among the media, only print may be read, reread, and mulled over, reached for, picked up and put down again and again, always at the reader's bidding and convenience. Martin Luther, pondering "night and day," with his Bible open to Paul's Letter to the Romans, finally discovered the "connection between the justice of God and that statement that 'the just shall live by his faith'." He was reborn with this discovery and went joyfully "through the open doors of paradise." Recall Luther Burbank, who systematically searched the shelves of his hometown library for books on plants and found Darwin's work on the variations of plants and animals under domestication. The same plenitude of books that put Burbank on the way to spectacular success as a plant breeder, figured in the happy surprise of young Isaac Rabi, innocent of any knowledge of science, as he chanced on the astronomy books after going through the children's fiction in a Brooklyn Public Library branch. The treatment in depth of important subjects, with many points of view represented, is peculiar to collections of books. As Tolstoy dug into the diverse pile of material he had assembled on the Napoleonic period, and selected telling incidents, he enriched War and Peace with the vivid sense of being present at the cataclysmic events that make it one of the greatest books ever written. Esoteric volumes such as those Freud and Jung delved into to extend the boundaries of their pioneering explorations of the mind still attract bold thinkers who look beyond conventional writings for fresh insights. Such obscure, occult material is seldom treated in depth in any of the nonprint media.

The unique qualities of the books that met the needs of Saint Teresa, Luther, Burbank, Tolstoy, Freud, and Jung --availability in quantity and variety, compactness, portability, an image that does not fade from a screen to be brought back only with the aid of electronic gadgetry, and easy-to-use retrieval devices (numbered pages, tables of contents, and often indexes)--make books basic for those questing present-day men and women, who need, in their often lonely intellectual voyages, the inspiration and enlightenment to be found in the books of wise, unorthodox, and venturesome thinkers of earlier times and far places, as well as in the writings of their brilliant contemporaries. These unmatched qualities of the book give it a clear edge over all the other media as a store and transmitter of the infinitely varied knowledge, facts, and speculation needed for the stimulation of inquiring minds.

And let us remember the research reported in Chapter 2, showing that reading activates the brain waves more than TV watching. This effect surely must give reading an advantage in stimulating original thought.

But the question remains: Will the great timebinder-- the book--serve and inspire the intellectual leaders of the future, struggling to think in the midst of a cacophony of communication, much of it mindless, as it has served and inspired those of a quieter past? I believe, on the basis of the evidence we have seen, and because of the peculiar qualities of print, that it will.

Time will tell.

NOTES

Chapter 1

1. Baltimore Evening Sun, October 7, 1975, p. B1.

Chapter 2

1. Caryl Rivers, Aphrodite at Mid-century (New York: Doubleday, 1973), p. 33.
2. Ibid., p. 194.
3. Ibid., p. 35.
4. Baltimore Sun, April 25, 1974, p. A8.
5. Ibid.
6. Ibid.
7. Modern Maturity, April-May, 1977, p. 9.
8. Tucson Citizen, April 8, 1978, p. 9.
9. Ibid.
10. Shana Alexander, Talking Woman (New York: Delacorte, 1976), p. 214.
11. Donald Bowie, Station Identification.... (New York: M. Evans, 1980), pp. 14-15.
12. Ibid., p. 16.
13. Ibid., p. 13.
14. Ibid.
15. Ibid.
16. Ibid.
17. Ibid., p. 20.
18. Ibid., p. 22.
19. Ibid.
20. Ibid., p. 24.
21. Ibid.
22. Ibid., p. 214.
23. Ibid., p. 215.
24. Baltimore Sun, January 20, 1978, p. A7.
25. International Herald Tribune (Paris), October 5, 1977, p. 3.
26. Baltimore Sunday Sun, August 26, 1979, p. A3.
27. Baltimore Sunday Sun, November 12, 1975, p. A21.
28. Ibid.
29. Ibid.
30. Ibid., March 23, 1979, p. B4.
31. American Libraries, Vol. 10, No. 8, September 1979, p. 493.

Chapter 3

1. Dante Alighieri, The Divine Comedy ("Great Books of the Western World," Vol. 21) (Chicago: Encyclopaedia Britannica, 1952), p. 2.
2. Ibid., p. 22.
3. Francis Ferguson, Dante (New York: Macmillan, 1966), p. 11.
4. Dante, op. cit., p. 8.
5. Ferguson, op. cit., p. 106.
6. John Gardner, The Life and Times of Chaucer (New York: Knopf, 1977), p. 200.
7. Ibid.
8. Ibid.
9. Geoffrey Chaucer, The Canterbury Tales ("Great Books of the Western World," Vol. 22) (Chicago: Encyclopaedia Britannica, 1952), p. 189.
10. Gardner, op. cit., p. 201.
11. Dante, op. cit., p. 2.
12. Marchette Chute, Geoffrey Chaucer of England (New York: Dutton, 1946), p. 67.
13. Gardner, op. cit., p. 77.
14. Ibid., p. 199.
15. Chaucer, Legend of Good Women. In The Works of Geoffrey Chaucer, 2nd edition. F. N. Robinson, editor. (Boston: Houghton, Mifflin, 1961), p. 500.
16. Percy Van Dyke Shelley, The Living Chaucer (New York: Russell and Russell, 1940), p. 102.
17. Francisco Navarro y Ledesma, Cervantes: The Man and the Genius (New York: Charter House, 1973), p. 219.
18. Miguel Cervantes, The History of Don Quixote de la Mancha ("Great Books of the Western World," Vol. 29) (Chicago: Encyclopaedia Britannica, 1952), p. xi.
19. Ibid.
20. Navarro, op. cit., p. 10.
21. Cervantes, op. cit., p. 21.
22. Kenneth Muir and S. Schoenbaum, editors, A New Companion to Shakespeare Studies (Cambridge: Cambridge University Press, 1971), p. 66.
23. Kenneth Muir, The Sources of Shakespeare's Plays (New Haven: Yale University Press, 1978), p. 166.
24. Ibid.
25. Ibid.
26. Ibid.
27. Karl J. Holzknecht, The Backgrounds of Shakespeare's Plays (New York: American Book Co., 1950), pp. 235-36.
28. Ibid., p. 236.
29. Ibid.
30. Ibid.
31. Johann Wolfgang von Goethe, Goethe's Literary Essays: A Selection in English.... (New York: Frederick Ungar, 1921), p. 145.
32. _____, Goethe's Autobiography: Truth and Poetry from My Own Life. Translated by R. O. Moon (Washington, D.C.: Public Affairs Press, 1949), p. 23.

33. Ibid.
34. Ibid., p. 24.
35. Ibid., p. 62.
36. Ibid., p. 64.
37. Ibid.
38. Ibid., p. 73.
39. Ibid., p. 297.
40. Ibid., p. 272.
41. George Henry Lewes, The Life of Goethe (New York: Frederick Ungar, 1965), p. 56.
42. Ibid.
43. Goethe, op. cit., p. 272.
44. Ibid., p. 592.
45. Lewes, op. cit., p. 563.
46. Walt Whitman, Leaves of Grass.... (New York: Aventine Press, 1931), p. 55.
47. Gay Wilson Allen, The Solitary Singer: A Critical Biography of Walt Whitman (New York: Macmillan, 1955), p. 125.
48. Lucretius, On the Nature of Things ("Great Books of the Western World," Vol. 12) (Chicago: Encyclopaedia Britannica, 1952), p. 58.
49. Whitman, op. cit., p. 100.
50. Ibid., p. 108.
51. Ibid., p. 280.
52. Allen, op. cit., p. 123.
53. Ibid., pp. 53-54.
54. Whitman, op. cit., p. 66.
55. Allen, op. cit., p. 129.
56. Ibid.
57. Whitman, op. cit., p. 10.
58. Allen, op. cit., p. 117.
59. Whitman, op. cit., p. 92.
60. Edwin Haviland Miller, Melville (New York: George Braziller, 1975), p. 34.
61. Ibid., p. 35.
62. Ibid., p. 36.
63. Ibid.
64. D. E. S. Maxwell, "Melville, Herman," Encyclopaedia Britannica (Chicago: Encyclopaedia Britannica, 1975), Vol. 11, p. 874.
65. Philip Spencer, Flaubert: A Biography (London: Faber and Faber, 1952), p. 29.
66. Ibid., p. 19.
67. Ibid., p. 151.
68. Henri Troyat, Tolstoy (New York: Doubleday, 1967), p. 57.
69. Ibid., p. 90.
70. Ibid., p. 48.
71. Ibid., p. 49.
72. Ibid., p. 276.
73. Ibid., p. 316.
74. Mark Twain, Autobiography.... (New York: Harper and Row, 1955), p. 98.
75. Cyril Clemens, Young Sam Clemens (Portland, Me.: Leon Tebbetts Editions, 1942), p. 37.

182 / Notes

76. Ibid., p. 71.
77. Ibid., p. 85.
78. Ibid., First unnumbered page of Foreword.
79. Ibid., Second unnumbered page of Foreword.
80. Lewis Leary, "Twain, Mark," Encyclopaedia Britannica (Chicago: Encyclopaedia Britannica, 1975), Vol. 18, p. 805.
81. James Joyce, A Portrait of the Artist as a Young Man (New York: Viking, 1969), p. 62.
82. Richard Ellmann, James Joyce (New York: Oxford University Press, 1959), p. 78.

Chapter 4

1. Saint Augustine, The Confessions ("Great Books of the Western World," Vol. 18) (Chicago: Encyclopaedia Britannica, 1952), p. 5.
2. Ibid., p. 13.
3. Ibid., p. 14.
4. Ibid., p. 15.
5. Ibid.
6. Ibid.
7. Ibid., p. 26.
8. Ibid., pp. 60-61.
9. Thomas Pittenger, Saint Thomas Aquinas: The Angelic Doctor (New York: Franklin Watts, 1969), p. 28.
10. Ibid., p. 64.
11. Herbert B. Workman, John Wyclif: A Study of the English Medieval Church. 2 vols. in 1 (Hamden, Conn.: Archon Books, 1966), Vol. 1, p. 103.
12. Ibid., Vol. 1, p. 119.
13. Ibid.
14. Ibid., Vol. 2, p. 21.
15. Ibid., Vol. 2, p. 22.
16. Matthew Spinka, John Hus' Concept of the Church (Princeton, N.J.: Princeton University Press, 1966), p. 36.
17. Ibid., p. 41.
18. Ibid., p. 94.
19. Ibid., p. 137.
20. Ibid., p. 195.
21. Roland H. Bainton, Erasmus of Christendom (New York: Scribner's, 1969), p. 31.
22. Ibid., p. 45.
23. Ibid., p. 141.
24. Ibid.
25. Ibid., p. 65.
26. Ibid., p. 202.
27. Ibid.
28. Bainton, Here I Stand: A Life of Martin Luther (New York: Abingdon Press, 1950), p. 65.
29. Ibid.
30. Ernest Gordon Rupp, "Luther, Martin," Encyclopaedia Britannica (Chicago: Encyclopaedia Britannica, 1975), Vol. 11, p. 190.

31. Saint Ignatius, The Testament of Ignatius Loyola. Translated by E. M. Rix (London: Sands and Co., 1900), pp. 44-45.
32. Ibid., pp. 46-47.
33. Francois Wendel, Calvin: The Origins and Development of His Religious Thought. Translated by Philip Mairet (New York: Harper and Row, 1963), p. 46.
34. Saint Teresa, The Autobiography of St. Teresa of Avila. Translated and edited by E. Allison Peers (Garden City, N.Y.: Image Books, 1960), p. 34.
35. Ibid., p. 66.
36. Ibid., p. 69.
37. Ibid.
38. Ibid.
39. Ibid., p. 76.
40. Ibid.
41. Ibid., p. 88.
42. Ibid.
43. Ibid., p. 118.
44. Ibid., p. 247.
45. Ibid.
46. Ibid., p. 365.
47. John Bunyan, Grace Abounding to the Chief of Sinners (Oxford: Clarendon Press, 1962), p. 5.
48. Ibid., p. 8.
49. Ibid., pp. 8-9.
50. Ibid., p. 77.
51. Ibid.
52. Ibid.
53. Ibid.
54. Ibid., p. 102.
55. Bunyan, The Pilgrim's Progress (New York: New American Library, 1964), p. 17.
56. _____, Grace Abounding.... pp. 40-41.
57. Ibid., p. 76.
58. Ibid., p. 183.
59. Jonathan Edwards, Puritan Sage: Collected Writings of Jonathan Edwards (New York: Library Publishers, 1953), p. xiv.
60. Ibid., p. 129.
61. Ibid., p. 234.
62. Edwards, The Works of Jonathan Edwards, A.M. 2 vols. (London: Ball, Arnold, 1840), Vol. 1, p. liv.
63. Ibid.
64. Ibid., Vol. 1, p. lv.
65. Ibid.
66. John Wesley, The Journal of the Rev. John Wesley, A.M.... Edited by Nehemiah Curnock. 8 vols. (London: Robert Culley, n.d.), Vol. 1, p. 83.
67. Ibid., p. viii.
68. Ibid., Vol. 1, pp. 466-67.
69. Ibid., Vol. 1, p. 467.
70. Ibid., Vol. 1, p. 472.
71. Ibid.
72. Ibid., Vol. 1, pp. 475-76.

73. Wesley, The Works of John Wesley (Grand Rapids, Mich.: Zondervan Publishing Co., n.d.), vol. 1, p. 315.
74. Robert Southey, The Life of Wesley.... 2 vols. (London: Humphrey Milford, 1925), Vol. 1, p. 359.
75. Donna Hill, Joseph Smith, the First Mormon (Garden City, N.Y.: Doubleday, 1977), p. 10.
76. Ibid., p. 47.
77. Ibid.
78. Ibid., p. 52.
79. Ibid., p. 51.
80. Ibid., p. 52.
81. Ibid., p. 74.
82. Ibid.
83. Ibid., p. 78.
84. Ibid.
85. Mary Baker Eddy, Retrospection and Introspection (Boston: Joseph Armstrong, 1891), p. 20.
86. Ibid.
87. Ibid., pp. 38-39.
88. Eddy, Christian Science Journal (June, 1887), n.p.
89. _____, "Miscellaneous Writings, 1883-1896," in Prose Works Other than Science and Health with Key to the Scriptures (Boston: Trustees ... of Mary Baker Eddy, 1925), p. 24.
90. Teresia de Spirito Sancto, Edith Stein (New York: Sheed and Ward, 1952), p. 57.
91. Ibid., pp. 64-65.
92. L. D. Reddick, Crusader Without Violence: A Biography of Martin Luther King, Jr. (New York: Harper, 1959), p. 18.
93. Ibid.
94. Ibid., p. 80.
95. Ibid., p. 81.
96. Ibid.

Chapter 5

1. Charles Darwin, The Autobiography of Charles Darwin.... Edited by Francis Darwin (New York: Dover Publications, 1928), p. 9.
2. Ibid.
3. Ibid.
4. Ibid., p. 10.
5. Ibid.
6. Ibid., p. 11.
7. Ibid., p. 24.
8. Ibid., p. 29.
9. Ibid., p. 42.
10. Ibid., pp. 54-55.
11. Ibid., p. 55.
12. Ibid.
13. Darwin, "The Darwin Reading Notebooks (1838-1860)," Journal of the History of Biology, Vol. 10, No. 1 (Spring, 1977), p. 124.

14. Ibid., p. 148.
15. Alfred Russel Wallace, My Life: A Record of Events and Opinions. 2 vols. (New York: Dodd, Mead, 1905), Vol. 1, p. 20.
16. Ibid., Vol. 1, p. 74.
17. Ibid.
18. Ibid., Vol. 1, p. 75.
19. Ibid., Vol. 1, p. 109.
20. Ibid., Vol. 1, p. 232.
21. Ibid.
22. Ibid.
23. Ibid.
24. Ibid.
25. Ibid.
26. Ibid., Vol. 1, p. 264.
27. Ibid., Vol. 2, p. 253.
28. Ibid., Vol. 2, p. 285.
29. Ibid.
30. Ibid.
31. Ibid.
32. Ibid., Vol. 1, p. 372.
33. Francis Galton, Memories of My Life (London: Methuen, 1908), p. 287.
34. Ibid., pp. 287-88.
35. Ibid., p. 290.
36. Ibid.
37. Gavin de Beer, Charles Darwin: Evolution by Natural Selection (New York: Doubleday, 1964), p. 157.
38. Wilhelm Bölsche, Haeckel: His Life and Work (London: T. Fisher, Unwin, 1906), p. 133.
39. Ibid.
40. Ibid., p. 140.
41. Ibid., p. 189n.
42. Peter Dreyer, A Gardener Touched With Genius (New York: Coward, McCann and Geohegan, 1975), p. 80.
43. Ibid., p. 77.
44. David Brewster, Memoirs of the Life, Writings and Discoveries of Sir Isaac Newton. Reprinted from the Edinburgh Edition of 1855. (New York: Johnson Reprint Corp., 1955), Vol. 1, p. 142.
45. Nicolaus Copernicus, On the Revolution of the Heavenly Spheres ("Great Books of the Western World," Vol. 16), (Chicago: Encyclopaedia Britannica, 1952), p. 508.
46. Ibid.
47. Ibid., p. 511.
48. Galileo Galilei, Discoveries and Opinions of Galileo.... Translated by Stillman Drake (New York: Doubleday Anchor Books, 1957), pp. 28-29.
49. Johannes Kepler, Epitome of Copernican Astronomy ("Great Books of the Western World," Vol. 16), (Chicago: Encyclopaedia Britannica, 1952), p. 850.
50. Ibid.
51. Brewster, op. cit., p. 21.

186 / Notes

52. Ibid., pp. 21-22.
53. Ibid., p. 22.
54. Ronald W. Clark, Albert Einstein: The Life and Times (New York: World, 1971), p. 10.
55. Ibid.
56. Ibid.
57. Ibid., p. 17.
58. Ibid., p. 38.
59. Jacques Nicholle, Louis Pasteur.... (New York: Basic Books, 1961), p. 8.
60. James D. Watson, The Double Helix: A Personal Account of the Discovery of DNA (New York: The New American Library, 1969), p. 31.
61. Baltimore Evening Sun, October 13, 1978, pp. A1, A3.
62. Paul Brooks, The House of Life: Rachel Carson at Work.... (Boston: Houghton, Mifflin, 1972), pp. 5-6.
63. Ibid., p. 6.
64. Milton Lehman, This High Man: The Life of Robert H. Goddard (New York: Farrar, Straus, 1963), p. 23.
65. Ibid.
66. Ibid.
67. Jeremy Bernstein, "Profiles: Physicist--1," The New Yorker, October 13, 1975, p. 49.
68. Ibid., pp. 49-50.
69. Henry S. F. Cooper, Jr., "Profiles: A Resonance With Something Alive--1," The New Yorker, June 21, 1976, pp. 74-75.
70. Henry E. Baker, "Benjamin Banneker: The Negro Mathematician and Astronomer," Journal of Negro History, Vol. III, No. 2, (April, 1918), p. 104.
71. James B. Conant, My Several Lives: Memoirs of a Social Inventor (New York: Harper and Row, 1970), p. 86.
72. Ibid.
73. Burrhus Frederick Skinner, Particulars of My Life (New York: Knopf, 1976), p. 291.
74. Ibid.
75. Karl Shapiro, "Library, Asylum, Platform for Uninhibited Leaps," Wilson Library Bulletin, (April, 1963), p. 669.

Chapter 6

1. J. Malgaigne, Surgery and Ambroise Paré. Translated by Wallace B. Hamby (Norman, Okla.: University of Oklahoma Press, 1965), pp. 317-18.
2. Ibid., p. 318.
3. Ibid., p. 394.
4. C. D. O'Malley, Andreas Vesalius of Brussels (Berkeley: University of California Press, 1964), p. 31.
5. Ibid., p. 111.
6. Ibid., p. 121.
7. Ibid., p. 178.
8. Ibid., p. 323.
9. Geoffrey Keynes, The Life of William Harvey (Oxford: Clarendon Press, 1966), p. 95.

10. Ibid.
11. Ibid., pp. 420-21.
12. John Kobler, The Reluctant Surgeon: A Biography of John Hunter (Garden City, N.Y.: Doubleday, 1960), p. 9.
13. Ibid., p. 26.
14. Ibid., p. 27.
15. Ibid.
16. Ibid., p. 94.
17. F. Dawtrey Drewitt, The Life of Edward Jenner: Naturalist and Discoverer of Vaccination (London: Longmans, Green, 1931), p. 87.
18. Ibid., p. 88.
19. Cecil Woodham-Smith, Florence Nightingale (New York: McGraw-Hill, 1950), pp. 44-45.
20. Dorothy Clarke Wilson, Lone Woman: The Story of Elizabeth Blackwell, the First Woman Doctor (Boston: Little, Brown, 1970), p. 67.
21. Ibid., p. 122.
22. Ibid., p. 139.
23. Ibid.
24. Ibid.
25. Ibid.
26. Ibid., p. 140.
27. Erwin H. Ackerknecht, Rudolf Virchow: Doctor, Statesman, Anthropologist (Madison, Wisc.: University of Wisconsin Press, 1953), p. 166.
28. Ibid., p. 83.
29. Ibid., p. 135.
30. Richard B. Fisher, Joseph Lister: 1827-1912 (New York: Stein and Day, 1977), p. 28.
31. Ibid.
32. Ibid., p. 121.
33. Ibid., p. 294.
34. Harvey W. Cushing, The Life of Sir William Osler. 2 vols. (Oxford: Oxford University Press, 1929), Vol. 1, pp. 504-05.
35. Ibid., Vol. 1, p. 505.
36. Ibid., Vol. 1, p. 81.
37. Ibid.
38. Ibid., Vol. 1, p. 448.
39. Ibid., Vol. 2, p. 81.
40. Ibid., Vol. 2, pp. 454-55.
41. Ibid., Vol. 2, p. 455.
42. Simon Flexner and James Thomas Flexner, William Henry Welch and the Heroic Age of American Medicine (New York: Viking, 1941), p. 421.
43. Ibid., p. 362.
44. Ibid., p. 435.
45. Ibid., p. 60.
46. Ibid., p. 66.
47. Helen Buckler, Daniel Hale Williams: Negro Surgeon (New York: Pitman, 1968), pp. 11-12.
48. Ibid., p. 16.
49. Ibid., p. 17.

50. Ibid., p. 86.
51. Ibid., p. 87.
52. Ibid.
53. Ibid., pp. 90-91.
54. Havelock Ellis, <u>Dance of Life</u> (Boston: Houghton, Mifflin, 1929), pp. 215-16.
55. Ibid., p. 216.
56. Ibid., p. 217.
57. Ibid., pp. 216-17.
58. Ibid., p. 218.
59. Ruth Hall, <u>Passionate Crusader: The Life of Marie Stopes</u> (New York: Harcourt, Brace, Jovanovich, 1977), p. 102.
60. Ibid., p. 29.
61. Ibid., p. 90.
62. Ibid.
63. Ibid.
64. Ibid., p. 113.
65. Ibid.
66. Jack L. Rubins, <u>Karen Horney: Gentle Rebel of Psychoanalysis</u> (New York: Dial, 1978), p. 14.
67. Ibid., pp. 133-34.
68. Ibid., p. 298.
69. Ibid.

Chapter 7

1. Sigmund Freud, <u>An Autobiographical Study</u>. Translated by James Strachey (New York: Norton, 1963), p. 14.
2. Ibid.
3. Fritz Wittels, <u>Freud and His Time</u> (New York: Liveright, 1931), pp. 31, 34.
4. Ibid., p. 34.
5. Ernest Jones, <u>Sigmund Freud</u> (New York: Basic Books, 1961), p. 117.
6. Ibid.
7. Ibid., p. 227.
8. C. G. Jung, <u>Memories, Dreams, Reflections</u>. Recorded and edited by <u>Aniela Jaffé</u>; Translated by Richard and Clara Winston. Revised edition (New York: Pantheon, 1973), pp. 146-47.
9. Ibid., p. 147.
10. Ibid.
11. Ibid., p. 149.
12. Ibid., p. 17.
13. Ibid.
14. Ibid., pp. 56-57.
15. Ibid., p. 59.
16. Ibid.
17. Ibid.
18. Ibid., p. 60.
19. Ibid., p. 61.
20. Ibid.

21. Ibid., p. 63.
22. Ibid., p. 68.
23. Ibid.
24. Ibid., pp. 68-69.
25. Ibid., p. 69.
26. Ibid.
27. Ibid., p. 70.
28. Ibid.
29. Ibid.
30. Ibid., pp. 108-09.
31. Ibid., pp. 162-63.
32. Ibid., p. 204
33. Ibid., pp. 204-05.
34. Ibid., p. 205.
35. Ibid., pp. 205-06.

Chapter 8
1. Carl von Clausewitz, On War. Translated by J. J. Graham. New revised edition. 3 vols. (London: Routledge & Kegan Paul, 1962), Vol. 1, p. 113.
2. Ibid., Vol. 1, p. 114.
3. Ibid.
4. A. R. Burn, Alexander the Great and the Hellenistic World (London: The Universities Press, 1947), pp. 19-20.
5. Plutarch, "Alexander," in The Lives of the Noble Grecians and Romans. Translated by John Dryden, revised by Andrew Hugh Clough ("Great Books of the Western World," Vol. 14) (Chicago: Encyclopaedia Britannica, 1952), p. 544.
6. Burn, op. cit., p. 19.
7. Plutarch, op. cit., p. 544.
8. Ibid., p. 581.
9. Walter Gérard, Caesar: A Biography (New York: Scribner's, 1952), p. 8.
10. Napoleon Bonaparte, The Mind of Napoleon: A Selection from His Written and Spoken Words. Edited and translated by J. Christopher Herold (New York: Columbia University Press, 1955), p. 155.
11. Ibid.
12. Ibid., p. 156.
13. Basil Henry Liddell Hart, Foch: The Man of Orleans (Boston: Little, Brown, 1932), p. 23.
14. Napoleon, op. cit., p. 6.
15. Ibid., p. 61.
16. Ibid., p. 62.
17. Ibid.
18. Ibid.
19. Ibid., p. 255.
20. Ibid., p. 280.
21. Ibid., p. 154.
22. Philip Guedalla, Wellington (New York: Literary Guild, 1931), p. 21.

23. Ibid., p. 22.
24. Elizabeth Longford, "Wellington, Duke of," Encyclopaedia Britannica (Chicago: Encyclopaedia Britannica, 1975), Vol. 19, p. 755.
25. Guedalla, op. cit., p. 60.
26. Ibid., p. 56.
27. Ibid., p. 61.
28. Roger Parkinson, Clausewitz: A Biography (New York: Stein and Day, 1971), p. 28.
29. Ibid.
30. Ibid., p. 35.
31. Ibid.
32. Douglas Southall Freeman, R. E. Lee: A Biography. 4 vols. (New York: Scribner's, 1934-35), Vol. 1, p. 37.
33. Ibid., p. 454.
34. Ibid., p. 354.
35. W. E. Woodward, Meet General Grant (New York: Horace Liveright, 1928), p. 16.
36. Ibid., p. 45.
37. Ibid.
38. Ibid., p. 49.
39. Ibid.
40. Ibid.
41. Liddell Hart, op. cit., p. 8.
42. Ibid., p. 23.
43. Charles Carlisle Taylor, The Life of Admiral Mahan: Naval Philosopher (London: John Murray, 1920), p. 23.
44. Ibid.
45. Ibid., p. 25.
46. Ibid.
47. Ibid., p. 27.
48. Ibid.
49. Ibid., p. 34.
50. Ibid., p. 45.
51. Ibid., p. 143.
52. Ibid., p. 117.
53. Ibid., p. 131.
54. William Manchester, American Caesar: Douglas MacArthur, 1880-1964) (Boston: Little, Brown, 1978), p. 5.
55. Ibid., p. 6.
56. Ibid.
57. Douglas MacArthur, Reminiscences: Douglas MacArthur, General of the Army (New York: McGraw-Hill, 1964), p. 17.
58. Ibid., p. 27.
59. Manchester, op. cit., p. 23.
60. Ibid., p. 324.
61. Ibid.
62. Kenneth S. Davis, Soldier of Democracy: A Biography of Dwight Eisenhower (Garden City, N.Y.: Doubleday, 1945), p. 72.
63. Ibid., p. 94.
64. Ibid., p. 95.

65. Ibid., p. 196.
66. Gerhard Ritter, *Frederick the Great: A Historical Profile* (Berkeley: University of California Press, 1968), p. 65.
67. Jasper Ridley, *Garibaldi* (London: Constable, 1974), p. 25.
68. Frank E. Vandiver, *Black Jack: The Life and Times of John J. Pershing*. 2 vols. (College Station, Texas: Texas A. & M. University Press, 1977), Vol. 1, p. 20.
69. Desmond Young, *Rommel, the Desert Fox* (New York: Harper, 1950), p. 76.
70. "Giap--The Victor of Dien Bien Phu," *The Sunday Times Magazine* (London), November 5, 1972, pp. 48-66.

SELECTIVE BIBLIOGRAPHY

The bibliography includes the most significant publications consulted and cited. A brief explanation: Sometimes it was not clear to which edition of a book reference was made or in what language it was written. And often writers were imprecise about titles and the names of authors who had influenced them. Complete bibliographic information was not always available. In each case I have listed the title that seemed closest to the one referred to, giving such information on place of publication, publisher, and title as I could find.

Ackerknecht, Erwin H. Rudolf Virchow: Doctor, Statesman, Anthropologist. Madison: University of Wisconsin Press, 1953.

Alexander, Shana. Talking Woman. New York: Delacorte, 1976.

Allen, Gay Wilson. The Solitary Singer: A Critical Biography of Walt Whitman. New York: Macmillan, 1955.

Anders, H. R. D. Shakespeare's Books. New York: AMS Press, 1903.

Aristotle. The Nichomachean Ethics. Translated by J. A. K. Thomson. London: Allen and Unwin, 1953.

Augustine, Saint. The City of God. ("Great Books of the Western World," Vol. 18.) Chicago: Encyclopaedia Britannica, 1952. 129-618.

──────. The Confessions. ("Great Books of the Western World," Vol. 18.) Chicago: Encyclopaedia Britannica, 1952. 1-125.

Bainton, Roland H. Erasmus of Christendom. New York: Scribner's, 1969.

──────. Here I Stand: A Life of Martin Luther. Nashville, Tenn.: Abingdon Press, 1950.

Baker, Henry E. "Benjamin Banneker: The Negro Mathematician and Astronomer," Journal of Negro History, (Vol. III, No. 2, April, 1918), n.p.

Banneker, Benjamin. Benjamin Banneker's Pennsylvania, Delaware,

Maryland, and Virginia Almanak and Ephemeris for the Year of Our Lord, 1792.... Baltimore: William Goddard and James Angel, 1792.

Barth, John. Quoted in Baltimore Evening Sun. (Oct. 7, 1975), B1.

Bayly, Lewis. The Practice of Pietie Directing a Christian How to Walke That He may Please God. London: I. Hodgets, 1613.

Beer, Sir Gavin de. Charles Darwin: Evolution by Natural Selection. Garden City, N.Y.: Doubleday, 1964.

Bellamy, Edward. Looking Backward, 2000-1887. Boston: Tichnor, 1888.

Bennett, Lerone Jr. What Manner of Man: A Biography of Martin Luther King, Jr. Chicago: Johnson Publishing Co., 1964.

Bernstein, Aaron David. Popular Books on Physical Science. New York: C. Schmidt, 1869.

Bernstein, Jeremy. "Profiles: Physicist--I, II," The New Yorker, (Oct. 13, 1975; Oct. 20, 1975), 47-110; 47-101.

Biedermann, Aloys Emanuel. Christliche Dogmatik. 2 vols. Berlin: Reimer, 1884-85.

Bölsche, Wilhelm. Haeckel: His Life and Work. London: T. Fisher Unwin, 1906.

Bowie, Donald. Station Identification: Confessions of a Video Kid. New York: M. Evans, 1980.

Brewster, David. Memoirs of the Life, Writings, and Discoveries of Sir Isaac Newton. Vol. 1. New York: Johnson Reprint Corp., 1965.

Brooks, Paul. The House of Life: Rachel Carson at Work, with Selections from Her Writings.... Boston: Houghton, Mifflin, 1972.

Browne, Sir Thomas. Religio Medici. London: E. Stock, 1642.

Bryant, Arthur. The Great Duke; or the Invincible General. New York: William Morrow, 1972.

Büchner, Ludwig. Kraft und Stoff: Empirisch-naturephilosophische Studien. Frankfort, A.M.: Meidinger, 1855.

Buckler, Helen. Daniel Hale Williams: Negro Surgeon. New York: Pitman, 1968.

Bunyan, John. Grace Abounding to the Chief of Sinners. Oxford: Clarendon Press, 1962.

_____. The Pilgrim's Progress. New York: Coward, McCann & Geohegan, 1975.

Burbank, Luther. His Methods and Discoveries and Their Practical Applications.... 12 vols. New York: Luther Burbank Press, 1914-15.

Burn, Andrew Robert. Alexander the Great and the Hellenistic World. London: Hodder, 1947.

Burnet, Gilbert. History of His Own Time. 2 vols. Oxford: Clarendon Press, 1897-1900.

Burroughs, Edgar Rice. A Fighting Man of Mars. New York: Metropolitan Books, 1931.

Carpenter, Edward. Love's Coming of Age: A Series of Papers on the Relation of the Sexes. New York: M. Kennerly, 1911.

Carson, Rachel. Silent Spring. Boston: Houghton, Mifflin, 1962.

_____. The Sea Around Us. New York: Oxford University Press, 1951.

Cervantes, Miguel de. The History of Don Quixote de la Mancha. Translated by John Ormsby. ("Great Books of the Western World," Vol. 29.) Chicago: Encyclopaedia Britannica, 1952.

Chute, Marchette. Geoffrey Chaucer of London. New York: E. P. Dutton, 1946.

Clarendon, Edward Hyde, 1st earl of. The History of the Rebellion and Civil Wars in England.... 3 vols. Oxford: 1717.

Clark, Ronald W. Albert Einstein: The Life and Times. New York: World, 1971.

Clausewitz, Carl von. On War. Translated by Colonel J. J. Graham. 3 vols. London: Routledge & Kegan Paul, 1962.

Clemens, Cyril. Young Sam Clemens. Portland, Me.: Leon Tebbetts, 1942.

Conant, James B. My Several Lives: Memoirs of a Social Inventor. New York: Harper & Row, 1970.

Cooper, Henry S. F. Jr. "Profiles: A Resonance with Something Alive--I," The New Yorker, (June 21, 1976), 39-83.

Copernicus, Nicolaus. On the Revolutions of Celestial Spheres....
3 vols. Annapolis, Md.: St. John's Bookstore, 1939.

Cowley, Malcolm, and Smith, Bernard. Books that Changed Our Minds. New York: Kelmscott Editions, 1939.

Creuzer, Georg Friedrich. Symbolik und Mythologie der Alten Völker.... 4 vols. Leipzig: C. W. Leske, 1810-12.

Crick, Francis H. C. Of Molecules and Men. Seattle: University of Washington Press, 1966.

Cushing, Harvey W. The Life of Sir William Osler. 2 vols. New York: Oxford University Press, 1925.

Dante Alighieri. The Divine Comedy. Translated by Charles Eliot Norton. ("Great Books of the Western World," Vol. 21.) Chicago: Encyclopaedia Britannica, 1952.

Darwin, Charles. The Autobiography of Charles Darwin and Selected Letters. Edited by Francis Darwin. New York: Dover, 1958.

──────. The Origin of Species by Means of Natural Selection.... London: J. Murray, 1859.

──────. "Reading Notebooks, 1838-1860." Journal of the History of Biology (Dortrecht, Holland), (Vol. 10, No. 1, Spring, 1977). n.p.

──────. Variations of Animals and Plants Under Domestication. 2 vols. New York: Orange Judd, 1868.

Davis, Kenneth S. Soldier of Democracy: A Biography of Dwight Eisenhower. Garden City, N.Y.: Doubleday, Doran, 1945.

Dent, Arthur. The Plaine Mans Path-way to Heaven. London: I. Legett, E. Bishop, 1617.

Dezallier d'Argentville, Antoine Joseph. Vie des Peintres Italiens et Français. 2 vols. Marseille: Barile, 1843.

Diakanissen-Anstalt zu Kaiserswerth am Rein. Das Erste Jahrzehnt. Kaiserswerth am Rein: 1847.

Dodge, Theodore Ayrault. Hannibal: A History of the Art of War Among the Carthaginians and Romans Down to the Battle of Pydnia, 168 B.C.... Boston: Houghton, Mifflin, 1891.

Downs, Robert B. Books that Changed America. New York: Macmillan, 1970.

──────. Books that Changed the World. Chicago: American Library Association, 1956.

Drewitt, F. Dawtrey. The Life of Edward Jenner, M.D., F.R.S.: Naturalist and Discoverer of Vaccination. London: Longmans, Green, 1931.

Dreyer, Peter. A Gardener Touched with Genius. New York: McCann & Geohegan, 1975.

Druzhin, Aleksander Vasil'evich. Polina Saxe.... Bruxelles: Blanche, 1872.

Eddy, Mary Baker. Christian Science Journal, (June, 1877).

———. Miscellaneous Writings, 1883-1896.... Boston: Trustees ... of Mary Baker Eddy, 1925.

———. Retrospection and Introspection. Boston: W. G. Nixon, 1891.

Edwards, Jonathan. Puritan Sage: Collected Writings of Jonathan Edwards. Edited by Vergilius Ferm. New York: Library Publishers, 1953.

———. The Works of Jonathan Edwards, A.M., with an Essay on His Genius and Writings by Henry Rogers.... 2 vols. London: Ball, Arnold, 1840.

Edwards, William Henry. A Voyage up the Amazon Including a Residence at Pará. London: J. Murray, 1847.

Ellis, Havelock. Dance of Life. Boston: Houghton, Mifflin, 1929.

———. Man and Woman: A Study of Human Secondary Sexual Characters. London: W. Scott, 1894.

———. Studies in the Psychology of Sex. 4 vols. New York: Random House, 1936.

Ellmann, Richard. James Joyce. New York: Oxford University Press, 1959.

Enfield, William. Institutes of Natural Philosophy.... London: J. Johnson, 1785.

Fabricius, Hieronymus. De Venarum Ostiolis, 1603.... Facsimile edition. Springfield, Ill. and Baltimore: C. C. Thomas, 1933.

Falls, Cyril. Marshal Foch. London: Blackie, 1939.

Fénélon, François de Salignac de la Mothe. Les Aventures de Télémark, Fils d'Ulysse. 2 vols. Paris: Florentin Delaulne, 1720.

Ferguson, Francis. Dante. New York: Macmillan, 1966.

Ferguson, James. <u>Astronomy Explained upon Sir Isaac Newton's Principles</u>.... London: A. Millar, 1764.

Fisher, Richard B. <u>Joseph Lister: 1827-1912</u>. New York: Stein and Day, 1977.

Flaubert, Gustave. <u>La Tentation de Saint Antoine</u>. Paris: E. Fasquelle, 1900.

———. <u>Madame Bovary</u>.... Paris: Revue de Paris, 1856.

Fletcher, Charles R. L. <u>Gustavus Adolphus and the Struggle of Protestantism for Existence</u>. New York: Putnam, 1897.

Flexner, Simon, and Flexner, Thomas. <u>William Welch and the Heroic Age of American Medicine</u>. New York: Viking, 1941.

Foch, Ferdinand. <u>Des Principles de la Guerre</u>.... Paris: Berger-Levrault, 1917.

Foster, John. "On Decision of Character," <u>Essays in a Series of Letters to a Friend</u>. 2 vols. London: Longmans, Hurst, Rees, and Orme, 1806.

Fox, James. "Giap--The Victor of Dien Bien Phu," <u>The Sunday Times Magazine</u> (London), (Nov. 5, 1972), 56-65.

Frazer, Sir James. <u>The Golden Bough: A Study in Magic and Religion</u>. 12 vols. London: Macmillan, 1914-17.

———. <u>Totemism and Exogamy</u>.... London: Macmillan, 1910.

Freeman, Douglas Southall. <u>R. E. Lee: A Biography</u>. Vol. 1. New York: Scribner's, 1934.

Freud, Sigmund. <u>An Autobiographical Study</u>. Translated by James Strachey. New York: Norton, 1952.

———. <u>The Interpretation of Dreams</u>. Translated by A. A. Brill. ("Great Books of the Western World," Vol. 54.) Chicago: Encyclopaedia Britannica, 1952. 135-398.

Galen. <u>De Anatomicis Administrationibus</u>.... Lugduni: Gilielmum Rovillium, 1551.

———. <u>De Ossibus ad Tirones</u>. Rome: I. Balami, 1535.

Galileo, Galilei. <u>Discoveries and Opinions of Galileo, Including The Starry Messenger (1610), Letter to the Grand Duchess Christina (1615), and Excerpts from Letters on Sunspots (1613), The Assayer (1623)</u>. Translated with an introduction and notes by Stillman Drake. New York: Doubleday Anchor Books, 1957.

Galton, Francis. Hereditary Genius: An Inquiry into its Laws and Consequences. London: Macmillan, 1869.

———. Memories of My Life. London: Methuen, 1908.

Gardner, John. The Life and Times of Chaucer. New York: Knopf, 1970.

George, Wilma. Biologist Philosopher: A Study of the Life and Writings of Alfred Russel Wallace. London: Abelard-Schuman, 1964.

Goethe, Johann Wolfgang von. Faust. Translated by George Madison Priest. ("Great Books of the Western World," Vol. 47.) Chicago: Encyclopaedia Britannica, 1952.

———. Goethe's Autobiography: Truth and Poetry from My Own Life. Translated by R. O. Moon. Washington, D.C.: Public Affairs Press, 1949.

———. Wilhelm Meisters Lehrjahre. 4 vols. Berlin: Bey Johann Friedrich Unger, 1795-96.

Goodsir, John. Anatomical and Pathological Observations. Edinburgh: Macphail, 1845.

Graham, W. Fred. The Constructive Revolutionary. John Calvin and His Socio-economic Impact. Richmond, Va.: John Knox Press, 1971.

Grant, Ulysses S. Personal Memoirs of U.S. Grant. 2 vols. New York: C. L. Webster, 1885-86.

Gregory, Olinthus Gilbert. A Treatise on Mechanics, Theoretical, Practical and Descriptive. London: G. Kearsley, 1807.

Grigorovich, Dmitrii Vasil'evich. Anton Goremyka. Moscow: 1954.

Guedalla, Philip. Wellington. New York: Literary Guild, 1931.

Haeckel, Ernst H. P. A. Generelle Morphologie der Organismen. Allgemeine Grundztige der Organischen Formen-wissenschaft, Mechanisch Begründet Durch die von Charles Darwin Reformirte Descendenz-theorie. Berlin: Reimer, 1866.

Hall, Ruth. Passionate Crusader: The Life of Marie Stopes. New York: Harcourt, Brace, Jovanovich, 1977.

Harvey, William. On the Motion of the Heart and Blood in Animals. Translated by Robert Willis. ("Great Books of the Western World," Vol. 28.) Chicago: Encyclopaedia Britannica, 1952.

Hauptmann, Gerhardt. Hanneles Himmelfahrt.... 2 vols. Berlin: S. Fischer, 1902.

Hawthorne, Nathaniel. Mosses from an Old Manse. 2 vols. Boston: Tichnor and Fields, 1954.

Herndon, William Lewis. Explorations of the Valley of the Amazon.... 2 vols. Washington, D.C.: R. Armstrong, 1853-54.

Herschel, Sir John Frederick William. A Preliminary Discourse on the Study of Natural Philosophy. London: Longmans, Rees, Orme, Brown and Green, 1831.

Hill, Donna. John Smith, the First Mormon. Garden City, N.Y.: Doubleday, 1977.

Hinton, James. Life in Nature. London: G. Allen & Unwin, 1932.

Holtzknecht, Karl J. The Background of Shakespeare's Plays. New York: American Book Co., 1950.

Homer. The Iliad. Translated by Samuel Butler. ("Great Books of the Western World," Vol. 4.) Chicago: Encyclopaedia Britannica, 1952.

Horton, William Thomas. A Book of Images. London: Unicorn Press, 1898.

Hubatsch, Walther. Frederick the Great of Prussia: Absolutism and Administration. Translated by Patrick Doran. London: Thames and Hudson, 1975.

Humboldt, Alexander von. Personal Narrative of Travels to the Equinoctial Regions of the New Continent During the Years 1799-1804. Translated by Thomasina Russ. 3 vols. London: Bell and Daldy, 1871-76.

Hyma, Albert. The Youth of Erasmus. Ann Arbor, Mich.: University of Michigan Press, 1930.

Ignatius of Loyola, Saint. The Testament of Ignatius Loyola, Being the "Sundry Acts of Our Father Ignatius, Under God ... Taken Down from the Saint's Own Lips by Luis Gonzales." Translated by E. M. Rix. London: Sands & Co., 1900.

Institoris, Henricus. Malleus Maleficarum.... Cologne: Johann Koelfhoff, 1494.

"It Happened 50 Years Ago. May 1977 is the Fiftieth Anniversary of the Fabulous Lindberg Flight...." Modern Maturity, (Apr.-May, 1977), 8-10.

Jacobus de Veragine. Legenda Aurea Sanctorum. Strassburg: Georg Husner, 1479.

Jahr, Gottlieb Henri Georg. New Manual of Homeopathic Practice. 2 vols. New York: W. Radde, 1851.

Jomini, Antoine-Henri baron de. Traité des Grandes Opérations Militaires.... 8 vols. Paris: Guigetet et Michaud, 1807-16.

Jones, Ernest. Sigmund Freud. 3 vols. New York: Basic Books, 1961.

Joyce, James. A Portrait of the Artist as a Young Man. New York: Viking, 1969.

Jung, Carl Gustav. Memories, Dreams, Reflections. Recorded and edited by Aniela Jaffé. Translated from the German by Richard and Clara Winston. New York: Pantheon Books, 1973.

Kant, Immanuel. The Critique of Pure Reason. Translated by J. M. D. Meiklejohn. ("Great Books of the Western World," Vol. 42.) Chicago: Encyclopaedia Britannica, 1952. 1-250.

Keynes, Geoffrey. The Life of William Harvey. Oxford: Clarendon Press, 1966.

Kobler, John. The Reluctant Surgeon: A Biography of John Hunter. Garden City, N.Y.: Doubleday, 1960.

Krafft-Ebing, Richard Freiherr von. Lehrbuch der Psychiatrie.... Stuttgart: Ferdinand Enke, 1890.

Kraft, Ken, and Kraft, Pat. Luther Burbank: The Wizard and the Man. New York: Meredith Press, 1967.

Krug, Wilhelm Traugott. Allgemeines Handvörterbuch der Philosophischen Wissenschaften.... Leipzig: F. A. Brockhaus, 1827-34.

Law, William. Practical Treatise upon Christian Perfection. London: W. Innys, 1741.

_____. Serious Call to a Devout and Holy Life. London: W. Innys, 1729.

Leadbetter, Charles. Astronomy of the Satellites of the Earth, Jupiter and Saturn ... Also New Tables of the Motions of the Satellites of Jupiter and Saturn, etc. London: J. Wilcox, 1729.

Lehman, Milton. This High Man: The Life of Robert H. Goddard. New York: Farrar, Straus, 1963.

Levine, Isaac Don. Mitchell: Pioneer of Air Power. New York: Duell, Sloan, and Pearce, 1943.

Lewes, George Henry. The Life of Goethe. New York: Frederick Ungar, 1965.

Liddell Hart, Sir Basil Henry. Foch: The Man of Orleans. Boston: Little, Brown, 1932.

Lohrer, Alice, editor. "Research in the Fields of Reading and Communications." Library Trends, (Vol. 22, No. 2, Oct. 1973).

Lowes, John Livingston. Geoffrey Chaucer.... Oxford: Clarendon Press, 1934.

Ludolph of Saxony. Vita di Giesv Christo Nostra ... Redentore. Venice: Iacapo Sansouino, 1570.

Lyell, Charles. Principles of Geology.... 3 vols. London: J. Murray, 1830-33.

MacArthur, Douglas. Reminiscences: Douglas MacArthur, General of the Army. New York: McGraw-Hill, 1964.

Mach, Ernst. Science of Mechanics. Chicago: Open Court Publishing Co., 1902.

McLuhan, Marshall. Understanding Media: The Extensions of Man. New York: McGraw-Hill, 1964.

Mahan, Alfred Thayer. Influence of Sea Power upon History. Boston: Little, Brown, 1890.

Mahan, Denis Hart. An Elementary Treatise on Advanced-guard, Outpost, and Detachment Service of Troops.... New York: J. Wiley, 1861.

Malgaigne, J. F. Surgery and Ambroise Paré. Translated and edited by Wallace B. Hamby. Norman, Okla.: University of Oklahoma Press, 1965.

Malthus, Thomas Robert. An Essay on the Principles of Population.... London: J. Johnson, 1798.

Manchester, William. American Caesar: Douglas MacArthur, 1880-1964. Boston: Little, Brown, 1978.

Martin, Henri. History of France from the Earliest Period. 2 vols. Boston: Walker, Wise, 1865.

Miller, Edwin Haviland. Melville. New York: George Braziller, 1975.

Mommsen, Theodor. The History of Rome. 5 vols. Translated by William Purdie. London: J. M. Dent, 1911.

Muir, Kenneth. The Sources of Shakespeare's Plays. New Haven, Conn.: Yale University Press, 1978.

Muir, Kenneth, and Schoenbaum, S., editors. A New Compendium of Shakespeare Studies. Cambridge: Cambridge University Press, 1971.

Napier, Sir William Francis Patrick. History of the War in the Peninsula and in the South of France.... 4 vols. Philadelphia: Carey and Hart, 1842.

Napoleon Bonaparte. Considérations sur l'Art de la Guerre. Paris: n. d.

──────. The Mind of Napoleon: A Selection from His Written and Spoken Words. Edited and translated by J. Christopher Herold. New York: Columbia University Press, 1955.

Navarro y Ledesma, Francisco. Cervantes: The Man and the Genius. New York: Charterhouse, 1973.

Nicholle, Jacques. Louis Pasteur: A Master of Scientific Inquiry. New York: Basic Books, 1861.

O'Malley, Charles Donald. Andreas Vesalius of Brussels, 1514-1564. Berkeley: University of California Press, 1964.

Osler, Sir William. Principles and Practice of Medicine. New York: Appleton, 1892.

Papasogli, Giorgio. Saint Ignatius of Loyola. Translated from the Italian by Paul Garvin. New York: Society of St. Paul, 1959.

Parkinson, Roger. Clausewitz: A Biography. New York: Stein and Day, 1971.

Pasteur, Louis. Memoire sur les Corpuscles Organisés Qui Existent dans l'Atmosphere, Examin de la Doctrine des Générations Spontanées. Paris: Mallet-Bachelier, 1862.

──────. Examin de Rôle Attribué au Gaz Oxygène dans la Destruction des Matières Animales et Végétables Aprés la Morte. Paris?: n. d.

Peel, Robert. Mary Baker Eddy. New York: Holt, Rhinehart & Winston, 1966.

Pittenger, Thomas. Saint Thomas Aquinas: The Angelic Doctor. New York: Franklin Watts, 1969.

Plutarch. "Alexander." In The Lives of the Noble Grecians and Romans. Translated by John Dryden, revised by Arthur Hugh Clough. ("Great Books of the Western World," Vol. 14.) Chicago: Encyclopaedia Britannica, 1952. 540-76.

──────. "Caesar." In The Lives of the Noble Grecians and Romans. ("Great Books of the Western World," Vol. 14.) Chicago: Encyclopaedia Britannica, 1952. 577-604.

Reddick, Lawrence D. Crusader Without Violence: A Biography of Martin Luther King, Jr. New York: Harper, 1959.

Ridley, Jasper. Garibaldi. London: Constable, 1974.

Ritter, Gerhard. Frederick the Great: A Historical Profile. Translated by Peter Paret. Berkeley: University of California Press, 1968.

Rivers, Caryl. Aphrodite at Mid-century. New York: Doubleday, 1973.

Roberts, John Bingham. Paracentesis of the Pericardium with an Analysis of Forty-one Cases. New York: Appleton, 1877.

Rousseau, Jean-Jacques. The Confessions. London: "Printed for the Trade," n.d.

Rubins, Jack L. Karen Horney: Gentle Rebel of Psychoanalysis. New York: Dial, 1978.

Russell, Bertrand, 3rd Earl Russell. Philosophical Essays. London: Longmans, Green, 1910.

―――――. The Problems of Philosophy. New York: Holt, 1912.

Saint-Simon, Claude. Nouveau Christianisme.... Paris: Bossange père, A. Sautelet, 1825.

Salvandy, Narcisse Achille, Comte de. Seize Mois: ou la Revolution et les Revolutionnaires. Paris: Chez L. Advocat, 1831.

Schrödinger, Erwin. What is Life?.... New York: Macmillan, 1945.

Schweitzer, Albert. Philosophy of Civilization. London: A. & C. Black, 1923.

Sedgwick, Henry Dwight. Ignatius Loyola: An Attempt at an Impartial Biography. New York: Macmillan, 1923.

Shannon, Edgar. Chaucer and the Roman Poets. New York: Russell & Russell, 1964.

Sheahan, Henry Beston. The Outermost House. New York: Viking, 1956.

Shelley, Percy Van Dyke. The Living Chaucer. New York: Russell & Russell, 1940.

Skinner, Burrhus Frederic. Particulars of My Life. New York: Knopf, 1976.

―――――. The Shaping of a Behaviorist: Part Two of an Autobiography. New York: Knopf, 1979.

Smith, Hamilton O. "Nucleotide Sequence Specificity of Restriction Endonucleases," Science, (Vol. 205, 3 Aug. 1979), 455-62.

Smith, Jack. "How to be Brash, Childlike and Maudlin--and Love It," Tucson Citizen, (Apr. 8, 1978), 9.

Smith, Joseph. The Book of Mormon. Palmyra, N.Y.: E. B. Grandin, 1830.

Sneed, Laurel Crone. "Peter Crown: Tending TV's Fireplace." American Libraries, (Sept. 1979), 492-95.

Spencer, Philip. Flaubert: A Biography. London: Faber and Faber, 1952.

Spieker, Theodor. Lehrbuch der Ebenen Geometrie. Potsdam: A. Stein, 1881.

Spinka, Matthew. Jan Hus' Concept of the Church. Princeton, N.J.: Princeton University Press, 1966.

Sullaway, Frank J. Freud, Biologist of the Mind: Beyond the Psychoanalytic Legend. New York: Basic Books, 1979.

Symons, Arthur. The Symbolist Movement in Literature. London: W. Heinemann, 1899.

Taylor, Charles Carlisle. The Life of Admiral Mahan, Naval Philosopher.... London: John Murray, 1920.

Taylor, Jeremy. The Rule and Exercises for Holy Living.... London: Richard Royston, 1652.

Teresa of Avila, Saint. The Life of Teresa of Jesus: The Autobiography of St. Teresa of Avila. Translated and edited by E. Allison Peers. Garden City, N.Y.: Image Books (Doubleday), 1960.

Teresia de Spiritu Sancto. Edith Stein. Translated by Cecily Hastings and Donald Nicholl. New York: Sheed and Ward, 1952.

Thiers, Louis-Adolfe. Histoire du Consulat et de l'Empire.... Paris: Paulin, 1845-62.

Thomas Aquinas, Saint. The Summa Theologica.... Translated by Fathers of the Dominican Province. Revised by Daniel J. Sullivan. 2 vols. ("Great Books of the Western World," Vols. 19, 20.) Chicago: Encyclopaedia Britannica, 1952.

Troyat, Henri. Tolstoy. Translated from the French by Nancy Amphoux. New York: Doubleday, 1967.

Twain, Mark. Autobiography, Including Chapter Now Published for the First Time. New York: Harper and Row, 1959.

Vandiver, Frank E. Black Jack: The Life and Times of John J. Pershing. 2 vols. College Station, Texas: Texas A. & M. University Press, 1977.

Vesalius, Andreas. De Humani Corporis Fabrica Libri Septum. Basil: Johannis Oporini, 1543.

Virgil. The Aeneid. ("Great Books of the Western World," vol. 13.) Chicago: Encyclopaedia Britannica, 1952, 101-379.

Wallace, Alfred Russel. My Life: A Record of Events and Opinions. 2 vols. New York: Dodd, Mead, 1905.

Walsh, Frances. That Eager Zest: First Discoveries in the Magic World of Books. Philadelphia: J. B. Lippincott, 1961.

Walter, Gerard. Caesar: A Biography. New York: Scribner's, 1952.

Waples, Douglas, Berelson, Bernard, and Bradshaw, Franklyn. What Reading Does to People: A Summary of Evidence on the Social Effects of Reading and a Statement of Problems for Research. Chicago: University of Chicago Press, 1940.

Watson, James Dewey. The Double Helix. New York: American Library, 1968.

Watson, John Broadus. Behavior: An Introduction to Comparative Psychology. New York: Holt, 1914.

Wavell, Sir Archibald Percival. Generals and Generalship. London: Times Publishing Co., 1941.

Welling, Georg von. Opus Mago-cabalisticum et Theologicum. Frankfort, A. M.: Anton Heinscheidt, 1719.

Wendel, François. Calvin: The Origins and Development of His Religious Thought. Translated by Philip Mairet. New York: Harper and Row, 1963.

Wesley, John. The Journal of the Rev. John Wesley, A. M. Edited by Nehemiah Curnock. 8 vols. London: Robert Culley, n. d.

White, Gilbert. The Natural History and Antiquities of Selborne. London: J. and A. Arch, 1822.

Wilcken, Ulrich. Alexander the Great. New York: Dial, 1932.

Williamson, Henry. Tarka the Otter. London: Putnam, 1945.

Wilson, Dorothy Clarke. *Lone Woman: The Story of Elizabeth Blackwell, the First Woman Doctor.* Boston: Little, Brown, 1970.

Wittels, Fritz. *Freud and His Time: The Influence of the Master Psychologist on the Emotional Problems of Our Lives.* New York: Liveright, 1931.

The Wonders of the World. Dublin: Joseph Blundell, 1833.

Woodham-Smith, Cecil. *Florence Nightingale, 1820-1910.* New York: McGraw-Hill, 1951.

Woodward, W. E. *Meet General Grant.* New York: Liveright, 1928.

Workman, Herbert B. *John Wyclif: A Study of the English Medieval Church.* 2 vols. Hamden, Conn.: Archon Books, 1966.

Young, Desmond. *Rommel, the Desert Fox.* New York: Harper, 1950.

INDEX

Abraham, Karl 127
Académie des Inscriptions 28
Ackernknecht, Erwin 110
Addison, Joseph 32
<u>Adventures of Huckleberry Finn</u> 31
<u>Adventures of Telemachus</u> 20
<u>Adventures of Tom Sawyer</u> 31, 33
Aeneas 17
Aeschylus 148
Aesop 80, 152
Aëtius 99
Agamemnon 148
<u>Albert Einstein: The Life and Times</u> 88
Albert the Great 14, 41, 42
Alcott, Bronson 108
Alemán, Mateo 16
Alexander, Shana 7
<u>Alexander</u> (Plutarch) 148
Alexander the Great 148-49, 151, 171
<u>Alexander the Great and the Hellenistic World</u> 148
Allen, Gay Wilson 23, 24, 25
<u>Almanack and Ephemeris</u>.... 94, 95, 97
Alphonsus Liquori, Saint 34
<u>Amadís de Gaula</u> 17, 50, 53
<u>American Caesar: Douglas MacArthur, 1880-1964</u> 164
American Libraries 12
<u>Anatomical Procedures</u>.... 101
<u>Anatomy of the Human Gravid Uterus</u> 104
Anders, H. R. D. 17
Andreae of Bologna, John 43
<u>Andreas Vesalius of Brussels</u> 100
Anson, George Anson, Baron 20
Anthony 19
<u>Anthony and Cleopatra</u> 19
<u>Anton Goremyka</u> 28
Antony 19
<u>Aphrodite at Mid-century</u> 4
Apelles 100
Aquinas, Saint Thomas <u>see</u> Thomas Aquinas, Saint

Arber, Werner 90, 91
<u>Archives de Psychologie</u> 143
Arezzo Guittone d', 14
Aristotle 14, 17, 39, 42-44, 48, 52, 74, 87, 101-103, 148, 149, 171
Arnaut, Daniel 14
<u>Art of War</u> 157
<u>Artis Auriferae</u> 143
Aspasia 109
<u>Aspects of Nature</u> 84
Athenaeus 28
Atkinson 157
Augustine of Hippo, Saint 14, 38-41, 43, 44, 46-49, 52, 54-56, 74-76, 174
Augustus 149
<u>Aurea Catena Homeri</u> 21
Austen, Jane 32
"Author's Sonnet" (Paré) 100
<u>Autobiographical Study</u> (Freud) 134
<u>Autobiography</u> (Darwin) 77
<u>Autobiography</u> (Mark Twain) 31
<u>Aventures du Chevalier de Faublas</u> 153
Averröes 14, 43
Avicenna 43, 99

Babington, Robert S. 4-5
<u>Background of Shakespeare's Plays</u> 19
Bacon, Francis 32
Bainton, Roland H. 46, 48
Baker, Henry E. 94
<u>Baltimore Evening Sun</u> 3, 91
<u>Baltimore Sun</u> 4, 7, 11
Banneker, Benjamin 94-95, 97
Barrymore, John 7
Barth, John 3, 12, 174, 175
<u>Battle Studies</u> 167
<u>Battlestar Galactica</u> 10
Bayle, Pierre 22
Bayly, Lewis 57, 74
Beda, Noel 47
Bell, John 154
Bellamy, Edward 82

"Benjamin Banneker: The Negro Mathematician and Astronomer" 94
Berelson, Bernard 1
Bernard of Clairvaux, Saint 41
Bernhardi 159
Bernstein, A. 88
Bernstein, Jeremy 92
Beston, Henry 91
Bever, Thomas G. 11
Bevis of Hampton 56
Bhagavad-Gita 95
Bible 17, 25, 26, 36, 39, 41-43, 45-50, 52, 56-60, 62, 66, 68, 70, 71, 76, 89, 92, 99, 109, 134, 166, 175
Biedermann, Aloys E. 138
Billroth, Theodor 121
Bixby, Horace 31
Blackstone, Sir William 120, 153, 169
Blackwell, Elizabeth (first woman M.D. in U.S.) 107-10, 129, 130
Blackwell, Elizabeth (first Scotswoman doctor so named) 110
Blanc, Louis 111
Boccaccio 15
Boethius 14, 15
Bogart, Humphrey 7
Bolingbroke, Henry St. John, 1st Viscount 153
Bölsche, Wilhelm 84
Bonaventure, Saint 14
Boniface VIII, Pope 43
Bonnal 159
Book of Images 35
Book of Martyrs 56, 59
Book of Mormon 68
Book of the Courtier 34
Books That Changed America 1
Books That Changed Our Minds 1
Books That Changed the World 1
Boston Post 92
Bowie, Donald 8-10, 175
Boyle, Robert 87, 103
Bradshaw, Franklyn 1
Brahe, Tycho 87
Brahma 138
Breitinger, Johann Jakob 21
Brewster, David 87
Briefve Collection de l'Administration Anatomique 99
Bright, Timothy 18
British Theatre 154
Brooks, Paul 91
Browne, Sir Thomas 113, 117, 131

Browning, Robert 125, 133
Brühl, Carl 134
Bryant, Arthur 152
Büchner, Ludwig 88
Buckler, Helen 119
Buddha 30, 38
Budé, Guillaume 52
Buffalo Bob 8
Bulwer-Lytton, Edward see Lytton, Edward George Earle Bulwer-Lytton, 1st Baron
Bunsen, Chevalier 106
Bunyan, John 56-59, 74, 75
Burbank, Luther 85, 176
Burke, Sir Edmund 80
Burn, A. R. 148
Burnet, Gilbert 95
Burns, Robert 135
Burroughs, Edgar Rice 93, 96
Byron, Lord 26, 27, 36, 78, 135

Caesar, Julius 149-150, 152, 153, 157, 171
Caesar: A Biography 149
Cagney, James 7
Calvin, John 52-53
Calvin (Wendel) 52
Canterbury Tales 15
Canticles 61
Carlinski, Dan 5
Carlyle, Thomas 25, 26, 32, 114, 117, 131
Carpenter, Edward 125, 133
Carson, Rachel 91
Cassell, John 92
Castiglione, Baldassare 34
Cavalcante, Guido 14
Celestial Wonders of Philosophy 24
Cervantes, Miguel de 13, 16-17, 32, 35-37, 135, 136
Cervantes: The Man and the Genius 16
Chanute, Octave 163
Chaucer, Geoffrey 13-17, 35-37
Chemical Catechism 78
Chesterton, G. K. 95, 97
Children of Adam 23
Christian Pattern 63
Christian Perfection 64, 75
Christian Science 69, 70, 71, 74
Christian Science Journal 70
Christliche Dogmatik 138
Chronicles (Holinshed) 17
Chute, Marchette 15
Cicero 14, 39, 47, 52, 62, 86, 156

Clapperton, Hugh 80
Clarendon, Edward Hyde, 1st Earl of 95
Clark, Ronald W. 88
Clausewitz, Carl von 147, 155-56, 159, 160, 167, 171
Clausewitz: A Biography 155
Clemens, Cyril 31, 33
Clemens, Samuel see Twain, Mark
Clockmaker 32
Colbert, Jean-Baptiste 161
Coleridge, Samuel Taylor 59
College of the Book 114-15
Colonialism on Trial 170
Commedia see Divine Comedy
Commentaries (Blackstone) 120
Commentaries (Caesar) 153
Compleat Angler 80
Conant, James B. 95, 97
Confessions (Saint Augustine) 39, 41, 54, 55, 74
Confessions (Rousseau) 28, 29, 36, 157, 174
Confucius 30, 124
Connor, Fox 167
Conquest of Mexico 28
Considérations sur l'Art de la Guerre 157
Consolation of Philosophy 15
Consuelo 25
Consulate and the Empire 159
Cooper, Henry S. F., Jr. 93
Cooper, James Fenimore 158, 160
Cooper's Life 105
Copernicus 86, 87
Corneille, Pierre 159
Count of Monte Cristo 34
Countess of Rudolstadt 25
Courage to Be 128
Cousin, Victor 109
Cowley, Malcolm 1
Cowper, William 107
Crash Dive 7
Crébillon, Prosper 154
Creuzer, Georg Friedrich 142, 143
Crick, Francis 90
Crime and Punishment 166
Critical Art of Poetry (Breitinger) 21
Critical Art of Poetry (Gottsched) 21
Critique of Pure Reason 88, 140
Crown, Peter 12
Crusader Without Violence: A Biography of Martin Luther King, Jr. 72

Curtis, Tony 7
Cushing, Harvey 113
Cyrus the Great 168

Dana, Richard Henry 26
Dance of Life 121-23
Daniel Hale Williams: Negro Surgeon 119
Daniel in the Lion's Den 21
D'Annunzio, Gabriele 34
Dante (Ferguson) 14
Dante Alighieri 13-16, 34-37
d'Argentville see Dezallier d'Argentville, Antoine Joseph
Darwin, Charles 69, 77-85, 88, 91, 96, 97, 124, 125, 134, 174, 176
David Copperfield 28
Davis, Bette 7
Davis, Kenneth 166
De Anima 101
Declaration of Egregious Popish Impostures 17
De Clementia 52
Decline and Fall of the Roman Empire 32
Defoe, Daniel 80
Democratic Review 24
Demosthenes 52
De Motu Cordis 103
Denham, Dixon 80
Dent, Arthur 57, 74
Derby, George H. 32, 33
Descartes, René 29, 86, 87
Deserted Village 32
De Venarum Ostiolis 103
Dezallier d'Argentville, Antoine Joseph 21
Diary (Jonathan Edwards) 60-62
Dickens, Charles 28, 32, 95, 97, 135
Dictionary of National Biography 118
Dictionnaire Historique et Critique 22
Divine Comedy 13-14
Divine Names 42
Dodge, Theodore Ayrault 167
Don Quixote 16, 17, 53, 135
Dostoevski, Fyodor 166
Double Helix 90
Downs, Robert B. 1
Drewitt, F. Dawtrey 105
Dreyer, Peter 85
Druzhin, Aleksander Vasil'evich 28
Duns Scotus 43, 47

212 / Index

Eckhart, Meister 140
Eddy, Mary Baker 69-71, 74, 75, 76
Edith Stein 71
Edwards, W. H. 81
Edwards, Jonathan 59-62, 74, 75, 174
Einstein, Albert 88-89, 165
Eisenhower, Dwight 166-68, 171
Eliot, George 135
Ellicott, George 94
Ellis, Havelock 121-124, 129, 132, 133, 174
Ellman, Richard 34
Emerson, Ralph Waldo 25, 26, 108
Emile 28
Empedocles 140
Encyclopaedia Britannica 118
Encyclopaedia of Plants 81
Enfield, William 156
Engels, Friedrich 111
Ephesians 60
Epictetus 30, 62
Epistle of James 67
Epistle to the Romans 40, 49, 64, 74, 174, 175
Epitome of Copernican Astronomy 87
Erasmus, Desiderius 33, 46-48, 52, 74
Erasmus of Christendom 46
Essay on the Principle of Population 79, 81
Ethica see Ethics (Aristotle)
Ethics (Spinoza) 23
Euclid 87
Eugene Onegin 28
Euripides 148
"Examin de Rôle Attribué au Gaz Oxygèn dans la Destruction des Matières Animales et Végétables Après la Morte" 112
Explorations of the Valley of the Upper Amazon 31

Fabiola, Saint 109
Fabrica 101
Fabricius ab Aquapendente 103, 129
Falls, Cyril 159
Faraday, Michael 69
Faust 21, 27, 36, 139
Feldherr 170
Fénélon, François de Salinac de la Mothe 20, 169
Ferguson, Francis 14

Ferm, Vergilius 60
Fielding, Henry 32, 135
Fighting Man of Mars 93
Filial Indiscretion. . . . 154
Fisher, Richard B. 112
Flaubert, Gustave 13, 27-28, 35, 36, 132, 136, 174
Flaubert: A Biography 27
Fletcher, C. R. L. 168
Flexner, Simon, and Thomas Flexner 117
Florence Nightingale 106
Flournoy, Theodore 143
Flowers of the Saints 50, 74
Foch, Ferdinand 151, 159-60, 167, 171
Foch: The Man of Orleans 159
Force and Matter 88
Forest, Nathan Bedford 165
Foster, John 108
Fourier, Charles 109
Foxe, John 56, 59
Fragment upon Nature 135, 145
Franklin, Jon 91
Frazer, Sir James 136
Frederick the Great 151, 154, 155, 158, 169, 171
Frederick the Great of Prussia 169
Freeman, Douglas S. 156
Freud, Sigmund 64, 127, 134-38, 142, 145-46, 176
Freud in His Time 135
Froebel, Julius 111
From the Earth to the Moon 163
Front Page 5-6, 175
Fuller, Margaret 25, 108

Galathians see Galatians
Galatians 58, 59, 65, 75
Galen 99, 102, 103, 118, 129
Galileo 86, 87
Galton, Francis 83-84, 126, 174
Gandhi, Mahatma 73, 74, 75
Gardener Touched with Genius 85
Gardener's Chronicle 81
Gardner, John 14, 15
Garibaldi 169
Garibaldi, Giuseppe 169
Gassendi, Pierre 87
Gates, Frederick T. 115-16, 118, 131, 132
General Dictionary of the Philosophical Sciences 139
General Morphology of Organisms. . . . 84
Gentz, Friedrich von 154

Geoffrey Chaucer of London 5
Géométrie 87
George, Henry 30, 82
Gérard, Walter 149
Gerstäcker, F. W. C. 139
Giap, Vo Nguyen 170, 171
"Giap--The Victor of Dien Bien Phu" 170
Gibbon, Edward 34
Gilbert, William 87
Gilded Age 33
Goddard, Robert H. 91-92, 96, 97
Goethe, Johann Wolfgang von 13, 19-23, 25-27, 36, 37, 64, 84, 111, 132, 134, 135, 139, 145, 146, 174
Gogarty, Oliver St. John 34, 35
Gogol, Nikolay 28
Golden Bough 136
Golden Flower 143
Golden Legend 53
Goldsmith, Oliver 32
Goltz, (Wilhelm Leopold) Colmar, Freiherr, von der 159
Gonzales, Luis 50
Goodman, Benny 6
Goodsir, John 111, 130
Gospels 30
Gottsched, Johann Christoph 81
Grace Abounding to the Chief of Sinners 57
Grammar (L. Murray) 69
Grant, Cary 7
Grant, Ulysses S. 157-59
Gratian 43
Gray's Anatomy 120
Great Duke 152
Great Train Robbery 7
Greek Testament 152
Gregory, Olinthus G. 156
Gregory IX, Pope 53
Grey, Zane 126
Grigorovich, Dmitrii Vasil'evich 28
Grosseteste, Robert 43
Grotius, Hugo 168
Guedalla, Philip 152, 154
Guinizelli, Guido 14
Gunga Din 7
Gustavus Adolphus 168, 171
Gustavus Adolphus and the Struggle of Protestantism for Existence 168

Haeckel, Ernst 84-85, 96, 97
Haeckel: His Life and Work 84

Hall, Ruth 123, 125
Halliburton, Judge 32
Hamilton, Alexander 157
Hamlet 18
Hanley 161
Hanneles Himmelfahrt 35
Hannibal 157, 171
Harsnett 17
Harvey, William 103, 129
Hauptmann, Gerhart 34, 35
Hawthorne, Nathaniel 25-26, 174
Hawthorne and His Mosses 26
Heavens 113
Hegel, Georg Wilhelm Friedrich 25
Henry, William 78
Heraclitus 140
Here I Stand: A Life of Martin Luther 48
Hereditary Genius 83, 174
Herndon, William Lewis 31
Hero of Our Times 28
Herschel, Sir John F. W. 78
Hill, Donna 66
Himowitz, Michael J. 91
Hinton, James 121-23, 132, 174
Hippocrates 99, 118
History of France 161
History of His Own Time 95
History of Rome 161, 171
History of Sicily 148
History of the Rebellion 95
History of the War on the Peninsula 160
Ho Chi Minh 170, 171
Hoenig 159
Holbach, Paul Henri Dietrich, Baron d' 22
Holinshed, Raphael 17
Holzknecht, Carl J. 19, 25, 33, 149, 156
Homer 25, 33, 149, 156
Hooke, Robert 86
Horace 17, 47, 62
Horney, Karen 126-29, 133
Hortensius 39
Horton, William Thomas 35
House of Fame 15
House of Life: Rachel Carson at Work 91
Howdy Doody 9
Hubatsch, Walther 169
Hugo, Victor 27, 36
Humboldt, Alexander von 78, 81, 84, 85
Hunter, John 103-04, 129, 130
Hus, Jan 44-47, 50, 74

214 / Index

Husserl, Edmund 71
Huxley, Aldous 128, 133
Huxley, Thomas 69, 79, 84
Huysmans, Joris-Karl 34

Ibsen, Henrik 34, 37, 165
Ignatius of Loyola, Saint 50-53, 74, 75
Iliad 148
Illicit Love 154
Influence of Sea Power upon History 162
Influence of Sea Power upon the French Revolution and Empire 162
Ingersoll, Robert G. 120
Inquiry into the Causes and Effects of Variolae Vacciniae 105
Institutes of Natural History 156
Institutes of the Christian Religion 52
Interpretation of Dreams 137
Introduction to the Study of Natural Philosophy 78
Iron Heel 93
Irving, Washington 158
Isaiah 67, 68
Island of Felsenburg 20
Ivan Ivanovich 28

Jack the Giant Killer 80
Jackson, Elizabeth 109
Jackson, Stonewall 165
Jahr, Gottlieb H. G. 69
James, Saint 67
James Joyce 34
Jan Hus' Concept of the Church 44
Jefferson, Thomas 105
Jenner, Edward 105, 129, 130
Jerome, Saint 47, 54
Jesus Christ 38, 40, 44, 59
Job 54
John, Gospel According to 58
John Wyclif 43
Johnson, Hildy 6
Johnson, Mordecai W. 73
Johnson, Samuel 32
Jolson, Al 7
Jomini, Antoine-Henri 157, 159, 161, 167
Joseph Lister: 1827-1912 112
Joseph Smith, the First Mormon 66
Joshua, Book of 57
Journal (Darwin) 81

Journal (Wesley) 62, 63, 75
Journal of Negro History 94
Journal of the Plague Year 80
Journey Around the World 20
Journey from the Earth to the Moon 92
Joyce, James 13, 34-35, 37
Jung, Carl Gustav 134, 137-146, 174, 176
Jure Belli ac Pacis 168
Juvenal 62

Kaiserswerth Year Book 106, 107, 130
Kant, Immanuel 30, 88, 124, 140, 146, 156, 171
Karen Horney: The Gentle Rebel of Psychoanalysis 126
Kempis see Thomas à Kempis
Kennedy, Robert 91
Kent, James 169
Kepler, Johannes 86, 87
Keynes, Geoffrey 103
Kierkegaard, Sören 127
King, Martin Luther, Jr. 72-75
King Lear 27
Klopstock, Friedrich Gottlieb 21
Kobler, John 104
Kojac 10
Korzybski, Alfred 12
Krafft-Ebing, Richard 142, 145, 174
Krug, Wilhelm T. 139

La Bruyère, Jean de 159
Ladd, Alan 4
Lamartine, Alphonse de 27
Lamb, Charles 32
Land Nationalization Society 82
Land Tenure Association 82
Langley, Samuel P. 92, 163
Laocoön 21
Lao-tzu 30
Latini, Brunetto 14
Law, William 64, 75
Lee, "Light Horse Harry" 157
Lee, Robert E. 156-157, 165
Legend of Good Women 16
Lehman, Milton 92
Lehrbuch der Ebenen Geometrie 88
Lehrbuch der Psychiatrie 142, 145
L'Enfant, Pierre-Charles 95
Lenin 155
Leonora 153
Lermontov, Mikhail 28

Lessing, Gotthold Ephraim 21, 22
Lessons for Lovers 154
Letter to the Romans see Epistle to the Romans
Letters of Madame de Pompadour 154
Lever, Charles James 158
Levine, Isaac Don 163
Lewes, George Henry 21
Library Trends 2
Liddell Hart, Sir Basil 159
Life and Times of Chaucer 14
Life in Nature 121, 132, 174
Life of Admiral Mahan 160
Life of Christ (Ludolph) 50, 55, 74, 175
Life of Edward Jenner 105
Life of Goethe 21
Life of Hannibal 167
Life of St. Teresa of Avila 71, 76
Life of Sir William Osler 113
Life of Teresa of Jesus 53
Life of William Harvey 103
Lilienthal, Otto 163
Lincoln, Abraham 166
Lindbergh, Charles 6
Lister, Joseph 111-13, 130, 131
Little Red Riding Hood 80
Littleton, Sir Thomas 120
Lives (Plutarch) 153
Lives of the Painters 21
Lloyd, Major-General 154, 171
Locke, John 60, 153
Lohrer, Alice 2
Lombard, Peter 41, 44, 47, 48
London, Jack 93
Lone Ranger 9
Lone Woman: The Story of Elizabeth Blackwell, the First Woman Doctor 107
Longinus 156
Looking Backward 82
Loudon, John Claudius 81
Louis Pasteur: A Matter of Scientific Inquiry 89
Love at First Sight 154
Love's Coming of Age 125, 133
Lucan 14
Lucretius 23, 36
Ludolph of Saxony 55, 175
Luther, Martin 48-50, 58, 59, 64, 65, 74, 75, 175, 176
Lyell, Sir Charles 78, 79
Lysippus 100
Lytton, Edward Earle Bulwer-Lytton, 1st Baron 32, 158

MacArthur, Douglas 164-66, 168, 171
Macaulay, Thomas Babington, 32
Mach, Ernest 89
Machiavelli, Niccolò 151, 156, 157, 171
McLaglan, Victor 5
McLuhan, Marshall 2
Madame Bovary 27
Mahan, Alfred T. 160-63, 171, 172, 174
Mahan, Denis Hart 167
Malay Archipelago 82
Malgaigne, J. 98
Malleus Malificarum 136, 146
Malthus, Thomas Robert 79, 81, 97
Man and Woman 124, 133
Manchester, William 164, 166
Mao Tse-tung 155
Marcella 109
Marcus Aurelius 30
Married Love 126, 133
Marryat, Frederick 32, 158, 160
Marshal Foch 159
Martin, Henri 161
Mary Baker Eddy 69
Mather, Martha 11
Matthew, Gospel According to 28, 74
May, Karl 126
Mazzini, Giuseppe 169
Me Imperturbe 24
Measure for Measure 27
Mechanics Library (New York) 32
Medical practitioners and medical scientists, Reading of 98-146
Meet General Grant 157
Melville 26
Melville, Herman 13, 25-27, 35, 36, 174
"Memoires sur les Corpuscles Organisés qui Existent dans l'Atmosphere, Examin de la Doctrine des Générations Spontanées" 112
Memoirs (Elizabeth Jackson) 109
Memoirs (Grant) 158
Memoirs of the Life of Sir Walter Scott 103
Memoirs of the Life, Writings, and Discoveries of Sir Isaac Newton 87
Memoirs of the War in the Southern Department 157
Memories, Dreams, Reflections (Jung) 137
Memories of My Life (Galton) 83

Mencken, Henry L. 133
Messiah (Klopstock) 21
Metamorphoses 15
Meyer, F. A. A. 80
Military leaders, Reading of 147-72
Mill, John Stuart 82
Miller, Edwin Haviland 26
Milton, John 21, 26, 135
Mind of Napoleon 150
Miscellaneous Writings (Mary Baker Eddy) 70-71
Mr. Midshipman Easy 32
Mr. Wizard 11
Mitchel, O. M. 24, 36
Mitchell, Billy 163-64
Mitchell, Pioneer of Air Power 163
Mitscherlich, Eilhardt 89
Moby Dick 26
Modern Maturity 5
Mohammed 38
Mommsen, Theodor 161, 171
Montaigne, Michel (Eyquem) de 27, 33
Montesquieu, (Charles-Louis de Secondat, Baron de La Brède et de) 156
Morals of St. Gregory 54
More, Henry 88
Möser, Justus 21
Moses 38, 59
Mosses from an Old Manse 25-26, 36, 174
Movies 4-7, 173, 175, 176
Muir, Kenneth 17, 18
Murray, Lindley 69
My Life (Alfred Russel Wallace) 80
My Several Lives (James B. Conant) 95

Napier, Sir William 160, 174
Napoleon 150-52, 157-59, 161, 166, 167
Narrative of Travels on the Amazon and Rio Negro 81
Nathans, Daniel 90
Nation 119
National Dispensatory 120
Natural History and Antiquities of Selborne 78
Naturegeschichte der Haustiere 80
Navarro y Ledesma, Francisco 16, 17
Navigation 157

Nepos, Cornelius 169
Nester 148
Nevsky Prospect 28
New Companion to Shakespeare Studies 17
New Manual of Homeopathic Practice 69
New Poetry (Vinsauf) 15
New Testament 20, 61, 95
New Yorker 92, 93
Newcomes 96
Newton, Sir Isaac 56, 60, 86-88, 92, 94, 96, 156
Nicetus 86
Nicholle, Jacques 89
Nietzsche, Friedrich 141
Nightingale, Florence 106-07, 110, 130
Nouveau Christianisme 169
Nouvelle Héloïse 28, 153

Old Curiosity Shop 95
Old Testament 60
O'Malley, C. D. 100-02
On Bones 101
On the Heavens 87
On the Nature of Things 23
On the Revolution of the Heavenly Bodies 86
On War 147, 156
Oppenheimer, J. Robert 93
Opus Major Cabalisticum 21, 147, 156
Orbis Pictus 138
Origin of Species 83, 84, 96
Osler, Sir William 113-19, 131, 132
Outermost House 91
Outpost 167
Overcoat 28
Ovid 14, 15, 17, 36, 152

Paine, Thomas 25
Panorama of Human Life 16
Paradise Lost 21
Paré, Ambroise 98-100, 129
Park, Mungo 80
Parker, Theodore 108
Parkinson, Roger 155
Parliament of Fowls 15
Particulars of My Life (B. F. Skinner) 95
Passionate Crusader: The Life of Marie Stopes 123-25
Pasteur, Louis 89, 97, 112-13, 130

Paul III, Pope 86
Paul IV, Pope 48
Paul the Apostle, Saint 40, 49, 64, 65, 74, 174, 175
Paula 109
Pauline Saks 28
Pauling, Linus 90
Pavlov, Ivan Petrovich 95
Peel, Robert 69
Peers, E. Allison 53
Pendennis 32
Peninsular War 174
Perennial Philosophy 128
Pershing, John J. 169-71
Personal Narrative of Travels to the Equinoctial Regions of the New Continent 78, 105
Personal Recollections of Joan of Arc 32
Peter Pan 10
Petrarch 15, 36
Philistus 148
Philosophy of Civilization 127-28, 133
Philoxenos 148
Phoenixiana 32
Pickwick Papers 32
Picq, Ardant du 167
Pilgrim's Progress 56, 58, 59
Pittenger, Thomas 41, 42
Plaine Mans Path-way to Heaven 57, 74
Plant and its Life 84
Plato 43, 44, 52, 102, 140, 166
Plautus 17
Pliny the Elder 28, 99
Plotinus 39
Plutarch 17, 19, 28, 62, 86, 148, 149, 153
Police Woman 10
Politics (Aristotle) 148
Polybius 27
Popular Books on Physical Science 88
Popular Educator 92
Population see Essay on the Principal of Population
Portrait of the Artist as a Young Man 34
Power, Tyrone 7
Practices of Piety 57, 74
Prescott, William H. 28, 32
Pride and Prejudice 32
Priestley, Joseph 154
Priestly Peru 80
Principia Mathematica 92, 156
Principle and Practice of Medicine 115-16, 131

Principles de la Guerre 160
Principles of Geology 78
Principles of War 167
Progress and Poverty 82
Proudhon, Pierre-Joseph 111
Ptolemy 86
Puritan Sage 60
Pushkin, Aleksandr 28
Pythagorus 140

Quadripeds of Paraguay 103
Quintillian 47

R. E. Lee: A Biography 156
Rabelais, François 27
Rabi, Isaac I. 92-93, 97, 176
Racine, Jean 21, 159
Radio 8
Rafinesque, C. S. 24
Reading 1-3, 53-54, 173-77
Reading Notebooks (Darwin) 79
Reagan, Ronald 7
Reddick, L. D. 72
Reed, Walter 118
Reflections on the General Principles of War 154, 171
Religio Medici 113, 131
Religious leaders, Reading of 38-76
Reluctant Surgeon: A Biography of John Hunter 104
Remak, Robert 111, 130
Reminiscences (MacArthur) 164
"Research in the Fields of Reading and Communication" 2
Retrospection and Introspection (Mary Baker Eddy) 69
Revolution of the Heavenly Bodies 111
Rhazes 100
Ribicoff, Abraham 91
Ridley, Jasper 169
Rin Tin Tin 7
Rivers, Caryl 4
Robbers 28
Roberts, John Bingham 120-21
Robinson Crusoe 20
Rockefeller, John D. 115-18, 131-32
Rommel, Erwin 170, 171
Rommel, the Desert Fox 170
Roosevelt, Theodore 162
Rousseau, Jean-Jacques 25, 27-29, 36, 150, 152, 153, 157, 171, 174
Rubin, Jack L. 126

218 / Index

Rudolf Virchow: Doctor, Statesman, Anthropologist 110
Rules for Holy Living and Dying 63, 75
Russell, Bertrand 95

Sagan, Carl 93-94, 96, 97
Saint-Simon, Claude 169
Saint Thomas Aquinas 41
Salammbô 27
Sallust 169
Salvandy, Narcisse Achille, Comte de 23
Samuel, Books of 58
Sand, George 25
Sandford and Merton 80
Schiller, (Johann Christoph) Friedrich von 28
Schleiden, Matthias Jakob 84
Schoenbaum, S. 17, 30
Schopenhauer, Arthur 84, 140, 141, 146
Schrödinger, Erwin 90
Schwartz, Bernie see Curtis, Tony
Schweitzer, Albert 91, 127, 128, 133
Science of Mechanics 89
Scientists, reading of 77-97
Scipio Africanus 28
Scott, Sir Walter 27, 32, 36, 78, 80, 108, 135, 158
Seasons 78
Seize Mois, ou la Révolution et les Révolutionnaires 23
Selborne see Natural History and Antiquities of Selborne
Seneca 17, 47, 52
Sentences 41
Sentimental Journey 28
Serious Call 64, 75
Servetus, Michael 53
Seven Books on the Structure of the Human Body see Fabrica
Seven Champions of Christendom 56
Shadow 8
Shakespeare, William 13, 17-19, 20, 25, 26, 27, 32, 35-37, 63, 78, 104, 125, 133, 159, 166
Shakespeare (Bell) 154
Shakespeare's Books 17
Shapiro, Karl 97
Shaw, Artie 6
Shaw, George Bernard 165
Shelley, Percy Bysshe 25
Shiva 138

Silent Spring 91
Silius Italicus 28
Six Lectures on Astronomy 24
Skinner, B. F. 95-97
Smith, Adam 153
Smith, Bernard 1
Smith, Hamilton O. 90-91
Smith, Jack 5-6, 175
Smith, Joseph 65-69, 75
Social Statistics 82
Socrates and Jesus Compared 154
Soldier of Democracy: A Biography of Dwight Eisenhower 166
Solitary Singer: A Critical Biography of Walt Whitman 23
Song of Myself 23-25
Song of Solomon 174
Sonnets (Shakespeare) 125, 133
Sophocles 148
Sources of Shakespeare's Plays 18
Spencer, Herbert 82
Spencer, Philip 27
Spieker, Theodor 88
Spinka, Matthew 44
Spinoza, Benedict de 22, 23
Sporting Magazine 154
Sportsman's Sketches 28
Starry Messenger 86
State of Europe Before and After the French Revolution 154
Station Identification 7, 10
Statius 14
Stein, Edith 71-72, 75, 76
Sterne, Laurence 28, 156
Stopes, Marie 123-26, 129, 133, 174
Struve, Gustave von 111
Studies in the Psychology of Sex 124, 133, 174
Summa Theologica 42
Summary Account and Military Character of the Several European Armies that have Been Engaged During the Late War 154
Sunday Times Magazine (London) 170
Surgery and Ambroise Paré 98-99
Swedenborg, Emanuel 109, 124
Swift, Jonathan 153
Swinburne, Charles 125, 133
Symbolik und Mythologie der Alten Völker 142
Symbolist Movement in Literature 35
Symons, Arthur 35
Système de la Nature 22

Tacitus 156, 169
Talking Woman 7
Talmey, Max 88
Tarka the Otter 91
Taylor, Charles C. 160
Taylor, Jeremy 63, 75
Télémark 169
Telestes 148
Television 173, 175, 176
Temptations of Saint Anthony 135
Tenures 120
Terence 47, 62, 152
Teresa Benedicta of the Cross see Stein, Edith
Teresa of Avila, Saint 53-56, 71, 72, 74, 75, 174-76
Teresia de Spiritu Sancto, Sister 71-72
Terman, Lewis 174
Testament of Ignatius Loyola 50
Thackeray, William Makepeace 32, 96, 135
That Eager Zest 2
Thiers, Louis-Adolfe 159
This High Man: The Life of Robert H. Goddard 92
Thomas à Kempis 63, 64
Thomas Aquinas, Saint 14, 38, 41-44, 47, 74, 76
Thomson, James 78
Thoreau, Henry David 73, 74, 85, 108
Thoughts Out of Season 141
Thus Spake Zarathustra 141
Tillich, Paul 128, 133
Time 12
Times (London) 84
Tippoo 153
To a Person Sitting in Darkness 33
Tolstoy, Leo 13, 28-30, 34-37, 174, 176
Tolstoy (Troyat) 29
Totem and Tabu 136
Totemism and Exogamy 136
Traité des Grandes Opérations Militaires 157
Treatise of Melancholie 18
Treatise on Mechanics 156
Tristram Shandy 156
Troilus and Cressida 15
Trotula 109
Troublesome Reign of King John 18
Troyat, Henri 29, 37
Truth and Poetry from My Life 20

Tucson Citizen 5
Tully 39
Turgenev, Ivan 28
Twain, Mark 13, 30-36, 133, 166
Two Years Before the Mast 26
Typee 26

Udall, Stewart 91
Ulysses 35
Uncle Tom's Cabin 28, 160
Understanding Media 2
Universal Magazine 154
"Urim and Thummim" 68

Van Loon, Hendrik W. 33
Variations of Animals and Plants Under Domestication 85
Venus and Adonis 125, 133
Verlaine, Paul 34, 35
Verne, Jules 92, 163
Vesalius, Andreas 100-03, 129
Vicar of Wakefield 32
Vigo, Giovanni da 99
Vii 28
Vinsauf, Geoffrey de 15
Virchow, Rudolf 110-11, 129, 130
Virgil 13, 14, 16, 17, 36, 62
Vishnu 138
Vita Nuova 14
"Volksbücher" 21, 37
Voltaire 150, 152, 156, 169, 171
Voyage up the Amazon 81
Vulgate 196

Walden Two 95
Wallace, Alfred Russel 80-83, 97
Walsh, Frances 2
Walton, Izaak 80
Wandlungen und Symbole der Libido 143
Waples, Douglas 1
War and Peace 29, 30, 176
War of the Worlds 92, 96
Warner, Jack 7
Washington, George 95
Waterhouse, Benjamin 105
Watson, James Dewey 90
Watson, John Broadus 95
Wavell, Sir Archibald 170, 171
Wayne, John 4-5
Wealth of Nations 153
Welch, William Henry 117-19, 132
Welling, Georg von 21
Wellesley, Sir Arthur see Wellington, Duke of

Wellington 152
Wellington, Duke of 152-55, 171
Wesley, John 62-65, 74, 75
Westminster Catechism 69
What Is Life? 90
What Is Man? 33
What Price Glory? 5
What Reading Does to People 1
When I Heard the Great Astronomer 24
White, Gilbert 78
Whitman, Walt 13, 23-25, 35-37
Wilhelm, Richard 143
Wilhelm Meister 20
Wilhelm II, Emperor 162
Wilkins, Maurice H. F. 90
William of Ockham 47, 48
William Welch and the Heroic Age of American Medicine 117
Williams, Daniel Hale 119-21, 132

Williamson, Henry 91
Wilson, Dorothy Clarke 107
Wittels, Fritz 135
Woman of Pleasure 153
Wonders of the World 78
Woodham-Smith, Cecil 106
Woodward, W. E. 157
Workman, Herbert B. 43, 44
Writers, Reading of 13-37
Wyclif, John 38, 43-46, 50, 74

Xenophon 17, 28, 168

Young, Desmond 170
Young America Movement 24
Young Sam Clemens 31

Zola, Émile 34, 165

WITHDRAWN

Forsyth Library